Banished

Banished

The New Social Control in Urban America

KATHERINE BECKETT

and

STEVE HERBERT

OXFORD

UNIVERSITY PRESS

OXFORD
UNIVERSITY PRESS

Oxford University Press, Inc., publishes works that further
Oxford University's objective of excellence
in research, scholarship, and education.

Oxford   New York
Auckland   Cape Town   Dar es Salaam   Hong Kong   Karachi
Kuala Lumpur   Madrid   Melbourne   Mexico City   Nairobi
New Delhi   Shanghai   Taipei   Toronto

With offices in
Argentina   Austria   Brazil   Chile   Czech Republic   France   Greece
Guatemala   Hungary   Italy   Japan   Poland   Portugal   Singapore
South Korea   Switzerland   Thailand   Turkey   Ukraine   Vietnam

Published by Oxford University Press, Inc.
198 Madison Avenue, New York, New York 10016
www.oup.com

First issued as an Oxford University Press paperback, 2011

Oxford is a registered trademark of Oxford University Press

Library of Congress Cataloging-in-Publication Data
Beckett, Katherine, 1964–
Banished : the new social control in urban
America / Katherine Beckett and Steve Herbert.
    p. cm.—(Studies in crime and public policy)
Includes bibliographical references and index.
ISBN 978-0-19-539517-4; 978-0-19-983000-8
1. Seattle (Wash.)—Social policy.
2. Marginality, Social—Washington (State)—Seattle.
I. Herbert, Steven Kelly, 1959–   II. Title.
HN80.S54B43 2009
307.3'41609797772—dc22   2009005367

Printed in the United States of America
on acid-free paper

Acknowledgments

It is difficult to complete a project of this scope without incurring numerous debts. The list of those from whom we have drawn some measure of support is long indeed. At the risk of omitting someone, we wish to acknowledge the contributions of the following individuals and institutions.

For financial support, we thank the Open Society Institute and two organizations at the University of Washington—the Institute for Ethnic Studies in the United States and the Simpson Center for the Humanities.

We received research assistance from a number of individuals. The most notable of these was Matt Wilson, who performed superb work with an impressively cheerful and constructive demeanor. We are also grateful for the work of a group of similarly well-motivated (and unpaid!) undergraduate students, including Christian Brown, Nicholas Case, Jessy Van Horn, Carmen Wong, and Christopher Zentz. Suzanna Ramirez and Juliet Scarpa did extensive and excellent data coding, and Erin Powers provided numerous interview transcriptions.

Attorneys at The Defender Association and Associated Counsel for the Accused helped us in many ways: alerting us to banishment in the first place; educating us on its particulars; and helping us find banished subjects for interviews. Of particular importance were the contributions of Lisa Daugaard, which included a careful reading of an earlier version of this manuscript, one that helped us clarify our arguments in multiple ways.

A wide range of people consented to be interviewed for this project. We thank them for helping us understand banishment from varied perspectives. We express special thanks to those who are banished who shared their difficult experiences and thoughtful reflections.

Others provided us with other kinds of data or useful background information, including Bob Scales, Robert White, Keri-Anne Jetzer, Tricia Lapitan, and Lorri Cox.

Our colleagues at the University of Washington who provided bibliographic, intellectual, and other forms of moral support are too numerous to mention, but we do wish to single out Sarah Elwood, Angelina Godoy, Judy Howard, Michael McCann, Jamie Mayerfeld, Katharyne Mitchell, Matt Sparke, and Stewart Tolnay. We especially thank Katharyne Mitchell for encouraging us to keep the manuscript publicly oriented.

Colleagues at other institutions—University of California at Berkeley, University of Toronto, Vassar College, University of Oregon, University of British Columbia—invited us to present some of the story included here, and we thank them for their support and helpful feedback.

Michael Musheno, Nick Blomley, Daniel McCarthy, and three anonymous reviewers read full versions of the manuscript. Their suggestions improved the work notably. Michael Tonry's support for this project was sizable, welcome, and deeply appreciated. As ever, Joe Nevins stood firmly in our corner, a place we hope he never leaves.

Jesse and AnnaRose Beckett-Herbert tolerated the prolonged presence of this project in their parents' lives with their usual grace and humor. Though they did little to contribute directly to the work, their ability to make everyday life rich and compelling helped us stay grounded. Our appreciation and love for them are boundless.

Contents

Banished

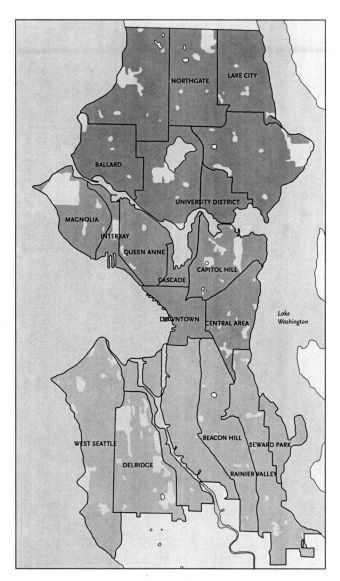

Seattle and its neighborhoods.

Introduction

Three Stories

One drizzly Seattle day, a young African American woman named Rhonda dropped off her boyfriend at a local community college. While he was in class, Rhonda went to find her mother. Frequently homeless, Rhonda's mother used drugs and suffered from poor health. Concerned, Rhonda regularly looked for her mother to try to ensure that her basic needs were met. She usually began her search downtown, near the corner of 2nd and Pike, an intersection known to host an outdoor drug market and thus attract significant police attention.

After reaching her destination, Rhonda approached a male acquaintance to ask if he had seen her mother recently. He had not. As she turned to continue her search, she told us:

> The police were comin' down the street, so I just kinda stood there lookin' around and they started approachin' on me and the gentleman....I had known the officer before, and he said that I was goin' to the jail for drug traffic loitering. He said, "Did you know where you're goin'?" and I'm like, "What?" And he goes, "You're goin' to jail." And he cuffed me. They arrested me and they took me to the precinct and strip searched me and took all my money and took me to jail.

The basis of Rhonda's arrest was Seattle's drug traffic loitering ordinance, adopted in 1990. The ordinance defines loitering with the intent to engage in illegal drug activity as a gross misdemeanor.[1] In addition to defining loitering with the intent to sell or procure drugs as a crime, the ordinance served as the vehicle for the introduction of another new social control technique, namely, Stay Out of Drug Area (SODA) orders. These orders are often imposed by judges as a condition of a sentence or deferred prosecution. They may also be issued by probation or community corrections officers as part of community supervision. SODA orders require recipients to stay out of specified neighborhoods that are defined as high-drug areas, maps of which are provided to recipients. SODA orders were modeled on already existing Stay Out of Areas of Prostitution (SOAP) orders, often imposed on those charged with prostitution-related offenses. To be under a SODA or SOAP order is to be banished from specified zones. Failure to comply with the exclusion order leaves one vulnerable to arrest.

Insisting on her innocence, Rhonda took her case to trial, where, she claimed, the officer testified, "He seen me talking to a fifty-year-old woman and it looked like I took somethin' from my mouth and gave it to her." On the basis of this testimony, and in the absence of any corroborating physical evidence, Rhonda was convicted of drug traffic loitering.[2] Her sentence included a requirement that she remain out of SODA Zone 1 for twenty-four months. SODA Zone 1 encompasses nearly all of downtown, including the area where her mother lived in her new apartment. As Rhonda explained: "I have to carry this [paper] around with me because if the officer stops me and I don't have it he could take me to jail. So I have to keep this paper with me all the time to show that where my zone is, it's a big zone. This is the, Zone 1—all this. I cannot go."

At the time of sentencing, Rhonda protested the imposition of the SODA order, primarily because it includes the area in which her ailing mother lives.

RHONDA   She lives now on 2nd Avenue and Stewart Street, and the judge, it was a big problem, because the judge was like, "No way. I don't care if that's your mother or not, there's no way. That's a drug area, that's around the area you got caught in, so we don't want you in there." I'm like, "That's my mom, I mean, either you're gonna have to just keep taking me to jail and give me SODA violations, because I'm not gonna stop seeing my mom. So he gave me an exception between 6 and 6. From 6 am to 6 pm I can only be at her house, and I can't leave her house. And I told him, "Well I have to catch the bus, I have to walk through that area." And he said,

"Well if you get caught and the officer wants to take you in, they're gonna take you in." I'm like, "What if I'm on my way to my mother's house?" and he said, "Well you better go there and straight back."

INTERVIEWER So how do you prove that that's what you're doing if they stop you?

RHONDA I dunno. I dunno.

Tom is a tall, sometimes homeless Native American man in his thirties. One unusually pleasant March evening, Tom sat with a group of friends enjoying the view across Puget Sound from Seattle's Victor Steinbrueck Park, a small grassy area adjacent to the tourist-friendly Pike Place Market. Several members of the group shared a bottle of spirits, a violation of a park rule that prohibits alcohol consumption. Two police officers approached and issued a parks exclusion order to all members of the group, despite their protestations that not all present were imbibing.

Tom's banishment was enabled by Seattle's parks exclusion ordinance, adopted after much controversy in 1997.[3] Prior to its adoption, individuals could only be removed from public parks if police officers possessed probable cause of a criminal offense that warranted arrest. More minor violations of park rules (such as littering, being present after hours, or possessing an open container of alcohol) resulted in a citation. The parks exclusion law authorized police officers and parks officials to immediately remove persons for committing crimes or minor infractions of park rules and to ban them from some or all public city parks for up to one year, depending on the type of violation and the number of prior violations. The legislation creating the exclusion orders defined them as civil in nature. Yet the violation of such an order is a misdemeanor criminal offense.

Tom's exclusion order stipulated that he could not return to Victor Steinbrueck Park for one week. Although he resented it, he signed the order and made an effort to comply. This was not easy, as many of his friends gathered in the park, and another friend brought meals for the group to share. In addition, the park offered important amenities, such as a public restroom and a waterfront view.

Before the week was out, Tom sought the company of his friends in the park. In an effort to comply with the exclusion order, he sat on a short ledge that surrounds the park's green space. He kept his body facing the street while maintaining contact with his friends. Before long, an officer approached and informed him that he was in violation of his exclusion order. Tom protested, arguing that he was outside the park boundary. He did not prevail in this dispute and was issued another parks exclusion notice that extended his banishment to ninety days and expanded it to include all downtown parks. He was incensed: "I mean, that was ridiculous. I was trying to comply and the asshole didn't even give me a chance to explain. I was on the wall! My feet were on the sidewalk! I was not in the park!"

Furious, Tom decided he would not comply with his second exclusion order and continued to visit city parks. Before long, he was excluded from all city parks for one year. This led to several arrests and many nights in jail. He was also, he told us, banned from using the metro bus system (for carrying alcohol in his backpack) and from the downtown public library (for sleeping).

At the time of our interview, Tom reported that he could no longer stay in Seattle and was preparing to head back to "the Rez" in his native Nebraska where, he reports, "There ain't nothin'":

> I mean, what can I do? I can't go anywhere. Just bein' anywhere I'm committing a crime. I can't even ride the bus to get somewhere else! I don't see how I can stay here. I mean, what will it be next? I'll be arrested for being here [in a coffee shop] talking to you? And this is supposed to be America, the land of the free and all that bullshit.

José is a Latino man in his late thirties. A native Texan, he struggles with bipolar disorder and alcohol addiction. Despite these challenges, for several years he was able to support himself with day jobs, most of them secured through a downtown social services agency, Casa Latina. Unfortunately for José, some of the men who stand outside Casa Latina sell drugs. This led to his trespass exclusion from Casa Latina:

> The guys [who sell crack] stand in front of Casa Latina in order to blend in. I'm standin' here because I'm lookin' for a job! And every once in a while the police will do a raid. I don't know where they got the cameras or how they're watching, but they're watching. They pull up in their cars, and then the bicycle cops come down the hill, and they come in, and they line everybody up along the fence. "Okay, IDs." I didn't have ID, blah blah. "Okay, you don't have any warrants, but what are you doing down here, are you selling dope?" And I said, "No, I'm only looking for work." "How come you're always talking to these guys? These guys are known crack dealers." I said, "Hey, man, you know, I'm socializing." I didn't have a crack pipe on me. I don't use

crack. So they don't arrest me. But they tell me, "Now you can't come
to Casa Latina anymore because you have a tendency to be out here
socializing with the crack dealers and we think you're selling crack."
But I never had any crack on me, no pipe, nothing. So now I can't go
over there to Casa Latina.

Jose's banishment was made possible by a creative new application
of trespass law. In Seattle and other municipalities, property owners are
encouraged to authorize law enforcement to determine who can be on
their property; they do so through contractual agreements that share their
trespass authority with the police. Some of these properties, such as malls
and historic districts, are normally open to the public. Officers are thereby
enabled to trespass admonish individuals who they believe lack legitimate
purpose for being on any property with such a contract. Other individuals,
such as transit police and private security officers, are also authorized to
issue trespass admonishments. If admonished, individuals must remain
off the property for a specified period of time, often a year, or risk arrest.[4]
In some cases, multiple properties are bound together in a single trespass
program; if one is admonished from one of the included properties, one is
forbidden from all. Notably, these trespass exclusions are defined as civil
in nature. In Seattle, officers are not required by the police department to
record the grounds for a trespass admonishment. The trespassed lack any
official means to contest their admonishment.

As a result of his trespass exclusion, Jose avoided Casa Latina and was
therefore unable to secure day jobs. He resorted to selling single bottles of beer
to those who could not afford a six-pack, and to making connections between
local drug dealers and young professionals who frequent downtown bars. This
occupational shift was quite unfortunate: it put Jose in serious jeopardy of
being arrested for drug delivery and triggered intense feelings of guilt and acts
of self-harm.

JOSÉ   I don't feel good when I hustle. It gives me a bad feeling.
Because I prefer to work for my money. When I'm out there hustling
people, it degrades me, okay. And, let me show you something [pulls
up sleeves and shows many scars on wrists]. I do this kind of shit
to punish myself. Okay, see right there? I took a piece of glass and I
stabbed myself.

INTERVIEWER   To punish yourself?

JOSÉ   To punish myself for the things that I do.

The Return of Banishment

Seattle is arguably one of the most progressive cities in the United States. Its political leaders are almost uniformly Democratic. It boasts one of the most robust efforts at forward-thinking environmental policies. It is home to several icons of the postindustrial economy, such as Microsoft, Amazon.com, Starbucks, and Costco. It sits in a region of stunning natural beauty. As James Fallows once wrote about the city, "If the climate were not so dark and rainy, everyone would want to live there."[5] Yet Seattle is not an urban utopia for everyone. As the stories of Rhonda, Tom, and Jose reveal, the city currently deploys a social control regime that lies in sharp contrast to its progressive image.[6]

At the core of this regime lie practices of banishment. Increasing swaths of urban space are delimited as zones of exclusion from which the undesirable are banned. The uniformed police are marshaled to enforce and often delineate these boundaries; they use their powers to monitor and arrest in an attempt to clear the streets of those considered unsightly or "disorderly."

Seattle is not alone in its deployment of social control tactics that entail banishment. In many other U.S. cities, exclusion orders that make mere presence in public space a crime are regularly imposed. Although it is not well known, New York City, Los Angeles, Portland, Las Vegas, Cincinnati, Honolulu, and many other municipalities employ one or more banishment strategies. These new legal tools are rarely debated publicly; they are largely deployed without much fanfare against individuals, such as the homeless, whose daily travails are not especially well chronicled. This lack of attention to banishment is unfortunate, because it is an increasingly consequential reality in the lives of many.

For example, public housing authorities across the United States regularly employ trespass enforcement to address concerns about crime and disorder. Specifically, newly created trespass programs permit authorities to trespass admonish unwanted individuals for extended periods of time. Such programs are in operation in New York City,[7] Boston,[8] Richmond (Virginia),[9] and many other cities.[10] Some public housing trespass programs ban those who have been arrested for or convicted of particular crimes from public housing buildings and grounds; this can even include residents. Other no-trespass policies ban nearly all nonresidents.[11]

The adoption of new trespass policies in New York City is increasingly controversial. New York state law explicitly prohibits trespassing in public housing and other locations. Yet prior to 1991, public housing was considered a public space; no one could be arrested for entering lobbies or public hallways in these buildings. In the early 1990s, however, the trespass statute was amended to give public housing authorities the same capacity to exclude unwanted members of the public that is enjoyed by owners of private dwellings.[12] Moreover, a recent executive order enables housing authorities and police officers to *permanently* exclude people from public housing property for a variety of reasons. Although the city's Operation Safe Housing program specifies that only those arrested for selling drugs on public housing property may be excluded indefinitely, others—including residents and their guests—may be excluded for significant periods of time as well.[13] This policy is enforced through vertical sweeps. Such sweeps are now also conducted in private buildings as a consequence of the Trespass Affidavit Program (TAP).[14] TAP allows building owners in private buildings to sign an affidavit that gives police permission to enter buildings and arrest individuals who are not tenants for trespassing. As a result, trespass arrests have skyrocketed in New York City.[15]

Off-limits orders are also increasingly popular. In numerous U.S. cities, including Cincinnati, Portland, and Fort Lauderdale, judges and correctional officers regularly require those convicted of certain offenses to stay out of particular sections of the city as a condition of their community supervision sentence.[16] In some cases, off-limits orders are imposed on defendants who are not convicted of a crime. In Portland, for example, orders to remain outside drug-free zones and prostitution-free zones may be imposed by police officers at the time of arrest or in lieu of arrest.[17]

Many U.S. cities now deploy other new social control tools that involve spatial exclusion and, like the innovations just described, fuse civil and criminal law. These include gang injunctions, juvenile curfews, and "no contact orders."[18] Civil gang injunctions, widely used by such California cities as Los Angeles, mobilize the civil power of the injunction to address what is typically thought of as a crime problem.[19] In these municipalities, prosecutors and other officials request that judges use injunctive power to prohibit alleged gang members from, among other things, being within a specified target area.[20] In many cases, judges comply with these requests. As is the case with trespass exclusions, a violation of these civil orders is a criminal offense.[21]

In short, cities across the United States increasingly employ novel social control mechanisms that entail spatial exclusion and fuse civil and criminal legal authority. Other cities of the global North deploy similar tactics.[22] In the United Kingdom, for example, new control measures are increasingly employed to reduce "antisocial" behavior and thereby enhance "security." In particular, Anti-Social Behavioral Contracts and Anti-Social Behavioral Orders cover a wide range of unwanted behaviors, fuse civil and criminal law, and often lead to the imposition of place-based restrictions.[23]

It thus appears that Seattle is on the leading edge of an emerging trend. It is therefore important to tell its story to enable an understanding and evaluation of strategies that are steadily becoming more common.

Analyzing Banishment's Return

Banishment is hardly new; imposing exile to encourage conformity dates back to ancient times. Banishment was featured extensively in the Old Testament and was employed in ancient Babylon, Greece, and Rome, as well as by British authorities throughout the colonial empire.[24] In the new republic of the United States, banishment was thought by many to be repulsive but was nonetheless practiced widely. When miscreants proved troublesome, many towns forced them away.

As a result of this history, today banishment is considered an archaic and even primitive form of punishment by many scholars and legal experts.[25] Although the appeal of banishment to people living thousands of years ago and lacking alternative mechanisms for dealing with disruptive behavior makes retrospective sense, most countries now prohibit the banishment of their citizens.[26] In the United States, too, most states disallow interstate banishment. As one legal scholar noted, banishment "would seem more appropriate to *Romeo and Juliet* or *Great Expectations* than to the solution of problems in a modern society."[27]

Nonetheless, the new legal tools we analyze here entail banishment: the legal compulsion to leave specified geographic areas for extended periods of time. Banishment's return raises a number of questions. Why is it reemerging with such blunt force in Seattle and many other cities of the global North? How is it justified? How is it practiced? Who are its targets? How are they targeted? What does it mean for them to be banished? What does its practice suggest about Seattle as a city? What does it reveal about the contemporary politics of public space and democratic inclusion? Can banishment be justified, or should it be rejected as a solution to urban social problems? Our task in this book is to address these questions by chronicling and assessing the return of banishment in one of America's iconic cities.

Of course, some might object to our use of the term *banishment*. After all, to be banished historically meant to be excluded from a town, county, state, or country. In the common law tradition, banishment is defined as "a punishment inflicted upon criminals, by compelling them to quit a city, place or country for a specified period of time."[28] Understood this way, banishment is rarely allowed. Courts now prohibit interstate banishment, and only five states permit intrastate banishment, that is, the legal expulsion of a citizen from a town or county.[29]

Furthermore, courts generally do not consider expulsion from a neighborhood or area within a city to constitute banishment.[30]

Given this, our use of *banishment* to describe the exclusion of persons from relatively small geographic areas requires some explanation. It is certainly the case that some of the spaces from which people are banned in Seattle are small in scale—city parks from which expulsions spring can be minuscule, as are some private businesses from which one may be trespassed. It is thus perhaps better to use the term *exclusion* to describe the practices we evaluate.

We prefer to use the term *banishment* for four reasons. First, we want to underscore the strong role of the coercive power of the state in accomplishing this form of spatial segregation.[31] The word *exclusion* often describes more informal practices, such as ostracism from a peer group. Banishment, by contrast, provides a stronger implication of overt state policy, as a policy emerging by dint of "official decree."

This leads to a second motivation behind our use of *banishment*. Banishment is a punishment, meted out to those condemned as deviant or criminal. The practices that entail banishment rest on the assumption that the social problems to which they are frequently a response—homelessness, addiction, mental illness—may be understood and treated as criminal problems. This is true even to the extent that banishment results from the application of civil rather than criminal law. For reasons we explore later, basing expulsion in civil law only enhances the scope and authority of criminal law and does not alter the fact that these exclusions compel their targets to "quit" a place or risk arrest and incarceration.

Indeed, the deployment of the new control tools—touted by proponents as alternatives to arrest and punishment—has a "net-widening" effect: it creates crimes and criminal cases that would not otherwise exist. Taken together, these techniques represent a dramatic extension of the state's authority and surveillance capacity throughout the urban landscape. The punitive city of twenty-first-century America is one in which an increasing number of acts are regulated and criminalized; the state's ability to search, detain, regulate, and monitor is expanded; and a system of invisible yet highly consequential gates and barriers increasingly constrains the movement of some urbanites in public space.[32]

Third, we believe the term best describes what the ostracized say they experience. Historically, banishment imposed social separation and deprived the exiled of the rights that accompany membership in a political community. Similarly, those who experience banishment in Seattle describe their social and spatial marginalization in sharp terms, not just as a complication in their everyday lives but an expulsion from the body politic. They understand themselves to be cast aside and punished daily for their transgressions, no matter how minor. They also report that their rights as citizens and community members are severely weakened as a result of their banishment, and their exclusion order serves as a kind of "master status"[33] that govern their interactions with authorities. As Bauman writes,

> Estrangement is the core function of spatial separation. Estrangement reduces, thins down, and compresses the view of the other; individual qualities and circumstances which tend to be vividly brought within sight thanks to the accumulated experience of daily intercourse, seldom come into view when the intercourse is emaciated or prohibited altogether.[34]

Fourth, through the use of the term *banishment*, we wish to highlight the extent to which the zoning logic is expansionary. Although any given zone of exclusion may be small, some zones are not, and the cumulative effect of creating multiple exclusion zones is to render much of the city a "no go" area for many residents. Those who are homeless or otherwise considered disreputable are quite likely to be the subject of numerous exclusionary bans, to the point where their mobility through the city is severely limited.

Granted, people today are not banned from extensive areas as in the past. We are nevertheless compelled to use the term *banishment* to describe the consequence of the legal tools we analyze. These exclusionary practices rest on the coercive capacity of the state, create crimes and punishments that would not otherwise exist, and deprive their targets of political rights. Moreover, the spaces from which people are banished are growing. Although it may look different from previous iterations, banishment is indisputably back.

Reconstituting Police Power

Banishment is not the only archaic legal practice now back in operation. Throughout the nineteenth century, the police were engaged in ambitious projects aimed at "moral regulation" in cities across the country.[35] Historically, the police were able to target attention to presumptively disreputable people through invocation of vagrancy laws. For hundreds of years, vagrancy and loitering laws in the United Kingdom and United States made it a crime to wander without destination or visible means of support.[36] A number of events shaped the emergence and implementation of these laws, including the enclosure movement, the dissolution of monasteries, and the shift toward industrialized production and associated migratory processes.[37] Early vagrancy legislation sought to control a new kind of poverty—that experienced by "masterless men."[38]

Similarly, vagrancy laws were used by Southern authorities in the United States to control the black population and prevent the collapse of the sharecropping system following the abolition of slavery. Mississippi's Black Code, for example, defined vagrants as "runaways, drunkards, pilferers; lewd, wanton, or lascivious persons...those who neglect their employment, misspend their earnings, and fail to support their families; and...all other idle and disorderly persons."[39] Under the Black Codes, those without work contracts were obligated to hire themselves out to employers. Those who violated their contracts were then prosecuted as vagrants and sentenced to hard labor.[40]

Vagrancy laws were also an important weapon in urban battles against immorality and disorder.[41] As adapted and implemented in the United States, these laws reflected deeply held concerns about idleness; they primarily penalized those who did not appear to work. A 1901 news story published in the *Seattle Times* describes what appears to be a typical example of the use of Seattle's vagrancy law: "In the early morning hours of January 4, 1901, the Seattle Police arrested for vagrancy 28 suspicious characters considered by police to be a menace to the peace and safety of the citizens in the Tenderloin district." Despite the many derisive assertions cast on their character, those arrested were charged with no crime other than vagrancy.[42] The "professional hobos" arrested in this raid were given a choice of leaving town or serving time in the city jail and working on roads in the chain gang. Indeed, those arrested for vagrancy were often given the option of leaving town in lieu of jail time, a modified version of granting pardon to those willing to submit to banishment.[43] Civil nuisance abatement statutes were used in conjunction with vagrancy law to eradicate red-light districts in many cities.[44]

Vagrancy laws were quite broad and were therefore used toward other ends as well. For example, these laws were employed to suppress labor organizing efforts and manage workers in the first half of the twentieth century. In particular, labor organizers and harvest workers in the Northern plains faced arrest for vagrancy during the Depression.[45] Later, Southern authorities used these laws to police civil rights protest and protesters.[46] Vagrancy and related laws thus helped punish and regulate vice and maintain race, power, and property relations.

These laws came under disabling scrutiny in the 1960s and 1970s as part of the U.S. courts' short-lived "rights revolution." In a series of well-known decisions, the courts ruled that the vagueness and breadth of the vagrancy and loitering statutes enabled unjustifiable police discretion. For example, in one key Supreme Court case, *Papachristou v. City of Jacksonville*, a unanimous court ruled that a Florida loitering law "Furnishes a convenient tool for harsh and discriminatory enforcement by displeasure. It results in a regime in which the poor and unpopular are permitted to stand on a public sidewalk only at the whim of any police officer."[47] The vagueness of vagrancy and loitering laws, in other words, granted the street officer too much discretion in deciding whom to arrest.

Unsatisfied with this restriction on police power, many cities in the 1990s began to pass civility codes. Like the vagrancy laws, these ordinances criminalize behaviors deemed disorderly and are used to deal with nuisances rather than serious crime. Unlike vagrancy laws, however, these criminal laws proscribe specific behaviors (e.g., sitting) rather than status (being transient or homeless).[48] The most widely adopted civility laws made it a crime to sit or lie on sidewalks or in bus shelters, sleep in parks and other public spaces, place one's personal possessions on public property for more than a short period of time, drink alcohol in public, engage in public elimination, sell newspapers and other written materials in public spaces, and panhandle aggressively.

Because these laws criminalized many common behaviors (such as sleeping, lying down, sitting, and urinating) when those behaviors occur outdoors, the homeless and unstably housed bore the brunt of the codes. Indeed, the homeless make up a significant share of the court and jail populations. Nationally, roughly one of six jail inmates was homeless for at least some portion of the previous year. Jail inmates are seven to eleven times more likely than members of the general U.S. adult population to experience homelessness in a given year.[49] In Seattle and other cities, those moving through the municipal courts are even more likely to be homeless.[50] More broadly, these laws provide the police with an important set of order maintenance tools; police can now make stops and conduct searches they could not otherwise legally accomplish.[51]

Despite their significance, the behavioral specificity of the civility laws meant that they did not re-create the broad police discretion afforded by vagrancy and loitering laws. They were, moreover, subject to sometimes successful legal challenges. In light of these limitations, many cities developed an even more potent arsenal of legal tools. These new tools merge civil and criminal authority to enable banishment. They are also so sufficiently broad and flexible that they expand police discretion and authority. Even if vagrancy laws remain unconstitutional, the new legal tools that entail banishment function as their twenty-first-century replacement.

Placeless in Seattle

We seek here to document and analyze the rise of banishment in one American city. We focus on Seattle for two reasons. One is that it is our home, and therefore the city we know best. We are better positioned to tell its story than that of any other city. Second, and more important, Seattle is one of the pioneering cities in the use of banishment as a social control strategy. In focusing on this particular case, we seek to explain and assess what we consider to be a historically significant development, one that may be particularly mature in Seattle but is certainly not limited to it. Even if all of the particulars of the Seattle case are not present in other cities, it remains instructive to tell its story. The broad forces that compel banishment are undoubtedly at play in other places, and the consequences of its use are likely to be broadly similar. Although additional research in other locales would undoubtedly be instructive, the critical scrutiny we direct at the Seattle case illuminates important patterns and contradictions.

We focus on three mechanisms by which spatial exclusion is imposed, all of which are routinely deployed in Seattle: (1) off-limits orders, as detailed in Rhonda's story; (2) parks exclusion laws, the basis of Tom's arrest; and (3) new applications of trespass law, such as those experienced by José.[52] The adoption of these techniques, we argue, signals the return of banishment as a leading urban social control strategy: they exclude those deemed disorderly from particular urban spaces for significant periods of time.

These legal innovations are more far-reaching than the civility laws they increasingly supplant, for several reasons. First, as noted, the new social control practices entail banishment: they bar certain people from specified places from weeks, months, and even years. Second, the new techniques combine elements of criminal and civil law in ways that work to expand the authority of the criminal law. Indeed, the infusion of criminal law with other sources of legal authority does not undermine the logic of criminalization. Instead, it enhances the power of police and prosecutors to address behaviors and situations that do not otherwise constitute crimes. This includes mere presence in particular urban spaces. Some of these techniques can be so broadly employed that they essentially criminalize status for some urban residents; individuals may be targeted for how they look and what they symbolize rather than specific behaviors. Moreover, the legal hybridity of these techniques diminishes the rights-bearing capacity of their targets, further enhancing police and prosecutorial power. Finally, zones of exclusion tend to expand over time. When a zone of exclusion is established in one area, those in adjacent areas often follow suit, seeking to ward off the displacement of undesirables into their backyards.[53]

Together, these characteristics mean that many of those who spend time in public spaces are barred from an increasing number of urban places, many of which are normally open to the public. As a result, they encounter an often dizzying array of invisible legal barriers that impede their mobility. Moreover, for the banished, mere presence in increasingly large urban spaces may lead to arrest and (re)incarceration. In these ways, the new tools work as a functional replacement for traditional loitering and vagrancy laws.

Overview of the Book

We use this book to argue for greater recognition of banishment as an emerging and consequential social control practice. We draw on a range of data to chart the rise, implementation, and consequences of banishment in Seattle. In the process, we hope to substantiate four principal arguments.

The first is that banishment is indeed back; it is a practice of social control on which municipal governments increasingly rely. Although we focus on Seattle, similar techniques are now used in many U.S. cities and in a range of international settings, particularly the United Kingdom and Germany. Given this increased popularity, banishment deserves close attention in terms of both its structure and its implications.

Second, we suggest that the reemergence of banishment is explicable in sociohistorical terms and is in some ways a logical extension of trends established in many American cities beginning in the early 1980s. Rising inequality and the decline of affordable housing, due in part to rising land values spurred by gentrification, helped drive an increase in homelessness. At the same time, the broken windows theory—which posits that disorder fuels long-term crime—became enormously popular. These dynamics, in conjunction with the courts' invalidation of the vagrancy and loitering laws, propelled the implementation of both the civility codes and the newer legal tools that enable the banning of unwanted and disorderly urban residents.

Third, we demonstrate that banishment is consequential, even more so than the civility codes that they increasingly supplant.[54] Not only do these new tools enable banishment, they provide the police greater license to question and to arrest those who occupy public space. They place increased burdens on the courts and jails to accommodate those who are arrested. They make everyday life more onerous for the banished. More generally, the infusion of criminal law with civil legal authority works to expand the scope and power of the criminal justice system and reduce the rights that historically accompanied accusations of criminal wrongdoing. In this way, the citizenship status of the banished is quite significantly eroded. For this reason, the use of banishment strikes a discordant note in polities that are premised on democratic inclusiveness.

Finally, we suggest that banishment as policy is futile and counterproductive. Although its use serves many short-term interests—including those of police, prosecutors, and private capital—it is nonetheless a policy failure. Its futility lies in the reality that many of those pressured to relocate are hard-pressed to do so. They are deeply attached to the places from which they are banned, for multiple reasons. As a result, many do not comply with their exclusion orders, even though resistance enhances their vulnerability to criminal sanctions. Banishment is also counterproductive because it imperils efforts by the socially marginal to integrate with mainstream society. Their access to affordable housing, social services, and job opportunities are often compromised by their spatial limitations. Furthermore, banishment does nothing to resolve any of the underlying conditions that generate social marginality, such as poor employment prospects, inadequate affordable housing, or the challenges of addiction. To the extent that cities increasingly rely on banishment as a putative solution to disorder, they will succeed only in displacing some individuals from one location to another and in rendering the lives of the disorderly more difficult. Its increased use therefore deserves to be questioned and significantly curtailed.

To articulate and substantiate these arguments, we move through six chapters, each of which addresses a basic question about banishment. In chapter 1, we ask: Why did banishment reemerge as a leading social control strategy? We identify several developments that contributed to its rise. Some increased the population of the homeless and, consequently, public concern about disorder. These dynamics include the transformation of urban economies under global neoliberalism; the assault on the already weak welfare state, including diminished spending on low-income housing; the deinstitutionalization of the mentally ill (and the failure to ensure a viable alternatives for shelter and care); and the acceleration of gentrification. On the ground, these dynamics, combined with local planning and policy decisions, often worked to concentrate geographically the service-dependent in otherwise valuable and often gentrifying urban areas. These dynamics in turn generated significant political pressure on the police to "do something" about urban disorder.

At the same time, the rhetoric and imagery associated with broken windows policing undermined the notion that urban public space should facilitate encounters with difference. Instead, public places were increasingly defined as the conduit for the free circulation of goods, consumers, and workers.[55] Legal developments reinforced this cultural logic. The invalidation of vagrancy and loitering laws deprived cities of traditional social control tools precisely when homelessness increased and the service-dependent became ever more concentrated near urban centers. As the perceived need to crack down on disorder intensified, many city leaders began to search for alternative social control mechanisms. Civility codes were the first resort; banishment is its more muscular successor. These social control tools increase the power of the police to restore order to the urban landscape in a way that that, proponents hope, will pass constitutional muster.

In chapter 2, we ask: How did the social control practices that entail banishment emerge out of key legal and political dynamics? We suggest that banishment emerged in response to the Supreme Court's invalidation of traditional vagrancy and loitering laws and enabled a significant extension of the legal logic that underwrites the civility codes. Drawing on archival materials and interview data, we outline the legal evolution of the techniques that entail banishment. We then suggest that these techniques possess three distinguishing and consequential characteristics. First, they are resolutely territorial: they attempt to remove perceived disorder from particular geographic locations. Although the police have long acted as territorial agents,[56] displacement via banishment increasingly trumps rehabilitative and even punitive aspirations as a matter of policy. Second, by combining elements of criminal and civil law, the new social control tools enhance police and prosecutorial power and provide few (if any) avenues for contestation. Because the rhetoric surrounding the new tools typically invokes issues of neighborhood security, it often obscures how banishment diminishes the rights of many urban residents. Finally, by defining mere presence in certain urban spaces as a crime, the new tools broaden the range of behaviors that can lead to criminal justice intervention. In this sense, the new social control practices go beyond the civility laws and restore to the police the broad discretion historically bestowed by traditional vagrancy and loitering laws. Not surprisingly, these exclusions contribute substantially to the overcrowding of the courts and jails.

We use chapter 3 to ask: How, where, and against whom is banishment practiced? Here, we draw on police records and other data sources to identify central patterns. One such pattern, not surprisingly, is the predominant use of banishment to regulate the socially marginal—the banished are disproportionately homeless and people of color. Second, banishment is geographically concentrated in particular locales, especially in highly contested downtown spaces where poverty and gentrification are pronounced. The data further show that social exclusion is used to respond to people that are better understood as nuisances—drunks, the mentally ill, the aesthetically displeasing—rather than as serious criminal actors. In short, we provide empirical evidence that banishment is imposed on some of the most disadvantaged urban residents, particularly those living in contested downtown neighborhoods.

The central question in chapter 4: Why does banishment continue to grow in popularity, in terms of its use and spatial extent? We provide evidence of growth in both the use of banishment and in the spatial extent of zones of exclusion. We highlight several factors that help explain this spread in the use of exclusion. First, we describe various sources of political pressure on police and prosecutors to respond to concerns about crime and disorder. We draw on interviews and observations to explain why banishment is an attractive tool for police officers and correctional officers—it significantly increases their power to monitor, arrest, and search those who spend considerable time in public space. It is also attractive to prosecutors, who can add banishment orders as conditions of deferred prosecutions or as components of plea agreements. Defense attorneys, by contrast, find themselves with limited options in contesting the increasing popularity of banishment measures. It is therefore unsurprising that court records indicate that banishment contributes significantly to the ongoing expansion of the court, jail, and probation populations.

The evidence in chapter 4 demonstrates how the expanding use of the new tools contributes in important ways to the growth and overcrowding of the criminal justice system, even in an era of declining crime rates. This growth in turn triggers the quest for new institutions and technologies aimed at both helping and monitoring the expanding criminal justice population. Yet the help offered by criminal justice institutions is often accompanied by heightened surveillance and regulation. Thus, even as Seattle, like many other cities, develops "therapeutic" courts to address underlying social problems, the expansionary logic of banishment means that more people enter the criminal justice system due to their failure to comply with a growing number of spatial restrictions. Therapeutic courts and other progressive innovations thus appear to be largely unsuccessful in extricating people from an increasingly capacious criminal justice net.

In chapter 5 we ask: How does banishment impact the banished? To answer this question, we draw largely on data derived from interviews of those who find themselves banished from much of Seattle. We explore whether and how people alter their patterns in response to banishment, how their exclusions and restrictions affect their lives, and how they understand the use of social control techniques aimed at regulating their mobility. Although a few of our respondents found compliance with their bans to be insignificant or even beneficial, the majority experienced their exclusions as a consequential and counterproductive burden.

Some of those we interviewed did alter their spatial patterns to comply with an exclusion or off-limits order. Yet they paid a price for doing so. For example, those excluded from particular parks for sleeping after hours were pushed to locations where they felt more isolated and unsafe. Even more dramatically, some respondents reported diminished access to work or training programs, family members, community support networks, public transportation, and drug treatment programs or other social services. In these cases, respondents reported that the effect of the ban was not at all therapeutic but quite destructive physically, financially, socially, and psychologically.

Others we interviewed choose not to comply with their legally imposed spatial restriction(s). Many in this category live in the area from which they are banned. For these individuals, complying with the ban seems impossible, or at least far too costly. Their resistance also imposes significant costs. In particular, those who refuse banishment describe living in constant fear of detection. Many are unable to extricate themselves from the criminal justice system because they resist their banishment orders. Their refusal to be exiled, we suggest, reveals a mismatch between official understandings of problem areas and how the banished experience those same places. Officials tend to imagine these neighborhoods almost exclusively in terms of the degree to which they house and tempt the deviant. The banished, on the other hand, offer rich accounts of the historical and symbolic significance of those same areas, as well as the importance of the social networks and services they contain. For them, to be banished from these places only increases their social marginality; it is not a therapeutic measure but a strictly punitive one.

This finding prompts chapter 6, where we ask: Should we banish? Our analysis leads us to conclude that banishment works primarily to expand the criminal justice system and diminish both the life circumstances and rights-bearing capacity of those who are targeted. We see little evidence that these techniques reduce the individual and collective harm associated with homelessness, addiction, outdoor drug sales, unregulated prostitution, and inadequately treated mental illness. Worse, we find evidence that these measures intensify the pain and harm associated with these social problems. We also find that the new techniques are sometimes used to limit the mobility and rights of those whose principal offense consists of being poor and/or of color. As Leonard Feldman argues, the denial of citizenship rights to the homeless and other socially marginal urban residents both reflects and perpetuates their economic and cultural "misrecognition."[57] Although the new tools enhance state power and therefore serve the interests of the police and prosecutors, they nonetheless represent a policy failure.

We use chapter 6 to explore alternatives to banishment. We emphasize the need to reduce the social and economic inequality that underlies the current urban crisis. Other alternatives include investment in various types of low-income housing; job creation programs that include people with criminal records; comprehensive medical care, including mental health care and addiction treatment; the decriminalization of addiction; and harm reduction innovations, such as safe injection sites.

It is, of course, an open question whether any of these alternatives can acquire enough political traction to overcome the urge to exclude. The term *disorder* is symbolically powerful and not easily contested. As long as those who occupy public space are primarily defined in these terms, it is difficult to envision them as full-standing members of the body politic. Yet to be homeless or to otherwise appear disorderly should not mean that one loses basic rights. Furthermore, a compassionate society will take the meeting of basic needs as a core collective responsibility. Banishment represents an erosion of rights and a turn away from societal care for the needy. As we urge that banishment be reconsidered, we simultaneously urge a vision of political life that is more inclusive and hopeful, rather than exclusionary and punitive.

Throughout the book, we substantiate our arguments with reliance on a wealth of diverse data. These include ethnographic observations of police and Department of Corrections patrols; interviews with judges, lawyers, social service providers, police officers, private security officers, anticrime activists, and the banished themselves; police and court records; and a wide range of legal and archival materials. These data were collected and analyzed from 2005 through 2007. We use secondary data sources to situate our case study in the larger national context. As a consequence, we tell a contemporary story about the practice of banishment in a paradigmatic postindustrial city.

Our principal aim with this book is to draw widespread attention to the practice and consequences of banishment. In our attempt to reach a broad audience, we minimize discussion of more theoretical and methodological matters in the text. The conceptual underpinnings of our analysis are reviewed primarily in the notes. Interested readers should direct their attention there.[58]

Conclusion

It is clear that many urban residents possess real concern about street-level dynamics: they wish to traverse their daily paths with minimal fear and disruption, and many simply do not wish to see those who appear disorderly or who otherwise inspire trepidation.[59] Nor is it pleasant to be reminded of the deprivations associated with homelessness, severe poverty, addiction, or mental illness. Of course, this reaction is not a cultural universal. In some times and places, the nomadic tend to be romanticized rather than feared.[60] Strongly negative portrayals in political and media discourse, however, appear to have shaped reactions to persons who appear to be homeless.[61] Indeed, there is evidence that persons perceived as homeless or addicted are, in the contemporary United States, most likely to elicit disgust.[62] This collective aversion underwrites the new social control regimes on display in Seattle and elsewhere.

Banishment represents a quick fix to this widespread fear. It is, at root, an attempt to use the criminal justice system to solve a set of entrenched social problems. It renders the territorial authority of the police remarkably robust and largely free from challenge. As a consequence, those who are unwanted— which includes those who merely offend our aesthetic sensibilities—feel continually harassed and unwelcome. The moral division between the respectable and not-so-respectable is reinforced daily by a spatial division between the included and excluded.

Banishment is a short-sighted and ultimately counterproductive practice. It is, to borrow a phrase from Peter Andreas, a "politically successful policy failure."[63] Because it fails to address the underlying issues that generate social marginality, it does not make more secure those urban residents who live and work alongside the "disorderly." Rather, it increases the degree of social marginality experienced by the downtrodden; it makes their daily struggle for existence more treacherous, their path to the mainstream more arduous. Even if banishment provides a means by which the state can appear to be acting aggressively to clean up certain urban areas, it only exacerbates the conditions that generate social disadvantage in the first place.

All that said, we recognize that many urban social problems often cause real harm to those who live and work in shared spaces. Indeed, we wish to underscore this point: it is absolutely the case that addiction, unregulated prostitution, untreated mental illness, and homelessness diminish the health, safety, and well-being of many urban denizens. Yet these problems can be ameliorated, and the harms associated with them minimized, by effective social policy that does not entail reliance on the criminal justice system to generate either mass incarceration or banishment. What follows is an assessment of the effects, both intended and unintended, of employing banishment as a policy response to the problems of social and spatial marginalization.

1

Banishment's Reemergence

The practice of marking and enforcing a boundary between the respectable and the unrespectable is hardly a novel phenomenon. Social divisions like these are universal, and they are frequently reinforced through spatial barriers. From this historical perspective, the dynamics of banishment we analyze in Seattle are nothing new. They are yet another manifestation of age-old processes of inequality.

Yet one can still ask why banishment is currently reemerging in Seattle and other cities of the global North. In the not-so-distant past, Seattle—like many other U.S. cities—accommodated a large population of transient residents. Many of them lived in one of numerous single resident occupant hotels that were concentrated downtown, especially in the southern section in and around the Pioneer Square neighborhood.[1] As the original "skid row," the Pioneer Square neighborhood in particular possessed a reputation as a red-light district, a place where various forms of vice were sometimes tolerated. Even if "respectable" Seattle turned up its nose at skid row, there was grudging tolerance of its presence.[2] To be sure, chronic alcoholics and others who occupied public space frequently found themselves the subject of police attention. Laws prohibiting vagrancy, loitering, and public drunkenness authorized the police to intervene in such cases. As a result, skid row residents experienced many short-term jail stays.[3] The police possessed ample power to monitor vice-prone areas and sweep them of undesirables when either officers or their political superiors deemed it necessary.

However, the Supreme Court's invalidation of vagrancy and loitering laws in the 1960s and 1970s undermined the capacity of cities to use the police to respond to this kind of urban disorder. More broadly, these cases signaled a growing recognition of the ways in which the broad discretion afforded by the vagrancy laws could be misused. Even as police power diminished and the rights of the socially marginal were given greater recognition by the courts, various economic and political dynamics intensified pressure to clean up places like Pioneer Square. These forces combined to allocate to the criminal justice system the responsibility of dealing with the consequences of growing inequality, most notably the presence of visible homeless people. Continually pressed to clear the streets of undesirables, state agents responded in a fashion that led to embracing banishment.

We use this chapter to outline these dynamics and explain how they facilitated banishment's reemergence. Critical here was the rise of homelessness and the consequent clustering of disorderly people, primarily downtown. This increase in visible disorder was no accident but a result of economic shifts and government policies that reduced jobs, wages, and affordable housing.

Of course, the homeless are not the only populations targeted by banishment, but their increased visibility coincided precisely with growing concern with disorder. One particularly important manifestation of this concern was the ascendance of the broken windows philosophy. This theory of crime suggests that more serious criminals will eventually invade neighborhoods that tolerate the presence of disreputable individuals. According to the theory, police need increased tools to crack down on public behaviors that are perceived as disorderly. These behaviors are common to the homeless, who lack access to private space. The civility codes legitimated by the broken windows philosophy criminalized such behaviors as sitting or lying on a sidewalk, engaging in aggressive panhandling, or sleeping in parks. One of the leaders in implementing such codes, Seattle is now in the forefront of the embrace of banishment. Understanding how banishment emerged requires understanding how certain people and behaviors were framed as manifestations of disorder and then criminalized.

Manifestations of inequality, such as the visible homeless, are often discomfiting. It is thus understandable why the impulse to clear the streets is so frequently voiced. Yet the embrace of such a short-term solution fails to reckon with the larger structural dynamics that generate inequality in the first place. Any meaningful understanding of contemporary urban environments requires a consideration of the various processes through which poverty intensified in recent years. Even though our focus here is on Seattle, it is important to remember that the processes discussed are translocal in their origin and impacts. For this reason, it is perhaps unsurprising that other cities possess growing populations of the extremely poor, and they increasingly mimic Seattle in enacting banishment.

Homelessness and Concern about Disorder

> Punitive policies employ the false premise that if you hit a homeless person hard enough, or issue a big enough fine and then jail them when they don't have the money to pay, then that person will stop wanting to be poor and will stop having nowhere to sleep. The fallacy of this premise is that while the person may leave that park, doorway, neighborhood, or town, they will still be poor and homeless.[4]

As the Western Regional Advocacy Project notes, it is common to see homelessness as an individual choice. To use the criminal law to try and clean up the streets of a city like Seattle is to reinforce this individualistic logic. The threat of a fine or a jail stay is meant to deter individuals from sleeping on sidewalks or gathering in parks late at night. Criminal sanctions can thereby ostensibly serve as a hammer to prod individuals to make better choices.

Yet historical trends belie this emphasis on individual choice. The number of people without consistent shelter rose dramatically beginning in the early 1980s. Indeed, the rate of homelessness—measured per 100,000 members of the population—rose from 5 to 15 percent in the 142 largest U.S. cities from 1981 to 1989.[5] At present, up to 3.5 million Americans experience extended periods of homelessness each year.[6] More than 7 percent of persons living in the United States have been homeless (defined as sleeping in shelters, the street, abandoned buildings, cars, or bus and train stations) at some point in their lives.[7] About half of those who are homeless are members of families with children; this is the fastest-growing segment of the homeless population.[8] As with other ostracized populations, the homeless are disproportionately people of color.[9] In Seattle, for instance, African Americans constitute barely 8 percent of the population, but 35 percent of those found in homeless shelters.[10]

It is hard to fathom that such a large number of individuals in the early 1980s began choosing to eschew mainstream society and take to the streets. It seems rather more plausible that structural dynamics generated the sudden increase in visible homelessness. Although an exhaustive explanation of homelessness is not our goal, we do wish to make plain that the people who spend considerable time in public space—and in the process generate widespread ire—are not there simply as a matter of personal choice. As a result, policies like banishment that presume to change individual choices will fail to generate long-term benefits. For this and other reasons, it is misguided to rely heavily on the criminal justice system to address a social problem such as homelessness.

Explaining the Rise in Homelessness

No single factor accounts for the dramatic increase in homelessness that began in the 1980s and persists into the contemporary period. It is instead best explained as a consequence of several related dynamics, all of which combined to make housing beyond the reach of far too many people, especially those who live in cities. According to the National Low Income Housing Coalition, at least a third of those who live in central cities face an affordable housing problem.[11] Part of this is due to stagnant wages, increased joblessness, and associated poverty; part to shifts in housing markets fueled significantly by gentrification; and part to the withdrawal of government funding for housing and other forms of social support.

Joblessness, Poverty, and the Lack of Affordable Housing

The rise of homelessness is inextricably connected to certain economic transformations, most notably the shift to a postindustrial economy.[12] As the manufacturing sector declined in the United States, so did the factory jobs that once provided a reasonably comfortable existence for low-skilled workers. Service jobs became more prominent, but these were bifurcated. Those who worked largely with information—in the finance and high-tech sectors, for example— drew hefty salaries, whereas those who worked in the lower rungs of the service sector—in retail or restaurants—labored for minimum wages. In the 1980s, more than three-quarters of new jobs paid the minimum wage.[13] This wage level typically fails to generate sufficient income to escape poverty.[14]

This dynamic generated the "great U-turn" in the American income structure: the numbers at the higher and lower ends of the income spectrum grew, and the middle class declined.[15] It is thus not too surprising to learn that income inequality in the United States is now significantly greater than in other Western developed countries, and this fuels the emergence of homelessness on a large scale.[16] As Wolch and Dear put it: "Reduced to its essentials, homelessness is an expression and extension of poverty in the United States. Simply stated, personal income has declined to such an extent that people can no longer afford to purchase or rent a home."[17] Consistent with this argument is Martha Burt's discovery that a city's poverty rate was the strongest predictor of its rate of homelessness.[18] Like many cities, Seattle experienced a significant growth in income inequality in the 1980s and 1990s.[19]

As joblessness and reduced earnings increased inequality, changes in the housing market made acquiring inexpensive shelter more difficult. A key dynamic in many urban housing markets was the rise of gentrification. In this process, older, deteriorating city neighborhoods witnessed infusions of capital for remodeling and thereby attracted young professionals as residents.[20] Multiple factors drove the move toward gentrification: the enforcement of growth limits that reduced suburban home availability, the desire of urban professionals to avoid growing commutes by living close to their downtown producer-service workplaces, and the opportunity to generate significant home equity by sharply increasing the value of previously declining properties.

Gentrification often works to deplete the stock of affordable housing. Single resident only (SRO) hotels are an important example of this. Indeed, the loss of SROs decreased the stock of inexpensive housing by about one million units in urban America between 1970 and 1982.[21] Often, they were replaced by apartments or condominiums that typically lay beyond the means of the urban poor. This process generated a shortfall of affordable housing that persists today. As the Joint Center for Housing Studies at Harvard University notes, there is a substantial undersupply of rental dwellings available for low-income households, even those willing to devote a large fraction of income to rent.[22]

Seattle, for example, lost about half of its SROs between 1970 and 1985.[23] This represented a loss of more than 15,000 units of low-income housing. Such a drastic decline, not surprisingly, had significant consequences for the downtrodden population downtown. As Thrush explains, "As the hotels closed, the people who remained downtown tended to be poorer, sicker, more often homeless and unemployed, and less likely to be white."[24] Given the loss of SRO rooms and the continuation of gentrification,[25] the availability of low-income housing in Seattle continues to decline, despite the city government's stated desire to preserve it. At the dawn of the twenty-first century, there were almost certainly fewer than 6,000 units of low-income housing in downtown Seattle, nearly 2,000 fewer than existed in 1985.[26] Moreover, as rental housing was replaced by with condos, median house values and rents rose far more rapidly than median family income.[27]

As a result of declining jobs, wages, and affordable housing, visible homelessness increased. To be sure, emergency shelters arose to help keep people off the streets. As significant as these are, they do not represent a comprehensive solution to the need for housing for several reasons. First, there are almost never sufficient shelter beds. The most recent one-night count of homeless people in Seattle—an annual effort to canvas the city to determine the number of people who lack shelter—found 7,839 people without permanent shelter. Of these, 2,139 spent the night outside. These numbers are necessarily an undercount, because many people seclude themselves well enough to be uncountable. Moreover, even if homeless persons can access a shelter bed, some chafe under shelter requirements that they consider unnecessarily restrictive. Many homeless people find shelters noisy, disease-prone, and crowded, and they fear for the safety of their person or the security of their belongings.[28] Clients are invariably required to abstain from the use of illicit drugs or alcohol and may be required to attend church services, perform chores, or arrive before their other obligations permit.

Unsurprisingly, when those engaged in the one-night count interviewed people who lacked permanent shelter, they learned that for those individuals, "the lack of affordable housing and nearly complete absence of shelters and services were the most urgent problems."[29] These interviews also revealed that many homeless people were uncertain about the existence of social services for which they might be eligible. Others indicated difficulty in accessing services even when they knew of them. These realities are symptomatic of another important component in the homelessness story: the fraying of the public social safety net. Indeed, it is impossible to tell the story of American homelessness without taking into account the role of government.

Government (In)action: Neoliberalism and the Withdrawal of Public Support

Economic shifts helped generate a dearth of affordable housing by both limiting living wage jobs and fueling urban real estate redevelopment. Yet government policies were also deeply complicit in generating the housing crunch. Most significantly, federal government involvement in providing housing assistance dropped precipitously in the 1980s, as did funding for other forms of social support. This was part of a broader movement to lessen government obligations to those at the bottom of the economic ladder. The derogation of welfare is considered by many to be one of the components of the rise of neoliberalism.

This somewhat fuzzy term is used by many analysts to describe the reaction against Keynesian economic policy. Under Keynesianism, governments were actively involved in structuring markets, largely by stimulating demand with expenditures on infrastructure and social services. Neoliberal philosophy challenges such practices, urging that governments disengage from involvement in the markets for housing or any other good. Instead, the laws of supply and demand should be trusted to generate maximal societal good. To the extent that the state builds housing for poor people, from this perspective, it disrupts the "natural" workings of the ostensibly efficient market. Government support for low-income housing also allegedly deadens the initiative of the poor, thereby creating them as dependent subjects.[30]

Whatever their ideological underpinnings, neoliberal policies emaciated federal support for low-income people. In the three-year period from 1982 to 1985 alone, federal programs targeted to the poor were cut by $57 billion.[31] Housing assistance was particularly hard hit. From 1978 to 1983, the portion of the federal Housing and Urban Development (HUD) budget dedicated to low-income housing declined from $83 billion to $18 billion. Not surprisingly, federal authorizations for housing shifted from 7 percent of the federal budget in 1978 to 0.7 percent by 1988.[32] The resulting decline in government-built public housing was dramatic. In the six years between 1976 and 1982, HUD built more than 755,000 public housing units. In the twenty-two years between 1983 and 2005, it built only a third that number—256,000 units.[33]

Instead of building or subsidizing public housing, the federal government shifted to providing vouchers for those deemed sufficiently poor to require housing assistance. Those granted vouchers were then required to enter the private market to secure housing. This approach is consistent with neoliberalism's emphasis on markets. Yet vouchers failed to provide the same level of housing.[34] Furthermore, as residents in private apartments, impoverished citizens were less able to acquire access to health and other services that were typically found in public housing facilities. This withdrawal of the federal government from an active role in providing housing for low-income people is arguably the single greatest factor in the growth of homelessness.[35]

As noted, the rise of visible homelessness triggered marked growth in emergency shelters, which today receive some federal support.[36] Yet to the extent that government aid goes to the provision of temporary shelter rather than permanent forms of affordable housing, the underlying dynamic that generates homelessness remains largely unaffected.

It is a mistake to draw the conclusion that federal assistance for housing declined across the board. For those who can afford to purchase a home, federal assistance is robust. In 2003, for example, the federal government spent $57.2 billion in housing-related tax expenditures for those households in the top income quintile, with an average annual income of $148,138. This is nearly double what the federal government spent that year on housing subsidies for the lowest-income households, with incomes below $18,500.[37] In 2004, 61 percent of all federal housing subsides went to households earning over $54,000; only 27 percent went to those households earning less than $34,500. For every year since 1981, tax benefits for home ownership have been greater than HUD's entire budget.[38] Indeed, federal tax expenditures for mortgage interest deductions to upper- and moderate-income homeowners far outweigh direct federal assistance to low-income renters.[39] Furthermore, tax benefits are increasingly directed away from those who build low-income housing.[40]

It is also worth noting the degree of government support for redevelopment. The tidal force of reconstruction in places like downtown Seattle swamped the sites that once provided low-income housing. Much of this work received public funding. Timothy Gibson catalogs the range of new developments in downtown Seattle, such as the Seattle Art Museum, the Seattle Symphony's home of Benaroya Hall, a stadium for professional sports teams the Mariners (baseball) and the Seahawks (football), a new flagship Nordstrom store, and an expansion of the Convention Center. Of the $1.4 billion of investment that enabled these and other developments, about half—$700 million—came from public sources.[41] As Gibson notes, much of this development is aimed at making sure that downtown Seattle serves as a magnet for tourists and other consumers.

This large-scale, expensive effort at redevelopment is another implication of the postindustrial city that Seattle symbolizes so well: absent a robust industrial sector, municipalities seek to bolster themselves through commerce and tourism. In 2000, the city made an initial investment of $12.7 million to construct a terminal that would accommodate many more cruise ships. As a result, the number of cruise passengers visiting Seattle each year shot up, from fewer than 10,000 in 1999 to an estimated 835,000 in 2008.[42] The economic emphasis on retail and tourism increases the number of visitors and shoppers in downtown areas. This in turn generates pressures to ensure an aesthetically pleasing downtown landscape—one that the visible presence of homeless people arguably disrupts.[43] In this way, the project of banishment—insofar as it succeeds in actually displacing the unwanted—can be seen as a kind of public subsidy on behalf of downtown commercial interests.

Neoliberal policies, then, drove governments at multiple levels to abandon the goal of providing affordable housing even as they continued to make it easier for wealthier individuals to purchase homes and shop at attractive upscale downtown stores. The sharp rise of homelessness that began in the early 1980s coincided precisely with the steep decline of federal support for housing and other forms of welfare for the impoverished. Not surprisingly, by 1985, most poor renters who possessed shelter paid more than 60 percent of their income on housing.[44]

Impoverished people who suffered from mental illness and/or some form of chemical addiction were most hard hit by the sharp decline in affordable housing. Many in this population once lived in SROs; by some estimates, they constituted a quarter of those residents.[45] Others were housed in state hospitals. However, through the 1950s and 1960s, the population of these institutions declined significantly, from about half a million to 100,000.[46] This decline was fueled in part by lawsuits challenging the arguably too-common practice of involuntary commitment, particularly given the atrocious conditions in some state institutions.[47] This decline was also fueled by a burgeoning faith in community-based care. This philosophy held that individuals were more likely to remain tethered to mainstream society if they stayed outside a closed institution. Faith in this philosophy was buttressed by the emergence of psychotropic drugs, which many thought would prevent mental health symptoms from becoming overly debilitating.[48]

Yet the level of care never met the need.[49] Furthermore, during the welfare retrenchment of the 1980s, various forms of financial assistance were curtailed significantly. With their need for services less likely to be met, and their ability to afford housing increasingly weakened, the mentally ill were among the charter members of the new homeless. Although their personal struggles were not the sole or even primary cause of their homelessness, the mentally ill were especially vulnerable to shifts in the availability of housing and services. As Burt explains, "One can conclude with some confidence that more people who are mentally ill or chemically dependent became and remained homeless in the 1980s than was ever the case in American history since the Depression."[50]

To make matters more severe for those now cast to the streets, an emerging discourse about crime worked to further ostracize them from the body politic. This discourse was significant both politically and legally; it fueled a particular construction of the homeless and helped municipal governments overcome constitutional obstacles to their criminalization.

Crime, Politics, and Broken Windows

Even if homeless individuals became a more common sight in American cities, it was not inevitable that their presence or behavior would become a focus of criminal law enforcement. Just as the 1980s witnessed a sharp reduction in governmental support for public housing and other forms of social service, it also birthed a remarkable resurgence in criminal punishment. Since 1980, the rate of incarceration in the United States has increased sevenfold. As a consequence, the United States now confines a larger share of its residents than any other country in the world.[51]

The massive and unprecedented expansion of the U.S. penal system reflects, in large part, a shift in the significance and framing of the crime issue in American political discourse.[52] Beginning in the 1960s, politicians began to make the issue of crime central to their campaigns, a process that accelerated through the

1970s. To demonstrate that they were not "soft on crime," legislators at both the federal and state levels created laws that stripped judges of much of their discretion in sentencing and increased the severity of punishments.[53] The punitive engine was fueled largely by growing concern over illegal drugs and the belief that addiction could be reduced by getting tough on drug offenders.

The consequences of institutionalizing this approach to the drug problem were dramatic. Between 1980 and 1996, the number of annual drug arrests increased from about 500,000 to over 1.5 million.[54] The surge in arrests and related policy changes that ensued contributed significantly to the sharp increase in incarceration rates overall and for people of color in particular.[55] By 2007, nearly half a million U.S. residents were in jail or prison for committing a nonviolent drug offense.[56] Nearly 80 percent of those currently serving time in state prison for drug offenses are black and/or Latino.[57]

Drug crime was not the only poster child for the alleged decay of social order and the presumed need for a robust criminal law response. At the municipal level, other kinds of allegedly problematic behavior in public space also attracted political attention. In this hyperpunitive political environment, many local elected officials sought to demonstrate that they were doing something in response to disorder. Fortunately for them, a theory of crime emerged in the early 1980s to provide a palatable justification for expanding the criminal law in this arena.

This theory concentrated on the effects of so-called broken windows. Articulated initially by James Q. Wilson and George Kelling in a short *Atlantic Monthly* article in 1982, the theory suggests a connection between, on one hand, street-level behaviors engaged in by homeless people and other ostensibly disreputable people, and, on the other hand, more serious criminality.[58] This connection arguably occurs through a sequence of events that begins with an unrepaired broken window or some other sign of unaddressed disorder. For Wilson and Kelling, broken windows symbolize a neighborhood that does not care about itself. In places where symbols of disorder accumulate, residents become more fearful. They withdraw from public space and become increasingly unable to exercise informal social control. According to Wilson and Kelling, this serves as a cue for those interested in criminal acts; they lack fear of detection in places where disorder is evident. Crime thereby becomes more common. Residents withdraw even further, and a cycle of deterioration is set in motion. It is therefore considered necessary to fix broken windows quickly to prevent this cycle from ever commencing.[59]

For Wilson and Kelling, a corollary of this theory is that urban police departments should reorient themselves. Rather than waiting for serious crime to occur and trying to apprehend a suspect, police should be proactive and address those conditions in which crime allegedly incubates. To "fix" broken windows means, in large part, using the police's coercive power to remove undesirable people from public space. Advocates of broken windows policing therefore call for city governments to give the police broad and flexible means of regulating public spaces and removing those deemed disorderly. Although the theory ostensibly concentrates on the built environment, it principally focuses on unwanted human behavior—particularly that which is engaged in by "disreputable or obstreperous or unpredictable people: panhandlers, drunks, addicts, rowdy teenagers, prostitutes, loiterers, the mentally disturbed"—as a cause of serious crime.[60] The police are therefore encouraged to consider misdemeanor offenses, such as public drunkenness and panhandling, as very serious matters.

This implication of broken windows—that the police should make those deemed disorderly feel unwelcome—encourages a practice that is hardly new. Efforts such as these to police vagrants and other undesirables possess a very long history.[61] People who are not spatially anchored and who appear to contribute little to the collective economy have long been stigmatized and their behavior criminalized. Despite the absence of a centralized police state, nineteenth-century America was highly regulated and policed; much of this regulation was aimed at protecting public morality and combating what was perceived as disorder.[62] Vagrancy-type laws were central to these efforts, but they were largely invalidated by the courts in the 1960s and 1970s.

The broken windows theory helped cities solve an important legal problem generated by the constitutional scrutiny U.S. courts directed toward vagrancy laws in the 1960s and 1970s. The symbolic politics of disorder were displayed no more obviously than in New York City in the 1990s. There, Mayor Rudolph Giuliani and his police commissioner, William Bratton, embraced a particularly muscular version of the broken windows philosophy, one they characterized as "zero tolerance." That meant that all street-level misdemeanors—including the infamous squeegeeing of car windshields by sidewalk entrepreneurs—would generate a strong police response. Because crime dropped in the same period that zero-tolerance practices were implemented, Giuliani and Bratton claimed that broken windows policing worked. Although this is a widely disputed boast,[63] the political value of cracking down on disorder was obvious from Giuliani's experience and undoubtedly contributed to the popularity of the broken windows theory and its spread to many other cities.[64]

The civility codes brought the broken windows philosophy to life and enabled the shifts in policing that theory endorsed. They also helped enable cities to overcome the restrictions on police discretion that accompanied the invalidation of vagrancy and loitering laws. The civility codes solved this problem by providing greater specificity in outlining the behaviors they prohibited.

Vagrancy was no longer a crime, but sitting or lying on a sidewalk was. Loitering was not prohibited, but one could not camp in a park. The police were thus better protected from constitutional challenge by possessing a clearer behavioral focus for their law enforcement efforts.

Although this specificity may protect civility codes against some constitutional challenge, it also limits their applicability. We see the banishment practices now deployed in Seattle as an extension and broadening of the civility codes.[65] Because the enforcement of these codes was insufficient to the task of clearing the streets, police and other government officials struggled to respond to ongoing concerns about disreputable people in public space. The fact that the new tools are touted as "alternatives" to incarceration helps explain their political appeal to states and localities struggling under the financial burden caused by the drug war and mass incarceration.

Unfortunately, neither the civility codes nor banishment address the underlying conditions that generate poverty and homelessness. As inequality intensifies and affordable housing shrinks, there is little reason to expect banishment to decrease the presence of the homeless or others who spend considerable time in public space. Indeed, as we show in chapter 5, banishment is likely nothing but self-defeating; it only exacerbates the challenges of the downtrodden and makes their visible presence all the more likely.

Conclusion

The reinvigorated use of banishment as a social control strategy is not a historical accident. It emerged in Seattle as a consequence of several interrelated factors. The shift toward a postindustrial economy and away from a strong welfare state increased levels of poverty. Extensive gentrification coupled with a decline in public housing made affordable shelter increasingly scarce. Together, these structural dynamics generated a sizable increase in the visible homeless. Their presence in downtown public spaces caused widespread concern about the effects of disorder. This concern was particularly acute for commercial establishments reliant on shoppers and tourists, many of whom abhor visible evidence of social disadvantage. For those seeking to revive downtown and improve downtown aesthetics, the broken windows theory was a boon. The popularity of this theory legitimized various civility codes that targeted the everyday behaviors of those deemed disorderly.

The civility codes did not make homelessness disappear, however. This is not surprising, because these codes left the underlying dynamics of homelessness untouched. If anything, they made matters worse, through reinforcing the notion of the homeless as disorderly. As the Western Regional Advocacy Project puts it, "The negative stereotyping of homeless individuals as deviant outcasts has fed the tendency to respond to homelessness with inadequate local and temporary policies that fail to address the systemic cause of homelessness."[66]

The persistence of homelessness meant that municipal governments continued to face ongoing pressures to clean up areas like downtown Seattle. The faith that the civility codes implicitly placed in criminal law enforcement to reduce homelessness and related ills is robustly reinforced by the move toward banishment. These newer tools significantly increase the power of the police to place pressure on those who spend considerable amount of time in public space and otherwise extend the net of surveillance and control. We use chapter 2 to explain the emergence of these new tools and outline their scope and significance.

2

Toward Banishment: The Transformation of Urban Social Control

As we outlined in chapter 1, the rise of the visible homelessness in the early 1980s fueled concerns about disorder in cities like Seattle. This concern led to frequent calls for the police and other municipal agencies to clean up places said to be awash in disreputable people and their associated behavior. Yet the ability of the police to respond was limited, in significant part because of the U.S. Supreme Court's invalidation of conventional vagrancy and loitering laws in the late 1960s and early 1970s. These laws were one of the major traditional mechanisms the police used to exert territorial pressure on the unwanted to relocate. In response to these political and legal dynamics, many municipalities, including Seattle, adopted civility codes in the 1990s. Because these targeted more specific behaviors than the now-unconstitutional vagrancy laws, they were expressly designed to escape scrutiny by the courts.

More recently, many cities have gone further, innovating and adopting more broadly applicable and durable social control tools. These are the tools of banishment; they explicitly create and enforce zones of exclusion. Born of the same impulse that birthed the civility codes, they take those codes a notable step further. They enable a significant increase in the power of the police and other actors in the criminal justice system to monitor, arrest, charge, and jail those considered disorderly.

Indeed, the practices of banishment represent an intensification of Seattle's reliance on the criminal justice system to try to solve social problems rooted fundamentally in impoverishment. Part of this is accomplished through innovative forms of legal hybridity. The new social control practices rest on a combination of criminal and civil legal authority in a way that increases the power of criminal law. In the process, the rights-bearing capacity of those who are banished is eroded in a way that lessens their status as full-fledged citizens.

This chapter outlines how this happens. We begin by using archival materials to explain the context in which intensified social control emerged in Seattle. We review the rising popularity of the broken windows philosophy and its influence in providing political impetus for various ordinances that enable banishment. Although many of these innovations encountered robust political opposition, the power of the discourse of disorder ultimately held sway. We then review each of the specific instances of banishment in practice—off-limits orders, trespass admonishments, and parks exclusion orders—and outline their basic contours. Finally, we review the shared characteristics of these tools, and explain how, collectively, they notably enhance the power of the criminal justice system to respond to instances of alleged disorder.

This embrace of banishment is a perhaps understandable yet ultimately flawed attempt to use the criminal justice process to address social problems. On one hand, banishment provides the police greater legal capacity to place pressure on frequent users of public space, and hence to seem responsive to requests that they clean up areas targeted as disorderly. Yet the power the police can exert is ultimately a blunt and ineffective weapon against such widespread problems as poverty, chemical addiction, and mental illness. For this reason, banishment is a practice that deserves ongoing scrutiny.

Our effort at such scrutiny begins with a brief account of the political dynamics that triggered the quest for new social control tools in Seattle.

Seattle's Quest to Recriminalize Disorder

The Supreme Court's invalidation of vagrancy and loitering ordinances in the 1960s and 1970s was part of an important (if short-lived) "rights revolution" in which the rights of the accused were extended and protected. Although heralded as progressive and enlightened in criminal law textbooks, many of the rulings of this period were castigated at the time by those more concerned about law and order than the rights of the disenfranchised. In 1969, for example, the Seattle City Council received a fifty-five-page petition demanding greater enforcement of vagrancy and loitering laws.[1] According to the petition,

We registered voters are appalled by the lack of leadership in the
City of Seattle to meet the present urban crisis. We are cognizant
of an invasion in our city by the dregs of American Society. We are
cognizant of our children being exposed to drug addiction in school
or being termed squares. We are proponents of enforcing vagrancy
and loitering laws in the city. We will support our police and other
police officers in doing these things. These undesirable elements must
be driven from the city. THEY MUST BE MADE TO REALIZE THAT
THEIR PRESENCE IS NOT CONDONED IN THE NORTHWEST.
(emphasis in original)

In keeping with the times, the Seattle police chief's response to the petitioners
was fairly unsympathetic:

Petitioners should be advised that laws must conform to the
constitutional guarantees of our democratic society. Those of us
who enforce the law must protect these guarantees. This means that
the less desirable elements in our society are also protected from
infringement on their personal freedom. We cannot, in other words,
"drive this undesirable element from our city."

Like the petitioners lamenting the invalidation of vagrancy and loitering ordinances, proponents of broken windows policing argued that the Supreme
Court's invalidation of vagrancy laws intensified problems of neighborhood
crime and decay and rendered the traditional order maintenance role of the
police more difficult.[2] This perception also apparently came to be shared by
police officers and city officials in Seattle, who claimed they lacked the tools
needed to cleanse the streets. In 1988, a police sergeant sent the following
memo to the Seattle Police Department legal advisor:

Having been given the job of clearing the [downtown] area of drug
users, sellers, juveniles, and unwanted transients, I'm running into
some difficulties. One of the main complaints my officers have is that
they are not supplied with adequate ordinances to do the job. We can
no longer arrest people for urinating or loitering in the area. Would it
be possible (constitutional) to set up an ordinance that would limit
the hours a juvenile could loiter in a known high drug area? Secondly,
could this be extended to all known drug offenders? Third, if all
the above is possible, could the "known high drug activity area" be
worded in such as way as to be floating?[3]

As part of his effort to clear the downtown area of the unpopular and
unconventional, then, this police sergeant urged his superiors to search for

constitutionally viable alternatives to ordinances that prohibited vagrancy, loitering, and public urination. Similarly, a 1991 memo from the Seattle chief of
police urged the mayor to "review those portions of the Municipal Code that
decriminalized many offensive behaviors" and "develop alternatives in order to
address the cumulative effect of small but significant quality of life issues."[4]

The police department did not act in isolation in advocating these alternatives. Over the course of the 1980s and 1990s, the increased visibility of
socially marginal populations triggered fear and frustration on the part of
many (increasingly middle-class and professional) urban residents and business owners. In this context, concern about the rights of the accused attenu-
ated, and the felt need to enhance order intensified.[5]

This concern dovetailed with the rising popularity of the broken windows
theory. In fact, broken windows advocates helped many cities develop alternative mechanisms to address quality of life issues. These were designed to avoid
the legal problems associated with vagrancy and loitering ordinances. Kelling
and Coles described the evolution of these tools as follows:

> Legislation and corresponding legal doctrine applicable to the
> control of much disorderly behavior have passed through several
> phases in the United States: in the first, early vagrancy laws and other
> legislation making a status a criminal offense were passed; these
> were soon supplemented . . . by anti-loitering laws directed more
> specifically at certain acts or behaviors; . . . these laws were supplanted
> by more specific prohibitions against loitering "for the purpose
> of" some criminal activity. Today, in the face of legal challenges
> to "loitering for the purpose of" laws, legislation restricting or
> prohibiting specific behaviors, such as lying down on a sidewalk,
> asking for money aggressively or more than once, or intentionally
> blocking pedestrian movement on sidewalks, is being developed and
> tested in the courts.[6]

Kelling and Coles thus depict a broad shift from vagrancy and loitering laws
to more specific versions of them and to loitering-with-intent laws. (An example
of such new laws was Seattle's drug traffic loitering law, described shortly.) These
shifts in legislation are ostensibly aimed at enhancing civility in the city. Thus
was born the term "civility codes."[7] As many critics note, these laws criminalize
many common behaviors—such as drinking, sleeping, and urinating—when
those behaviors occur in public spaces. For this reason, they have a disproportionate impact on the homeless. In addition, these ordinances provide the
police with an important set of order maintenance tools and arguably enable the

police to make stops and conduct searches that they could not otherwise legally make.[8]

These police powers were aimed at new crimes defined with sufficient specificity to prevent those laws from being overturned by the courts. In Seattle and elsewhere, the quest for more expansive and unassailable social control mechanisms has been ongoing and quite successful. We now turn to a description of even newer social control tools that enable banishment and to an analysis of their novel characteristics. A first key move toward banishment came in the form of new loitering-with-intent laws.

From Loitering to Loitering-with-Intent Laws

Although most vagrancy and loitering laws have been removed from the books, some remain in effect. In New York state, for example, a loitering statute continues to be enforced despite a 1992 federal District Court ruling that it was unconstitutional.[9] Indeed, 16 percent of the 224 cities recently surveyed continue to prohibit loitering city-wide.[10]

The more typical trend, as Kelling and Coles both note and encourage, is for cities to render their loitering laws more specific.[11] For example, the aforementioned city survey found that 39 percent of the cities prohibited loitering in particular public places. Other ordinances place time restrictions on loitering. For example, in February 2005, the Los Angeles City Council unanimously passed a law that prohibits loitering outside of public facilities, such as libraries, between 9 p.m. and 9 a.m.[12]

Many states and cities went further, adopting laws that prohibit loitering *with the intent to commit criminal acts,* such as selling drugs or engaging in prostitution. In Minneapolis, for example, it is a crime to "lurk" or "loiter" with the intent to commit a crime.[13] To increase the likelihood that these laws will survive constitutional scrutiny, they prohibit loitering only when it is coupled with behaviors that ostensibly manifest the intent to commit a criminal act (or, in the case of gang loitering ordinances, with a stigmatized status).[14]

The courts' response to these loitering-with-intent laws is thus far decidedly mixed. Although some were rejected by courts, others remain on the books.[15] Where they exist, loitering and loitering-with-intent ordinances add an important tool to a city's law enforcement arsenal. In the case of Seattle, they also served as the vehicle for some of the newer tools that entail banishment. In this sense, loitering-with-intent laws represent a step in the continuum from vagrancy and loitering laws to the new, legally hybrid control mechanisms that make banishment possible. In what follows, we provide a brief overview of the development of Seattle's prostitution and drug loitering ordinances, and then explain how these laws paved the way for a key form of banishment.

Seattle's Prostitution and Drug Traffic Loitering Ordinances

Like many other port cities, Seattle has long hosted a bustling sex trade. Historically, prohibitions against vagrancy, loitering, public intoxication, and prostitution were used to manage vice. Indeed, it appears that the city's loitering ordinance was a key part of anti-vice efforts. As a result, the decriminalization of loitering created important implications for the city's effort to combat prostitution and attendant ills.

In 1968, Seattle Police Department Chief Frank Ramon argued to the city council that the invalidation of the city's loitering ordinance necessitated the adoption of an alternative mechanism for managing prostitution-related activity. Toward that end, he requested that the mayor's office sponsor a prostitution-loitering law:

> It is redundant to again recount the inability of the Police department to control prostitutes loitering and soliciting on the streets because of recent court decisions. Continued concerted police actions which have been very costly in police man-hours and money have succeeded in affecting some control over known prostitutes soliciting on the streets. However, the amount or extent of control has not been satisfactory. One result has been to move the problem. As you are aware, prostitutes soliciting on the public streets are now congregating in the area immediately adjacent to the principal shopping areas in the downtown business district. The police methods and tactics which had some success in other parts of the city cannot be used as effectively in the present area. It is, therefore, respectfully requested that an ordinance which will give the police the authority to take positive action be enacted.[16]

The ordinance proposed by Chief Ramon made it a crime to loiter *with the intent* to commit a prostitution-related offense. Many downtown business groups joined police officials in conveying their support for this proposed ordinance to city council members. The result was the 1973 adoption of Seattle Municipal Code 12A.10.020, which prohibits loitering "under circumstances manifesting the purpose of inducing, enticing, soliciting or procuring another to commit an act of prostitution." Although many women's and children's organizations subsequently expressed concern that the prostitution loitering ordinance (like the prostitution statute itself) was used primarily to arrest prostitutes rather than those who procured their services,[17] the ordinance was not challenged on constitutional grounds until the 1980s.

This challenge was unsuccessful. In 1989, Seattle's prostitution loitering ordinance was upheld by the Washington State Supreme Court in *Seattle v. Slack*.[18] In this decision, the Court ruled that loitering in a public place is constitutionally protected behavior, and that status alone (such as being a "known prostitute") cannot be a criminal offense. However, the Court concluded that the prostitution loitering ordinance's requirement of evidence of the intent to solicit, induce, entice, or procure another to commit prostitution was sufficiently narrow and specific: "This element of specific criminal intent saves [the ordinance] from being unconstitutionally overbroad."[19] The Court also argued that the wording of the ordinance—which forbids loitering "in a manner and under circumstances manifesting an unlawful purpose, the unlawful purpose being to induce another to commit an act of prostitution"—is clear and unambiguous (rather than vague), and that the "circumstances" clause of the ordinance successfully "demonstrate[s] some of the types of conduct which may be considered in determining whether an unlawful purpose or intent is manifested."[20] Finally, the Court rejected an equal protection challenge by Slack that attacked the police's ability to consider his status as a "known prostitute" in evaluating his alleged intent to commit prostitution. Said the Court: "It [Slack's identity as a 'known prostitute'] is only one circumstance which may be considered by a police officer in inferring intent or purpose."[21]

Thus the Court signaled that loitering-with-intent laws were not unconstitutionally broad or vague. Given this, attentive city officials saw an opportunity to expand them. As one such official noted, the court's ruling in *Slack* "substantially reduced constitutional questions surrounding a hypothetical drug loitering ordinance."[22] Yet the debate over Seattle's drug traffic loitering ordinance proved far more rancorous than its prostitution-oriented predecessor.

Throughout the 1980s, concern about crime and drugs intensified, particularly in the south end of the city. Rising crime rates, the spread of crack cocaine, and the emergence of seven regional crime prevention councils catalyzed attention to public safety issues.[23] The South Precinct Crime Prevention Council was especially effective in calling attention to crime and drug activity in the southern part of the city.[24] In this context, King County Council member Norm Rice proposed a drug traffic loitering ordinance. The law was intended to prohibit loitering in a public place "for the purpose of drug trafficking." This early effort was unsuccessful, apparently as a result of unresolved questions about the constitutionality of such a law.

After the *Slack* decision in 1989, and a similar Washington state Supreme Court 1990 ruling in favor of neighboring Tacoma's drug traffic loitering ordinance, the political climate became more favorable to such legislation. In Seattle, a drug traffic loitering ordinance was introduced again in 1990, this time by City Attorney Mark Sidran. The ordinance was meant to prohibit drug traffic loitering, which was defined as remaining in a public place and intentionally soliciting, inducing, enticing, or procuring another to engage in illegal drug activity.[25] Sidran promoted the ordinance on several grounds. First, he argued, the law

> will assist in cleaning up areas of high drug activity and the other crime that such activity brings with it. People can be sentenced for up to one year in jail if they are convicted of this crime. *In addition the court can order as a condition of probation that the offender not return to the area.* This will slow down the revolving door of justice for these people and *remove the offender from the community* [emphasis added].[26]

Thus, one of the main rationales for the introduction of the drug traffic loitering ordinance was to enable municipal court judges to impose off-limits orders on misdemeanor drug offenders. Sidran also argued that the law would provide officers with an alternative to trespass law, which, he suggested, was inappropriately being used to arrest people suspected of engaging in drug activity.[27]

Opposition to the proposed drug traffic loitering ordinance was intense. Critics such as the American Civil Liberties Union (ACLU), National Organization for Women, the National Association for the Advancement of Colored People, and the Seattle Human Rights Commission expressed concern that the law would give the police license to stop and harass youth of color.[28] Public health officials and members of AIDS Coalition to Unleash Power also feared that the law would frighten drug users away from newly established needle exchange facilities. On the other hand, supporters of the proposed law, including members of business and neighborhood organizations, offered lurid tales of the negative effects of drug activity in their neighborhoods. The proposed law was particularly divisive among residents of the south end, home to a large share of the city's population of color.[29]

Despite this opposition to the ordinance, Seattle City Council records indicate that written and phone correspondence ran slightly in its favor. Supporters and detractors alike offered passionate testimony. One council member reported that the day of the vote was "the hardest day I've had on the council," whereas another predicted the law could have "dangerous, far-reaching consequences."[30] On July 6, 1990, the proposed legislation was adopted in a vote of seven to two "amid boos from the audience."[31]

Seattle's prostitution and drug loitering-with-intent laws remain on the books and enhance police authority and discretion by providing a basis for stopping and questioning someone perceived as loitering with the intent to commit a drug- or prostitution-related crime. In addition, as was evident in the story told by Rhonda in the introduction, securing a conviction requires nothing other than an officer's testimony that the suspect engaged in one or more of the behaviors thought to manifest the intent to commit a drug crime.

Perhaps less well noticed at the time—but critical to the banishment practices we analyze—the passage of the drug traffic loitering ordinance served as the vehicle for the introduction of a new social control practice, namely, Stay out of Drug Area (SODA) orders.[32] Indeed, a few months after the adoption of the drug traffic loitering ordinance, the first SODA order was issued to someone convicted of drug traffic loitering.[33] These were modeled after a similar, preexisting scheme for creating off-limits orders, Stay Out of Areas of Prostitution (SOAP) orders.

SODA and SOAP orders are now frequently issued in Seattle. According to one assistant city attorney, it is "almost a certainty" that anyone facing a misdemeanor drug or prostitution charge in Seattle with be saddled with one of these restrictions. These off-limits orders thus constitute one of the forms of banishment on which we concentrate. We use the next section to outline how these operate.

Off-Limits Orders: SODAs and SOAPs

As suggested, off-limits orders are imposed by judges and/or correctional officers, and require those convicted of certain offenses to stay out of particular sections of the city as a condition of their probation or parole sentence,[34] typically for a two-year period.[35] Violations of these orders are typically defined as violations of sentencing conditions rather than new criminal offenses. A violation of a court order may trigger the imposition of the full sentence for the original charge and in Seattle is also treated as a new charge, "probation violation."[36] In some cases, off-limits orders are also imposed on defendants who have not been convicted of a crime. In King County, for example, SODA orders are sometimes imposed as a condition of pretrial release.[37]

Off-limits orders enable judges and others to order those suspected or convicted of drug or prostitution offenses to stay out of areas where drug sales and prostitution are believed to be common.[38] These zones are created, as least in theory, by order of the presiding judge of Seattle's municipal court after hearing evidence of sustained patterns of illegal activity. In some municipalities, off-limits orders are governed by ordinance;[39] in others, such as Seattle, neither SOAP nor SODA orders appear to have been explicitly created or authorized by city ordinance.

The areas from which people are banned often comprise significant parts of the city and may include the entire downtown core in which social and legal services are concentrated. In Seattle today, roughly half of the city's terrain, including all of the downtown, is defined as a drug area from which someone might be banned. Those subject to off-limits orders are generally prohibited from being in the proscribed areas for any reason; violations may lead to additional jail time. In some locales, exceptions may be granted if people live, work, or have other legitimate reasons to be there. In Seattle, however, the defense attorneys we interviewed report that judges' willingness to grant such exceptions varies significantly.

In Seattle, SOAP orders have been imposed on many of those arrested for or convicted of prostitution-related offenses for the past several decades. According to prosecutors with whom we spoke, most of those charged with prostitution offenses plead guilty and are issued a SOAP order as part of a suspended sentence.[40] In some cases, SOAP orders are imposed as part of a deferred prosecution. One way or the other, nearly all of those arrested for prostitution "get SOAPed."[41]

In short, the number of people living in the Seattle area and subject to SOAP and especially SODA orders is growing, as we document in more detail in chapter 4. Moreover, as we will see in chapter 3, the zones from which people are excluded are also expanding. Although King County and Portland are apparently unique in imposing off-limits orders on people not convicted of a crime, many municipalities ban probationers from entering certain neighborhoods as part of their criminal sentence.

Besides off-limits orders, two other innovations enable banishment. Each of these—parks exclusion orders and trespass admonishments—enhance the authority of the police to monitor and arrest those legally defined as "out of place."[42] They do so by making the police's ability to enforce trespass law notably more muscular. We describe each of these in turn.

Innovations in Trespass Law Enforcement

Trespass law has long enabled private property owners to restrict access to their property by authorizing them to request the removal of unwanted intruders. Currently, however, these laws are being enforced and implemented in ways that extend trespass authority—the authority to banish—across both space and time. Dubbed "trespass exclusion" laws by the American Prosecutors Research Institute, these innovations facilitate what they define as law enforcement's primary responsibility: "to make the problem go away."[43] Parks exclusion orders are one key mechanism to enable this effort in Seattle.

Parks Exclusion Laws

One of the most important innovations in trespass law has been the adoption in Seattle and other cities, such as Portland, Oregon, of "parks exclusion" laws.[44] Prior to the adoption of these laws, individuals could be removed from public parks only if there was probable cause that they had committed a criminal offense. More minor rule violations, such as being in the park after closing time, resulted only in a citation. Parks exclusion laws authorize police and parks officials to ban persons for committing minor infractions (such as being present after hours, having an unleashed pet, camping, urinating, littering, or possessing an open container of alcohol) from one, some, or all public city parks for up to one year (depending on the number and type of violations). Although parks exclusion orders are defined as civil and remedial rather than criminal and punitive, violation of such an order is a misdemeanor criminal offense (in Seattle, Trespass in the Parks).

Seattle's parks exclusion ordinance was adopted by the city council in 1997 in a vote of six to two. Although its initial adoption was controversial, the ordinance became even more hotly debated after City Council member Nick Licata sought the following year to modify the ordinance. In his communication with other council members and members of the public, Licata and his supporters articulated a number of concerns. These included the failure of the law to provide for due process; the breadth of the rule violations that could result in exclusion; the likelihood of selective enforcement, particularly vis-à-vis the homeless; inadequate notice of the kinds of violations that could lead to banishment; and the fact that many rule infractions did not constitute a threat to public safety. Judging from the available archival materials, his concerns were shared by a significant number of residents and organizations, many of whom expressed their views in hearings and letters to council members.

However, there was also energetic and often impassioned support for retaining the parks exclusion ordinance without any modifications.[45] Many of those who favored retaining the original law dismissed concerns about selective enforcement by emphasizing the offensive nature of the behaviors that could lead to exclusion. As one put it, "I fail to see the argument that this regulation violates civil rights. Is it a civil right to urinate in a park? Is it a civil right to drink alcohol in a park?" Similarly, the *Seattle Post-Intelligencer* opined that "the law in question focuses on behavior, not a class of people."[46] Others emphasized the need to protect the parks for all to enjoy and the futility of issuing citations for violations of parks rules.

This debate included discussion of data regarding just how parks exclusion orders were being enforced. Those data indicated that the most common grounds for exclusions were, according to the police, possession of an open container of alcohol (53 percent) and camping/being present after hours (19 percent).[47] According to an ACLU report released shortly thereafter, nearly half (45 percent) of those excluded were people of color. Almost as many, 42 percent, were obviously homeless.[48]

Two aspects of the debate over Seattle's parks exclusion ordinance are particularly noteworthy. The first is the question of due process. As many critics pointed out, the ordinance authorized the police to exclude an alleged rule violator without providing any evidence of wrongdoing. As one letter writer put it, the law authorizes "the police to act as prosecutor, judge and executioner." Technically, those who are excluded for more than seven days have the right to appeal their exclusion. There are several important barriers to submitting an appeal: the accused does not have the right to legal representation; the written appeal must be postmarked within one week of the exclusion order; and the phone number that is provided on the form for those who have questions about submitting an appeal is, at the time of this writing, the phone number of a community center, the staff of which knows nothing about appealing a parks exclusion. According to Parks Security, only ten to twelve of the thousands of people who have been excluded from city parks in the past decade have appealed their exclusion. A successful appeal occurred in just two of these cases.[49]

Proponents of the law in the Seattle Police Department and the Seattle city attorney's office insisted that the denial of due process rights was not significant because "under the ordinance individuals are excluded from a park, not arrested. Thus, due process is—and should be—less than for a criminal arrest."[50] Supporters of the law thus emphasized that the legal authority to exclude was based on civil law rather than criminal law. They also noted the noncriminal and "relatively minor" nature of the (initial) sanction imposed on violators.

However, as critics point out, this emphasis on the noncriminal nature of the exclusion itself obscures the fact that the ordinance creates a new crime—being present in a park in violation of exclusion order. As one of the few letter writers to address this issue wrote, "The advent of police 'exclusion' powers under this ordinance has not necessarily meant that fewer homeless 'trespassers' are booked into jail for jail stays at taxpayer expense. Indeed...the issuance of an 'exclusion' actually creates a crime that would not have existed otherwise."[51]

In the end, most of the substantial amendments to the law were rejected, and the ordinance remains both intact and widely enforced. Similar ordinances are in place in a number of municipalities, particularly in the Northwest.[52] As we show in chapter 4, the number of people excluded from Seattle parks and the length of their exclusions has increased over time. Because the excluded are subsequently subject to arrest for simply being in a public park during operating hours, hundreds of people are arrested every year for this offense. The parks exclusion law thus enhances police authority to stop and question "undesirables," leads to the exclusion of many people from groups of city parks for extended periods of time, and enables a significant number of arrests each year.

Parks exclusion orders are one means of enhancing the territorial authority of the police. We turn to another means by which trespass law is being adapted to make banishment more likely in Seattle and elsewhere.

Innovations in Trespass Law Enforcement

No longer limited to private property or parks, trespass law is increasingly used to regulate access to both private and publicly owned places normally open to the public. These include transportation facilities, social service agencies, libraries, public housing facilities, and commercial establishments (and the sidewalks adjacent to them). In practice, in Seattle, a person must be forewarned, either by posted regulations or in the form of a trespass warning or admonishment, before they can be arrested for trespass in a public space or on private property that is normally open to the public.[53]

Municipalities use a variety of tactics to facilitate the use of trespass law on sidewalks and other public property. For example, many cities now convey public streets and sidewalks to private property owners or housing authorities. This grants the new owners the right to enforce no-trespass orders.[54] This tactic has been used in Richmond, Virginia; Knoxville, Tennessee; Tampa, Florida; El Paso, Texas, and elsewhere. In particular, streets located within public housing facilities are increasingly being conveyed to public housing authorities. This endows those agencies with the power to exclude certain individuals from those streets.

This use of trespass power to address crime was facilitated by the 1998 Quality Housing and Work Responsibility Act, which gave local governments and housing authorities more discretion over operating policies and practices.[55] Some trespass programs ban those who have been arrested for or convicted of particular crimes (including residents) from public housing buildings and grounds. Other no-trespass policies ban nearly all nonresidents, not just those who are unwelcome or uninvited by residents. Still others allow law enforcement officers wide discretion in deciding who to trespass admonish from the facilities and arrest for trespass if they return.[56]

In New York City, housing authorities and police officers can permanently exclude people from public housing property for a variety of reasons. Although the city's Operation Safe Housing program specifies that only those arrested for selling drugs on public housing property may be permanently excluded, many others experience the same fate. The names of the excluded appear in a Not Wanted list published in a newspaper distributed to public housing residents. Those who violate their banishment order for any reason are subject to arrest for trespass.[57] As noted in the introduction, the NYPD also encourages apartment building owners to authorize officers to arrest nonresidents for trespass. Both of these trespass initiatives attracted criticism in the wake of recent reports that people—usually young men of color—with no arrest record and legitimate business on the property were being arrested for trespassing. Indeed, trespass arrests in New York City jumped 25 percent between 2002 and 2007, presumably as a result of these new initiatives.[58]

These trespass programs are touted by housing authorities as an effective means of reducing crime.[59] Although some residents undoubtedly agree, many residents and analysts object that these policies are overly broad, deny residents their right to free association, and in some cases, are permanent. As one survey of these trespass programs concluded:

> All too frequently under Public Housing Authority (PHA) no-trespass programs, "unwritten policies" without "written standards or time deadlines" and lacking "any guidelines that delineate how an individual may obtain permission to use the property" prevent tenants from exercising their right to have visitors. Officials have barred nonresidents without inquiry into the legitimacy of their reasons for being on their property and often in spite of their having legitimate business at the development. In fact, nonresident visitors have been banned from PHA property for literally just standing there.[60]

Trespass admonishments are used to limit access to other kinds of properties that are normally open to the public. In Seattle, for example, people are also trespass admonished from libraries and recreation centers, the public transportation system, college campuses, hospitals and religious institutions, social service agencies, and commercial establishments.[61] Because there is little regulation of the circumstances under which these admonishments are given, critics worry that their use and enforcement may be discriminatory.[62]

The expansion of trespass authority in Seattle is vigorously pursued by the police. A principal mechanism for doing this involves property owners' sharing of the (private) authority to exclude particular individuals with the police. In Seattle, this practice appears to have been initiated by a Seattle Police Department (SPD) precinct captain in 1987 who was reportedly concerned about alleged drug dealers frightening customers away from local businesses. After contacting the city attorney's office, he asked the owners of the affected businesses to sign an agreement authorizing the police to issue a trespass admonishment to anyone on their property that the police deemed suspicious and to go to court to support any trespass arrests that resulted from violations of these exclusion orders.[63]

Thus was born a major initiative by the SPD and a citizen-led anticrime organization, the Seattle Neighborhood Group,[64] to encourage business owners to grant the police department the authority to ban people from places normally open to the public, even in the absence of evidence of criminal wrongdoing.[65] To make this happen, property owners sign a contract with the SPD in which they authorize the police to act as their agents in revoking certain individuals' right to use the property. That contract enables the police to exercise trespass power without soliciting the owner's permission to do so in any given instance. Officers are thereby allowed to target individuals on a property whom they believe lack "legitimate purpose" for being there. When this happens, officers first issue a trespass admonishment. This is a formal notification that the individual is to stay off the property, typically for one year. In recent years, the SPD has issued tens of thousands of trespass admonishments restricting access to a range of places normally open to the public.[66] If an individual violates an admonishment, that person is vulnerable to arrest for the crime of trespass.

In some instances, similar and geographically proximate businesses are brought together in a single trespass program. Anyone banned from one of the participating businesses is banned from all of them. Seattle's Aurora Motel Trespass Program is one example. A state highway, Aurora Avenue hosts some twenty-five motels. Several of these are somewhat dilapidated and are reputed to be sites for ongoing sales of illicit drugs and sexual services. All of these hotels were grouped together in a single trespass program created by the SPD. Under this program, someone trespassed from one of the participating hotels is effectively trespassed from all of them for a period of two years. Similarly, the West Precinct Parking Lot Trespass Program includes 321 downtown parking lots.[67] Anyone excluded from one of the participating lots is simultaneously excluded from all of them and is thereby subject to arrest (for trespass) for walking through any one of them.

In some cities, including Seattle, police officers and others issuing these civil trespass admonishments are not required to record the reason for the exclusion. Nor does the banished person have an opportunity to contest his or her exclusion. Yet a violation of these civil exclusion orders is a criminal offense.

Although comparably difficult to contest, some trespass programs have been challenged in the courts. In a recent case in Hawaii, for example, a trespass exclusion program was successfully challenged by a plaintiff who alleged that he was banned from a public library for one year because he viewed gay-themed Web sites on the library computer. Other plaintiffs alleged that the Hawaiian statute (Act 50) was used to remove homeless people from public beaches and parks.[68] In most cases, plaintiffs have challenged trespass programs operating in public housing facilities. The response from the courts to these challenges is thus far decidedly mixed.[69] However, in a recent case (*Virginia v. Hicks*, 2002), the Supreme Court affirmed the right of local governments to enforce trespass exclusion programs, ruling that these programs reflect "legitimate state interests in maintaining comprehensive controls over harmful, constitutionally unprotected conduct."[70]

As we show in chapter 4, violations of trespass admonishments generate large numbers of criminal cases and many short-term jail stays in Seattle. Although some admonishments do not lead to arrest, they may nonetheless generate significant consequences for people's lives, consequences we explore in chapter 5. Moreover, our observations and interviews suggest that trespass admonishments significantly enhance police discretion to stop, question, and search people deemed out of place. As one assistant city attorney put it, "Officers want to have a reason to contact individuals who are loitering at night." The trespass admonishment, he reported, gives them a reason to contact them and "find out what's in their pockets." He further noted that a prosecution of a trespass arrest based on violation of a prior exclusion order is a "slam dunk."

In sum, innovations in trespass law and off-limits orders impose significant spatial restrictions on their recipients and significantly expand police officers authority to investigate people deemed out of place. At the same time, authorities' capacity to detect and enforce these spatial exclusions has been enhanced by the emergence of new police–Department of Corrections (DOC) patrols, described next.

Joint DOC–Police Patrols

In 1999, the Manhattan Institute released a report titled "Broken Windows Probation: The Next Step in Fighting Crime." Noting that the probation population is large (now more than four million U.S. residents) and many probationers are readmitted to prison or jail, the report advocated a reorientation of community supervision programs. Probation, the report urged, must be primarily seen as a mechanism for achieving public safety rather than rehabilitation.[71] To undermine probationers' expectation that they get two or more "free" violations, the report argues that "this permissive practice must be abandoned. All conditions of a probation sentence must be enforced, and all violations must be responded to in a timely fashion."[72] Furthermore, because effective supervision of probationers cannot arguably be achieved from within the probation office during normal business hours, the report urged that supervision should occur in the neighborhood and around the clock.

A number of analysts see merging corrections officers and police officers in single patrol units as a sensible way to enhance supervision of probationers and, in some cases, parolees. One typical advocate, noting that "Probation officers have broad authority to stop and question offenders and immediately revoke their probation if they violate its requirements," stressed the advantages of combining forces.[73] Toward this end, different versions of broken windows probation have been implemented in cities across the United States.[74] In Boston, for example, fifty police officers and fifty probation officers patrolled together seven nights a week for several years. In Seattle, a dedicated team of state DOC officers now patrols the city, and units consisting of one or more DOC officers and a police officer often ride together as part of the city's Neighborhoods Corrections Initiative (NCI). Indeed, NCI teams now operate in all five SPD precincts.

The NCI combines SPD officers and Washington DOC officer-specialists in one patrol vehicle. Each officer brings unique capacities to the enterprise. The SPD officer can access databases that search by name and vehicle for information regarding criminal wants or warrants and for such restrictions as suspended driver's licenses. SPD officers can also make an arrest for perceived violations of the law. The DOC officer's database is confined to those with any history with the department. The DOC officer seeks to determine whether anyone under supervision is in compliance with the various conditions of probation or parole. In the pursuit of such verification, the DOC officer can search anyone under supervision, as well as his or her vehicle and domicile. Discovery of a violation makes possible a DOC arrest. Given their respective databases and capabilities, the two possess an impressive combined power. The detection of violations of off-limits orders, parks exclusion orders, and trespass admonishments constitute a key component of the work of these patrol teams.

In sum, new patrol practices and legal innovations—off-limits orders, parks exclusions, and trespass admonishments—significantly enhance the state's power to exclude as well as stop, question, and prosecute those deemed out of place.[75] Although they differ, they share important distinguishing characteristics that deserve scrutiny.

Toward Banishment: The Transformation of Urban Social Control

The legal innovations just described differ in important ways. For example, parks exclusion laws and trespass admonishments sometimes banish people from relatively small spaces; off-limits orders, such as SODA orders, cover more extensive areas. Parks exclusions and trespass admonishments do not require criminal conviction or even arrest, whereas off-limits orders are typically imposed after conviction. These are clearly important differences, in terms of both their practical and legal implications. Nonetheless, these social control innovations share a number of important characteristics, and, taken together, represent the return of banishment as an urban social control practice and paradigm. As we will show, each of these techniques enhances the territorial power of the police, works to heighten the use of status as a marker of criminality, and combines forms of law in a hybrid fashion.

Removal and Displacement as Policy Goals

The new social control tools are resolutely territorial: they seek to remove those perceived as disorderly from particular geographic locations. The exercise of territoriality is a central component of police power,[76] and many of the banished we interviewed reported that the police had long sought to "move them along." Thus, the fact that the police seek to spatially regulate deviance is hardly novel. What is new, however, is that this spatial goal now arguably trumps rehabilitative and even punitive aspirations *as a matter of policy*. Historically, banishment was aimed neither at deterrence nor rehabilitation but at dislocation. Similarly, when defended publicly, contemporary banishment practices are couched in terms of geographic control. Although proponents also—and more quietly— note that banishment serves key institutional and political interests, removal/ displacement has become the primary stated (and, we believe, short-sighted) policy objective of many of the practices aimed at managing urban disorder.

Although practices of banishment are publicly defended in territorial terms, many of the prosecutors, police officers, and correctional workers we interviewed expressed ambivalence about this, openly admitting that the new techniques often just move people around. Yet several police and DOC officers appreciated the fact that civil admonishments and off-limits orders gave them the capacity to respond to complaints and deal proactively with those identified as potential troublemakers. As one former officer put it: "So I mean, you've got businesses trying to, asking you to clean the place up, right? You've got citizens, getting harassed walking down the street. And so at some point you've got to get rid of them. You've got to do something to these people." An officer observed on Aurora Avenue put this notion into practice. As he escorted two men he had just arrested for trespass to his police van, he made the following comment: "I don't care where you go. I don't care if you go downtown, to Tacoma, or to Shoreline. You need to be anywhere but Aurora." On the other hand, some officers recognize that simply moving people along does not provide any long-term relief. As the former officer just quoted subsequently noted, "So I'll give you a ride downtown, and then it can become a downtown officer's problem. It's just moving the problem around."

Some of the city officials and community prosecutors with whom we spoke also noted the problem of displacement. Nonetheless, these actors typically defended spatial exclusion on one of two grounds. One way was through reference to broken windows theory, described in chapter 1. From this perspective, to arrest somewhat unsightly people who spend time in public space is to improve a place's image and thus encourage the exercise of informal social control. Absent this "repair," the argument goes, more serious criminal problems will develop. Reliance on the broken windows theory, in other words, provides a justification for banishment. Some prosecutors legitimated the theory by giving anticrime activists copies of a chapter from Malcolm Gladwell's *The Tipping Point*. Gladwell's text celebrates broken windows thinking and its alleged "success" in New York City.[77]

A second response to the problem of displacement was simply to urge the intensification of the effort to banish. Some officials also suggested that people living and working in areas into which disorder was displaced could advocate for exclusion zones and trespass programs in their own neighborhoods. As one anticrime activist noted, "We need to hammer it everywhere." Indeed, this appears to occur with sufficient frequency that these exclusionary zones possess an expansionary logic, an argument we develop in chapter 4.

In short, the new legal tactics that entail banishment are defended as a means of achieving spatial control over those defined as disorderly; removal and even displacement are thus key policy objectives. Of course, there are other less publicly articulated rationales for these practices, as suggested by the prosecutor who noted that exclusion orders allow the police to "find out what is inside peoples' pockets." Still, the idea that policy can do anything more than monitor and spatially control the people who are labeled disorderly is given comparatively scant attention.[78]

Redefining Status as a Crime

The idea that possession of a certain status, such as being black or transient, must not be a crime was central to the Supreme Court's invalidation of loitering and vagrancy laws in the 1960s and 1970s. In striking down these laws, the Court ruled that only clearly defined and very specific behaviors may be treated as criminal acts. For this reason, the civility codes birthed in the 1980s and 1990s defined the behaviors they proscribed in fairly specific terms. Although some of the behaviors are common—such as sitting on sidewalks—these laws did not go so far as to criminalize simply being a person with a certain status in a particular space.

Yet the exclusionary practices now in place in Seattle and elsewhere essentially recriminalize possession of a certain status. Indeed, they create a new legal status—excluded—which is then the basis for criminal justice intervention. Of course, this status—unlike being a member of a certain racial group—is created by the legal system and is subject to change. Nonetheless, the possession of this status in particular spaces—not the commission of certain well defined and specific acts—often triggers subsequent contact with the criminal justice system. Thus, although the legally created status of "excluded" differs from other protected statuses that emanate from more general social processes, the creation and imposition of this legal status authorizes the police to focus on a class of people rather than specific behaviors. Indeed, exclusion orders ban only the "future lawful conduct" of their targets, as crimes are already proscribed.

This is most obvious in the case of trespass enforcement. The police can trespass-admonish a citizen based solely on an officer's assessment that the person is on a property with no legitimate purpose. These exclusion orders need not be based on a criminal conviction or even arrest. Indeed, the police frequently do not even provide any reason for the exclusion. The banned citizen not only possesses no venue to contest the admonishment but also now falls within the boundaries of a new status category. The same dynamic occurs with parks exclusion orders: officers decide in the field to create such an order and thereby empower themselves to mobilize the criminal law in the future. Once they are banned, the excluded possess a status. For them, simply being present in a certain space is a criminal act. Hence, subsequent arrests for being present in a prohibited area are based on that status rather than on conduct. Although the banished can arguably avoid possession of a stigmatized status by remaining outside of their zones of exclusion, we show in chapter 5 that this is often extraordinarily difficult for them to do.

The conferral of this new status—banished—lays the foundation for the denial of rights centrally associated with citizenship. In particular, the conferral of this status deprives recipients of the right to geographic mobility. In some cases, because of the significant spatial extent of the spaces from which many are banned, these individuals arguably lose their "right to the city."[79] As we explicate in chapter 5, many also report that their possession of this status fundamentally transforms how they are seen and treated by city authorities; they are seen as less than full citizens.

As a result of these quite consequential features, the new techniques represent a return to the traditional vagrancy and loitering laws. The new tools broaden definitions of crime to the point of criminalizing the mere presence of some in contested urban spaces. This obviously enhances the territorial and discretionary power of the police and makes more individuals subject to not only arrest but also ongoing monitoring by the police. As one retired Seattle cop explained,

> And then that [the trespass admonishment] gives you a year worth of, you know, being able to shake 'em, and pat 'em down.... I mean, technically, they're trespassed, once you stop them, they can be under arrest. And it's up to you whether you actually book them or just identify and release them. So every time I stop someone who's been trespassed, then I can completely search them.

In short, the new social control techniques allow legal actors to create a new status that does not depend on criminal conviction or even arrest and that makes it a crime for some people simply to be in certain places. As a result, they endow the police with the power they once possessed through vagrancy and loitering ordinances and undermine the ability of the banished to make rights claims vis-à-vis city authorities.

Legal Hybridity

Unlike vagrancy laws and the civility codes, the new social control mechanisms combine elements of criminal and civil law. For example, parks exclusions and trespass admonishments ostensibly rest on civil legal authority. Yet each of these notably enhances the power of criminal law. In each instance, a violation of a civil banishment order becomes a criminal offense. These new criminal offenses, as noted, then provide the police expanded means to monitor and arrest. They also give prosecutors new crimes with which to charge individuals and judges more opportunities to impose yet more spatial restrictions on those charged and convicted. For those who are targeted, the legally hybrid nature of the new banishment works to restrict their capacity to resist the force of criminal law. Even if violations of those orders are criminal offenses, their basis in civil law reduces the avenues citizens can use to contest them.

Consider trespass law. Trespass admonishments are defined as civil (and remedial) acts rather than punishments and cannot be contested. The diminution of due process rights, including the right to legal representation, is justified on the grounds that the original exclusion order is civil. The lack of due process is most evident in the case of trespass enforcement. The police are not required to record the reason for the trespass admonishment and regularly do not do so. Yet violation of the admonishment is a criminal act, subject to a penalty of up to one year in jail and a $5,000 fine.

Thus, by simultaneously defining these exclusions as civil and their violations as criminal, city authorities significantly expand their capacity to regulate those considered disorderly. The legal hybridity that characterizes these tools thus strongly reinforces the extent to which Seattle officials turn to criminalization as a solution to the problems and people defined as disorderly. This hybridity also makes these social control tools more difficult to challenge in the courts. Indeed, the popularity of the new tools is to a large extent the consequence of their ease of use and their imperviousness to challenge. As one legal scholar writes:

> Police and prosecutors have embraced civil strategies not only because
> they expand the arsenal of weapons available to reach antisocial
> behavior, but also because officials believe that civil remedies offer
> speedy solutions that are unencumbered by the rigorous constitutional
> protections associated with criminal trials. A persistent question
> remains regarding the use of civil remedies to check antisocial behavior:
> what constitutional limits constrain their use?[80]

The current and former police officers we interviewed indicated the attractiveness of such civil strategies of exclusion because of their ease of application, breadth, and at least for the time being, diminished opportunities for contestation. As one former SPD officer explained, "I mean, that's the thing about a trespass, you can still trespass anybody for anything. It's easy, it's like win-win. You know?" The difficulty in contesting these banishment orders further undermines the capacity of the banished to make the basic rights claims normally associated with citizenship.

Banishment: Democracy in Action?

The politics of punishment and social control are rarely dispassionate. Anger, racial tensions, concern about social change, fear of crime, misperceptions spawned by the media, and the desire for protection impel the drive for greater punitiveness. At the national level, these debates have been highly charged and enormously consequential.[81] Policy discussions at the local level often elicit the same passions. Yet many of the techniques described escape public attention. Many of the new social control techniques just discussed were not the result of the modification of law. As a result, they escaped the notice of much of the public, including scholars.

Sometimes, however, social control innovations do emerge from new ordinances. In other words, elected officials make an overt, conscious policy choice to make banishment easier. Such was the case when the Seattle City Council passed the parks exclusion ordinance in 1997. In an instance like this, public policy can be understood as democracy in action, as an expression of the public will as filtered through decision makers.

This conclusion oversimplifies matters, because it may overstate the degree of consensus surrounding this or any other policy choice. In the case of measures to increase the power of municipal officials to banish, the attendant public debate is often heated. Supporters of such policies typically include city authorities, law enforcement officials, business organizations, property owners associations, and crime councils.[82] Opponents typically include civil rights organizations, homeless advocacy groups, and minority groups and residents, although in some instances minority communities are divided. The political jousting over these ordinances is often quite intense and divisive. Thus, their adoption arguably signifies the (perhaps temporary) dominance of a particular set of political alliances and discourses rather than the will of the majority.

The debate over Chicago's gang loitering ordinance is instructive. In their analysis of the ordinance and its adoption, Dan Kahan and Tracy Meares argue that what they call the "new community policing" is democratic in nature: its adoption reflects the preferences of a recently empowered black community.[83] Specifically, they claim that the gang loitering ordinance was initiated and supported by the African American community. However, Dorothy Roberts provides evidence that the ordinance was actually driven by a single neighborhood federation in a predominantly white neighborhood, embraced by the mayor, and adopted by the mostly white city council. Roberts also demonstrates that support for the measure among African American residents and organizations was quite mixed. She concludes, "A more realistic view of the political process suggests that white support for tougher police supervision of Blacks helped to guarantee the law's passage, despite vehement opposition by many Black representatives."[84]

Roberts's analysis is an important reminder that passage by a local elected body may not be a meaningful measure of (deep) democracy and may not signify that the ordinance is an expression of widely shared value and preferences. Furthermore, any such preferences are complex, ambivalent, and shifting.

In short, the sight of increasing numbers of homeless and destitute people does not inexorably lead to widespread popular support for civility laws and broken windows policing. The critical issue is how homelessness and poverty are framed in political discourse, and how various constituencies organize to present their solutions to the problem. The relentless association of homelessness with (in)security and the accompanying dehumanization of persons without housing are crucial to the creation of popular support for civility laws in Seattle and elsewhere. The embrace of banishment, too, is not an inevitable expression of the democratic process but a contingent and contradictory response to the worsening of the problems we now call "disorder."

Conclusion

It is clear why the return to banishment is welcomed by police and prosecutors. Each of the social control tools we reviewed here notably increase the power of the police to monitor, arrest, and seek to displace those deemed disorderly. They enable officers to create a category of individuals—the excluded—and then mobilize the criminal law against those they place in that category. These new tools yoke civil law and criminal law in a way that enhances the reach and power of the criminal justice system. Vagrancy laws are back in spirit, if not name, with notable consequences.

It may seem overly bold for us to suggest that Seattle is witnessing a return to banishment. Most courts would not recognize the practices we describe here as banishment. They generally allow spatial restrictions when imposed as a condition of parole or probation, and do not consider exclusion from a neighborhood or area within a city to constitute banishment.[85] Yet we think the new social control tools are best described in this fashion. Those who are excluded are required to "quit" a place and face potentially punitive consequences if they refuse to do so. The weight of the criminal justice apparatus is brought to bear on banished individuals in a heavy and consequential fashion. This occurs despite the rooting of banishment in civil law. Indeed, the legally hybrid nature of banishment is central to its reach and power. The fact that banishment orders are imposed on people not convicted of a crime and without the capacity to contest their legitimacy renders these exclusions more rather than less problematic.

The infusion of criminal law with other sources of legal authority is a significant step beyond the so-called civility codes of the 1990s. These codes faced significant criticism from those who argued that the goal, at root, was to punish and control the homeless and others considered to be disorderly.[86] We share this concern and agree that these laws criminalize behaviors associated with homelessness and subject the unhoused to greater formal control and punishment. Yet these ordinances at least define the conduct they prohibit in relatively specific terms. Moreover, those suspected of violating them are entitled to legal representation, limited as that may be in some jurisdictions. This contestability is important; many have been challenged in the courts, in some instances successfully.

Ironically, the success of some of these challenges fueled the quest for more expansive and durable social control tools. The new techniques of banishment possess a number of novel characteristics. In particular, they are justified in terms of the very limited goal of displacement. They are also quite broad— so much so that they criminalize the mere presence of the banished in some urban spaces. Furthermore, the new techniques infuse criminal law with civil legal authority. They diminish the rights-bearing capacity of those they target, even as they create new crimes and criminal cases. Together, the new techniques broaden the range of existing criminal offenses; increase the power, authority, and discretion of the police; and decrease the rights-bearing capacity of their targets. In this sense, they represent a return to status-based prohibitions against vagrancy.

In the following chapters, we examine the consequences of adopting this approach to urban disorder. These empirical chapters are based largely on data from our case study of Seattle. We begin with an examination of the social geographies and circumstances of exclusion.

3

The Social Geographies of Banishment

Banishment is reemerging in cities across the United States, largely as a response to the "disorder" attendant to homelessness and other social problems, such as addiction and untreated mental illness. These problems were made visible by the socioeconomic and policy changes outlined in chapter 1: rising inequality, due significantly to the decline of the manufacturing sector and the associated stagnation of wages; the weakening of the welfare state; and the large-scale withdrawal of federal support for low-income housing. Policy initiatives that aimed at reducing these problems—the wars on disorder and drugs—did not succeed in reducing overall levels of evident social disadvantage in the streets of America's cities. Given both gentrification and urban redevelopment aimed at promoting tourism and shopping, the pressure to remove or relocate visible manifestations of these problems has remained intense. In chapter 2, we described how rising attention to what was increasingly described as disorder led first to the civility codes and second to the reemergence of banishment.

We use this chapter to assess banishment in practice. We are interested in exploring whether banishment is used primarily to manage those populations and situations considered disorderly or to deal with more significant criminal threats. The evidence from several data sources lead us to conclude that banishment is used primarily to manage people and situations that bother and disturb— but do not endanger—other urban residents. For example, we find thatbanishment orders are often used by the police to initiate contact with a homeless person or to respond to low-level issues such as disturbances, panhandling, and alcohol consumption. In this sense, the new social control tools restore to the police the capacity to exercise moral regulation previously endowed by vagrancy and related statutes. We also find that most of these encounters occur downtown or in other commercial centers. It is thus reasonable to see banishment, in significant part, as a response to concerns from the business community about the effects of disorderly people on consumption patterns. We also find that a significant percentage of those targeted by parks exclusion orders and criminal trespass admonishments appear to be unhoused and/or of color. Given the frequent association in U.S. society between minority status and poverty, people of color are overrepresented in the homeless population and in the banished population as well.

Our analysis is largely descriptive and seeks to identify the people, places, and situations most strongly associated with banishment. We do not seek to establish that wealthy people and white people in similar situations would be less likely to be banished, although this may be the case. Rather, the hypothesis explored here is that banishment is used to deal with troublesome situations that do not rise to the level of crime and that disproportionately involve marginalized people.

We begin with a brief overview of the demographics of those who experience banishment in Seattle. Ideally, our analysis would be based on police records of parks exclusion orders, trespass admonishments and arrests for trespass and Stay Out of Drug Area (SODA) and Stay Out of Areas of Prostitution (SOAP). Unfortunately, not all of these records are available to us. Although the Seattle Police Department (SPD) did provide nearly all trespass admonishments and parks exclusion orders issued by that agency during a four-month sample period of 2005, it was unable to provide trespass arrest records from that period.[1] Moreover, other entities within Seattle—including King County Metro Transit, private security officers, the Parks Department—issue their own trespass admonishments. Because we obtained records only of parks exclusion records and trespass admonishments issued by the SPD, our data understate the extent to which banishment is deployed in Seattle.

Despite these limitations, the data we did acquire are telling. Analysis of the parks exclusion notices and admonishment records enables us to assess both the demographic characteristics and geographic locations of Seattle's banished population. Unfortunately, many of the trespass admonishment forms do not include a narrative account of the circumstances leading up to the exclusion. We therefore supplement our analysis of admonishment records with incident reports published in a local newspaper, *Real Change*, which exists "to create opportunity and a voice for low-income people while taking action to end homelessness and poverty."[2] Much of the paper's content is focused on issues related to homelessness. It features a regular column titled "Street Watch." This column contains a summary of police records of encounters that occurred in the East and West Precincts (where the majority of homeless Seattle residents live) and involved transients as victims, suspects, or both. These summaries are available on the *Real Change* Web site.[3]

Because the "Street Watch" column only includes police encounters with persons identified as homeless, these data do not help identify the percentage of all exclusions or admonishments that are issued to homeless people. However, these narratives provide a sense of how trespass law is used to deal with transients. We begin, however, with the question of who experiences banishment in Seattle.

The Demography of the Banished

We collected a sample of admonishments and parks exclusion orders for four months in 2005—February, April, August, and November. We chose one month for each season to take into account the vagaries of Seattle's weather; though cold and drizzly in the winter months, Seattle is typically sunny and mild in the summer. These data are extrapolated to the calendar year 2005 and allow us to identify patterns in the imposition of trespass admonishments and parks exclusion orders.

Based on the numbers in our four-month sample, we estimate that the SPD issued between 9,000 and 10,000 criminal trespass admonishments and parks exclusion orders in 2005. For the reasons identified previously, this figure—dramatic as it is—understates the frequency with which trespass admonishments are issued in Seattle. In what follows, we describe what is known about the social characteristics of those who experience these forms of banishment in Seattle.

Banishment and the Homeless

Our data indicate that banishment is particularly targeted at those who lack stable housing. Indeed, trespass enforcement appears to be an important means by which the homeless come into contact with the police. We cannot be precise here, because police officers are not required to record the housing status of the banished on parks exclusion notices or trespass admonishment forms. As a result, this information was not systematically reported. Nonetheless, officers sometimes described the banished as homeless in their narrative account of events or wrote "transient" in lieu of an address on the admonishment/exclusion form.

Although only 14.8 percent of parks exclusion notice recipients were explicitly identified by officers as homeless, it is likely that the actual percentage of these orders issued to homeless people is substantially higher. In many cases, the police did not explicitly identify the suspect as homeless or transient, yet described the circumstances in a way that suggested the banished lacked stable housing. The following incident narratives are illustrative.

> *City Hall Park.* Subject found sleeping under blankets on a park bench inside City Hall Park. Subject ID'd and issued this exclusion.[4]

> *Occidental Park.* Observed defendant sleeping on the benches at approximately 1100 hours. Awoke the defendant and informed him not to camp out with all his blankets, laying on the park benches. Returned at 1135 hrs and found the defendant once again sleeping on the benches.[5]

> *Cal Anderson Park.* On 11/12/2005, at about 1408 hours, I was on uniform bicycle patrol conducting a premise check of Cal Anderson Park. I was within the northern most portion of the park near E. Denny Way, when I saw an individual sleeping near the concrete wall. The individual was bundled up within a blue blanket. Upon closer inspection, I could see the individual's face. I observed the individual to be sleeping. The individual was in violation of the City of Seattle's park ordinance of No Camping.[6]

In these incidents, the suspects were not described as homeless, but the narratives strongly suggest that this was the case. In other situations, too, we can plausibly infer that people are homeless if not necessarily labeled as such. For instance, many individuals either have no address provided or are listed as living at 3rd Avenue, the site of the city's largest shelter and service provider for the homeless. If these trespass recipients are also counted as homeless, the results of our analysis indicate that just over half (50.8 percent) of those excluded from parks were homeless. Of course, we may be wrongly including people in the homeless category who have permanent housing on 3rd Avenue. However, this error is probably small, as 3rd Avenue is overwhelmingly commercial. In addition, this method does not include unhoused people who provided officers with the address of other shelters, friends, or family. For these reasons, we doubt that even the 50.8 percent figure accurately captures the frequency with which parks exclusion notices are issued to people who lack stable housing.

It is even more difficult to identify the frequency with which trespass admonishments were issued to the unhoused. In this case, officers are not required to record the housing status of the banished—or even the officer's justification for issuing the admonishment. Indeed, officers offered no rationale for the admonishment in 59.8 percent of the records in our sample. As a result, there is no narrative in which a person might be described as homeless in the majority of trespass admonishment records included in our sample. However, if we group together those incidents in the sample involving admonishees who (1) were identified as homeless or transient in the police summary of events (when one is provided); (2) who had no address entered on the address line; or (3) whose address is listed as 3rd Avenue, the results indicate that 42.5 percent of trespass admonishments were issued to people without permanent housing. This figure, too, is likely an underestimate, as only a fraction of the homeless live at the shelter on 3rd Avenue.

Other data further suggest that trespass enforcement is targeted primarily at the homeless. Take, for instance, patterns at Seattle's Community Court. Trespass cases are very common there. In fact, they are the second largest category of cases adjudicated in this setting. According to court officials, 68 percent of those whose misdemeanor cases were processed in the Community Court were homeless.[7] Thus, if we assume that those arrested for trespass were as likely to be unhoused as those facing other charges frequently adjudicated in the Community Court (mainly theft and prostitution), it appears that roughly two-thirds of those arrested for trespass and processed through Community Court are homeless.[8]

In sum, our data indicate that many—perhaps most—of those who experience banishment in Seattle are homeless. The data also indicate that banishment is disproportionately imposed on people of color, especially blacks and Native Americans, a reality we document in the next section.[9]

The Racial Composition of the Banished

Officers issuing parks exclusion orders and trespass admonishments are required to record the perceived race/ethnicity of the banished. Analysis of these records suggests that people of color, particularly blacks and Native Americans, are substantially overrepresented among the banished. The share of parks exclusions notices issued to black people—38.4 percent—is nearly five times the black share of the Seattle population—about 8 percent. Moreover, the Native American share of those issued parks exclusion notices is more than ten times its share of the Seattle population. Similarly, the share of trespass admonishments that are issued to blacks and Native Americans is five and six times

TABLE 3.1. Race/Ethnicity of Parks Exclusion Order and Trespass Admonishment
Recipients, Seattle 2005

	Seattle Population (A)	Parks Exclusion Recipients (B)	Trespass Admonishment Recipients (C)	Parks Exclusion Disparity Ratio (B/A)	Trespass Admonishment Disparity Ratio (C/A)
Black	8.1%	38.4%	40.1%	4.7	5
Native American	.8%	8.2%	4.8%	9.8	6
Latino/ Hispanic	6.3%	4.5%	2.8%	.66	.44
Asian	14.2%	3.1%	5.6%	.22	.39
White	66.4%	45.8%	46.6%	.69	.70

Note: Sample includes trespass admonishments and parks exclusions issued in February, April, August, and November, 2005. Percentages refer to the share of each issued to persons of each racial background. Because people may have more than one admonishment/exclusion, the racial composition of all persons with at least one admonishment/exclusion is unknown.

Sources: U.S. Census Bureau, American Community Survey 2005, Table B03002; Seattle Police Department.

greater, respectively, than the share of the population that is black or Native American (see table 3.1).

On the other hand, Hispanics, Asians, and whites appear to be underrepresented among the banished relative to the general population. However, the figures reported in table 3.1 for Hispanics are probably an undercount, as SPD officers are generally instructed not to report ethnicity/Hispanic background. To the extent that Hispanics are identified by police officers as white, the figures shown in table 3.1 may underestimate banishment among Hispanics/Latinos and overestimate the incidence of banishment among whites.

Although we hoped to also assess the racial and ethnic composition of SOAP and SODA recipients, we were unable to obtain records of those off-limits orders, which are issued by both judges and Department of Corrections personnel in the field. However, data regarding the racial composition of those arrested for drug law violations are available. Analysis of these SPD records indicates that blacks are dramatically overrepresented among those arrested for drug law violations compared to the general population (see table 3.2). Specifically, these data show that the percentage of drug arrestees who are black—52.5 percent—is 6.5 times higher than the share of the city population that is black. Indeed, racial disparities in drug arrests are especially pronounced in Seattle. According to SPD arrest figures, the total black drug arrest rate was more than thirteen times higher than the white drug arrest rate in 2006. This rate of disparity is surpassed by only one of the other thirty-eight comparably sized cities in the nation for which data are available.[10]

TABLE 3.2. Seattle Drug Arrestees by Race, 2005–2006

	Seattle Population (A)	Drug Arrestees (B)	Drug Arrest Disparity Ratio (B/A)
Black	8.1%	52.5%	6.5
Native American	.8%	1.9%	2.4
Latino/ Hispanic	6.3%	3%	.48
Asian	14.2%	5.6%	.39
White	66.4%	40%	.60

Note: The arrest figures for Latinos are likely low as SPD officers are instructed not to report ethnicity in the Incident Reports.

Sources: U.S. Census Bureau, American Community Survey 2005, Table B03002; Seattle Police Department Narcotics Incident Reports for April and May of 2005 and 2006.

In short, our analysis of police records indicates that blacks and Native Americans are substantially overrepresented in the population of recipients of parks exclusion notices and trespass admonishments relative to the city population. Although the racial composition of those who receive SOAP and SODA orders is unknown, blacks are substantially overrepresented among Seattle drug arrestees. It is therefore likely that blacks are similarly overrepresented among recipients of SODA orders. The fact that both the homeless and people of color are predominantly members of the banished population is not surprising: an estimated 61 percent of the county's homeless are people of color.[11] It is thus poor people, and disproportionately poor people of color, who are most likely to experience banishment in Seattle.

The Geography of Exclusion

Geographic analysis of police records indicates that parks exclusion orders and, to a lesser extent, trespass admonishments are disproportionately issued in the downtown area (broadly defined). Indeed, more than 90 percent of all parks exclusion notices included in our four-month sample from 2005 were issued in the West Precinct, which includes the downtown commercial areas. Of these notices, almost all were served in Parks Zones 4, 5, or 6, all of which are located downtown (see figure 3.1). Criminal trespass admonishments were also concentrated in the downtown area, but to a lesser degree: one-third of the trespass admonishments were issued downtown.

Although gentrifying rapidly, downtown Seattle continues to be home to a large share of the city's poor, homeless, and disabled populations. Rates of

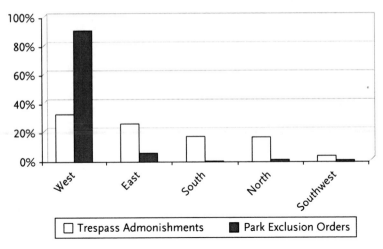

FIGURE 3.1. Trespass admonishments and parks exclusion. *Source*: Seattle Police Department.

poverty and unemployment are two to three times higher among those living downtown than in the city of Seattle as a whole. Nearly one-third of downtown Seattle's working-age population is disabled. Families living downtown are almost twice as likely to be headed by a single parent as is the case citywide (see table 3.3).

In short, downtown is both home to a sizable proportion of the socially disadvantaged population and the site of a disproportionate share of parks exclusion orders and trespass exclusions. The concentration of both social disadvantage and exclusionary practices downtown could be a coincidence. Yet as we already showed, people of color and people without stable housing disproportionately experience banishment. Taken together, these data suggest that banishment is employed in response to the problems associated with growing and increasingly visible poverty, inequality, and social marginality.

TABLE 3.3. Indicators of Social Disadvantage, Downtown Seattle vs. City of Seattle

	City of Seattle	Downtown Seattle
Poverty Rate	11.8%	29.9%
Unemployment Rate	3.6%	12.3%
Disability*	17.2%	30.5%
Single Parent Households	23.6%	56.3%

*Among adults aged 21–64.

Source: U.S. Census Bureau 2000; data for downtown Seattle were taken from http://www5.metrokc.gov/KCCensus/.

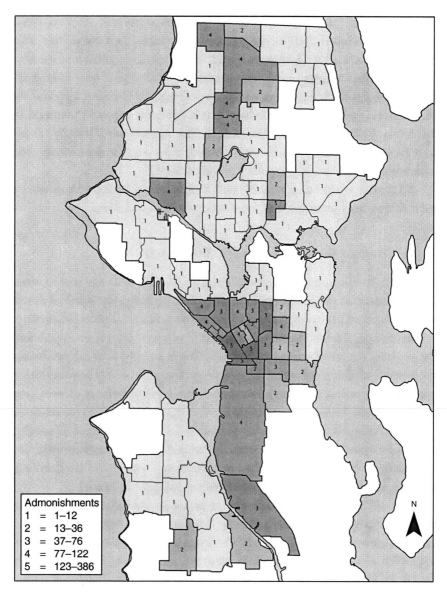

FIGURE 3.2. Admonishments by census tracts, Seattle, Washington. February, April, August, and November, 2005. Natural breaks (Jenks) classification (5 classes).
Source: Seattle Police Department.

Figure 3.2 provides a slightly more refined sense of the geographic distribution of criminal trespass admonishments, which are somewhat less concentrated than parks exclusion orders. Although a disproportionate share of trespass admonishments are issued downtown, they are used throughout the city, particularly along the Broadway corridor and southern end of the East Precinct and the Aurora corridor and University District in the North Precinct (see figure 3.2).

Seattle police in the South Precinct did not provide trespass admonishment records that included detailed geographic information. As a result, this map omits all trespass admonishments issued in the southeast portion of the city. Yet the data that were provided demonstrate that exclusion is used extensively in the South Precinct. Interviews with police officers, defense attorneys, and the banished themselves lead us to believe that exclusion is especially common in the Rainier Valley neighborhood in south Seattle. Indeed, one of the city's large-scale trespass programs includes several businesses along Rainier Avenue, clear evidence that banishment is regularly practiced there.[12]

To provide a better understanding of the dynamics that propel banishment, we provide a brief description of these other zones of exclusion.

The East Precinct: Broadway Avenue and Yesler Terrace

Broadway Avenue runs through the heart of Capitol Hill, the second most densely populated neighborhood in Seattle (after Belltown, just north of down-town). Historically the center of gay life in Seattle and a focal point for the city's counterculture, it is also home to a significant number of homeless youth and the second-most active syringe exchange facility in the city. SPD officers issued 175 trespass admonishments on the middle portion of Broadway Avenue during our sampling period; many more were issued in medical facilities, Seattle Central Community College, and at Seattle University, all of which lie at the southern end of this neighborhood. Of the trespass admonishments issued on Broadway, many were issued at commercial establishments, such as grocery stores and fast food restaurants, and were described by officers as a response to panhandling, loitering, and theft. (The majority identified no precipitating cause.)

In addition, a significant number of the exclusions issued in the East Precinct banned recipients from the city's oldest public housing development. Yesler Terrace, a twenty-two-acre development built 1941, was the state's first public housing facility. It was also the first racially integrated public housing development in the United States. Today, it is administered by the Seattle Housing Authority and is the city's only remaining large public housing development not yet converted into a mixed-income residential development. Yesler Terrace consists of several hundred two-story row houses and a small number of community buildings. Plans are currently in the works to convert Yesler Terrace to mixed-income use, a transition already completed at other Seattle sites. A resident organization is demanding that any plan for redevelopment enable the opportunity to remain. Many residents fear that they are being driven out of Yesler Terrace.[13]

Indeed, trespass enforcement is common there: officers issued forty-eight trespass exclusion notices during our four-month sampling period. Most of the admonishment forms banning people from Yesler Terrace did not offer a reason for the exclusion order or simply cited loitering. The remainder alleged that the banished were involved in or associated with drug activity. Interviews with people active in the Yesler Terrace community suggest that teenage residents are frequently banished for loitering. According to these accounts, their families' continued access to public housing may be jeopardized if the admonished are arrested for returning.

The North Precinct: Aurora Avenue and the University District

A state highway, Aurora Avenue was once the city's primary north–south arterial. For this reason, it is lined with numerous inexpensive motels, many of which are now run down and allegedly serve as sites for the exchange of drugs and sexual services. The neighborhoods that abut Aurora host numerous modest but often handsome single-family homes. In recent years, many young families moved into these neighborhoods. Perhaps because of the proximity to Aurora Avenue, these houses were comparatively affordable in the inflated Seattle housing market. Many residents are active in one of three anticrime organizations. Driven by intelligent and media-savvy leaders, these organizations succeeded in attracting attention from the mayor's office and the SPD. The SPD responded in part by creating one of the city's most extensive criminal trespass operations. Nearly every business on Aurora Avenue signed a trespass authorization with the SPD.[14] Furthermore, all of the twenty-five motels along Aurora were bound together in a single trespass program.

Given this, it is unsurprising to learn that the SPD issued 174 exclusion orders on Aurora Avenue North during our sampling period. These admonishments overwhelmingly banished recipients from motels. The reasons given for these exclusions largely parallel the reasons given citywide; disturbance, loitering, drug activity, and the ubiquitous "no reason" were most common.

Trespass admonishments were concentrated in another northern location as well: the University District. Adjacent to the University of Washington, the commercial establishments in the district cater to a young and less-than-affluent population. The youthfulness of the area contributes in part to its long history as an attractor for homeless teens, particularly along the major commercial thoroughfare, University Avenue, referred to colloquially as "the Ave." Homeless youth are a persistent source of complaints of business people in the area. Accordingly, 112 trespass admonishments were issued on the Ave during the sampling period. No reason was given for most exclusions issued in this neighborhood. When one was given, trespass, loitering, and disturbance were most commonly cited.

The South Precinct: Rainier Beach

Finally, a substantial share of the city's trespass admonishments, and the largest number of those involving black recipients, were issued in the South Precinct, mostly, we believe, in the Rainier Valley, home to a disproportionate share of Seattle's populations of color. According to 2000 census data, 26.8 percent of the southeast Seattle population is black, 29.3 percent is Asian or Pacific Islander, and another 6.1 percent is Hispanic. Although the South Precinct officers issued the second smallest number of admonishments, they issued more exclusion notices to black recipients than did officers from any other precinct. (As noted previously, the South Precinct declined to provide individual copies of its criminal trespass admonishment forms. It did, however, provide the total number of admonishments issued and identify the race of the excluded.) Interviews with youth living in the area suggest that most admonishments exclude people from neighborhood schools, bus shelters, apartment buildings, and commercial establishments where young people tend to gather and socialize.

On the basis of these findings, as well as our interviews with area residents, we suspect that the police use trespass admonishments primarily in their dealings with local youth of color rather than with the homeless. The South Precinct is home to one of the largest trespass programs in the city. Those banished from any of the commercial establishments included in this program are banned from all of them for one year. Participating businesses are outlined on the admonishment form and are listed in table 3.4. (The Othello Merchants Trespass Coalition is also located in the Rainier Valley and includes ten participating businesses.)

If someone is excluded from any of the establishments in this or other trespass programs, to return to any one of them is to commit a criminal offense. Thus, although exclusion from a particular commercial establishment may not appear significant, the creation of trespass programs like that in Rainier Beach means that a trespass admonishment can have significant implications. These programs significantly expand the zone of exclusion and underscore the strong role of the police. No single property owner could create such a program.

Places of Exclusion

Citywide, recipients of trespass exclusions were banned from a remarkable number and variety of locales. These include commercial establishments, such as stores, restaurants, shopping malls, and coffee shops; public housing facilities and other apartment buildings; Department of Transportation property (e.g., under viaducts and on-ramps); King County Metro Transit property, including

TABLE 3.4. Rainer Beach Trespass Program: Participating Businesses

Name of Business	Street Address
Vince's Enterprises, Inc.	8810, 8814, 8824 Renton Av S.
Allstate Insurance	9000 Renton Av S.
Gem Reality	9000 Renton Av S.
People's Translation Services	5013 S. Barton Place
G's Barbershop	5015 S. Barton Place
Video 4 You	5019 S. Barton Place
Komachi Beauty Salon	5027 S. Barton Place
Rany Food Mart	8600 Rainier Ave. S.
Rainier Photographic Supply	8728–8732 Rainier Ave. S
Payless Shoe Source	8824 Rainier Ave. S
Rite Aid Drug	9000 Rainier Ave. S
QFC	9000 Rainier Ave. S
Bank of America	9019 Rainier Ave. S
Southwest Mortuary	9021 Rainier Ave. S
Rainier Beach Dental	9040 Rainier Ave. S
Sub Shop #7	9050 Rainier Ave. S
SPD Storefront	9099 Seward Park Av. S.
Jack in the Box	9102 Rainier Ave. S
Pho Van Vietnamese Restaurant	9150 Rainier Ave. S
Rainer Beach Veterinary Hospital	9238 Rainier Ave. S
King Donut	9232 Rainier Ave. S
Vinson Brothers Corporation	9245 Rainier Ave. S
Safeway	9250 Rainier Ave. S
Key Bank	9255 Rainier Ave. S
Washington Dry Cleaners, Inc.	9252 Rainier Ave. S
Safeway	9262 Rainier Ave. S
McDonalds	9304 Rainier Ave. S
Rainier Beach Chiropractic	9305A Rainier Ave. S
Seattle Best Cleaners	9305C Rainier Ave. S
Washington Federal Savings	9325 Rainier Ave. S
Roscoe Energy Systems	9367 Rainier Ave. S
Hong Kong Seafood Restaurant	9400 Rainier Ave. S
KFC/Taco Bell	9401 Rainier Ave. S
Living Color Beauty Supply	9416 Rainier Ave. S
Larry Veldyke Building	9420 Rainier Ave. S
Morris Tax Service	9428 Rainier Ave. S
International Beauty College	9431–9437 Rainier Ave. S
Rainier Beach Cleaners	9432 Rainier Ave. S
Maya's Family Restaurant	9447 Rainier Ave. S
Rainier Beach Espresso	9471 Rainier Ave. S
R & R Real Estate Services	9258 57th Ave. S.
Hair Studio 57	9259 57th Av. S.
Lake Route Café	9261 57th Av. S.

buses, bus shelters, and bus tunnels; parks and recreation centers; Pike Place Market and the Historic District (including encompassed commercial establishments, social service agencies, and residential apartments); hospitals and other medical facilities; religious institutions; social service agencies; and government buildings. The distribution of parks exclusions and trespass admonishments across these locales is shown in table 3.5. As these figures make clear, banishment is not limited to any particular type of location in Seattle.

The overall story of the geography of banishment told by our data is, at root, fairly straightforward. One finding is that much of banishment practice occurs downtown. This is especially the case for parks exclusions and significantly true for criminal trespass admonishments as well. There are other locales where criminal trespass is heavily used; these are areas where many people—especially young people of color—gather in public space or that have recently experienced significant gentrification. In most cases, no reason is offered for a trespass admonishment. When reasons are given, our data suggest that recipients of exclusion orders are individuals who are associated with disorder and, less frequently, suspected of engaging in minor crime such as drug activity. The use of trespass and other forms of banishment appears especially welcomed by many business owners, presumably because of their fear that street-level activity will suppress commerce.

TABLE 3.5. SPD Trespass Admonishments and Parks Exclusion Orders by Type of Locale, Four Month Sample, 2005

	Trespass Admonishments (n = 2,615)	Parks Exclusions (n = 682)	All Exclusions (n = 3,297)
Commercial Establishments	47.2%	0	37.5%
Parks and Recreation Centers	2.7%	100%	22.8%
Public Housing/Apartment Bldg.	12.5%	0	9.9%
Hotel/Motel	8.2%	0	6.5%
Hospitals & Medical Facilities	4.2%	0	3.3%
Parking Lot	3.8%	0	3%
Pike Place Market/ District	3.4%	0	2.7%
DOT Property	3.3%	0	2.6%
Social Service Agencies/Shelters	1.9%	0	1.5%
Pier	1.8%	0	1.5%
Religious Institutions	1.4%	0	1.1%
Metro Property	1.2%	0	1%

Note: Based on a four month sample that includes February, April, August and November. Although the total number of admonishments shown includes exclusions issued in all precincts, figures for type of locale do not include trespass admonishments issued in the South Precinct, for which detailed information is unavailable.

In short, our evidence suggests that banishment is aimed at people who are considered disorderly and are gathered in places where concerns about disorder are expressed by local business owners and residents. This conclusion is further supported by an examination of the stories officers tell when they enforce banishment.

Accounting for Banishment

Officers issuing parks exclusion notices are required by ordinance to provide a reason for the exclusion order. This is not true of criminal trespass admonishments, however. As mentioned previously, officers failed to provide an explanation for such admonishments in nearly 60 percent of the records in our sample. This lack of accounting means we cannot comprehensively assess officers' reasons for issuing trespass admonishments. Table 3.6 summarizes the reasons most frequently provided for parks exclusion notices and criminal trespass admonishments issued during the four-month sample.

As table 3.6 shows, officers most commonly describe parks exclusion orders as a response to alcohol possession, suspected drug activity, or trespass (i.e., being in a park after hours or in violation of a previous exclusion order). In the 40 percent of cases where officers provided a reason, criminal trespass

TABLE 3.6. Reasons Given by SPD Officers for Parks Exclusions and Trespass Admonishments, 2005

	Parks Exclusion	Trespass Admonishment	All Exclusions and Admonishments
No Reason Given	0%	59.8%	45.7%
Suspected Drug Activity	29.5%	6.8%	11.6%
No Legal Access*/Trespass	14.8%	7.8%	9.4%
Possession of Alcohol	29.2%	3.5%	8.9%
Disturbance	1.5%	10.1%	8.6%
Theft/Shoplifting	0%	6%	4.9%
Loitering	0%	5.3%	4.2%
Sleeping/Camping**	17.6%	0%	3.6%
Other	6.2%	.7%	3.1%

* In the case of parks, this category included people who were present in violation of a prior exclusion order and/or who were in the park after closing time. Among trespass admonishment recipients, this category included people who were on property not open to the public, on public property in violation of a posted no trespassing sign (usually DOT property), and/or were on public or private property despite a prior admonishment.

**During park hours. If sleeping or camping took place after park hours, the event was coded as "no legal access."

admonishments were most commonly described as a response to either a disturbance or trespass. The latter category includes instances in which a person was somewhere he or she did not have legal authority to be, such as private property or public property in violation of a prior admonishment, a posted "No Trespassing" sign, or the city's prohibition of sleeping/camping in public place. Thus the available police records suggest that exclusions are typically issued in situations that do not involve the threat of serious crime.

Officers do not list mental illness as a reason for either parks exclusion orders or trespass admonishments. Yet trespass admonishments are one of the few tools available to officers who receive complaints about persons who are disturbing because they are mentally unstable.[15] We suspect that many of the exclusions prompted by a "disturbance" involve persons with untreated mental illness. We say this in part because trespass is one the most frequent charges levied against defendants in Seattle's Mental Health Court.[16] In addition, several narrative accounts provided by officers in the arrest records published by *Real Change* suggest the importance of mental illness. Some representative examples include the following.

Group Health. Group Health security officer called 911 to report that the suspect, a 40-year-old black male transient who had been previously trespassed from the Group Health campus, had returned. The suspect was loitering in the courtyard. He was detained and identified. Officers also verified the previous trespass admonishment provided by the security officer. The security officer requested the suspect be arrested, and he was. He was booked into King County Jail for trespass. The officer also noted that the man appeared to be mentally impaired, and was unsure if he had understood the trespass warnings, either in the past or currently. The officer thought it highly likely that the subject would return to the Group Health campus as soon as he could.

Starbucks on E. Madison St. The suspect, a white male 55 years of age, is a "chronic trespasser" in the 4000 block of Madison St. He was verbally warned by officers for criminal trespass in this area Thursday, December 7. A Starbucks employee called the police to report that the suspect was once again asked to leave, and would not comply. The man has mental problems, but his being a nuisance has not involved violent behavior. He was taken into custody, interrogated, and released. He was cooperative, and when warned not to return to Starbucks, he said he would not return.

3200 block W. Howe St., under City Bridge. The officer found the suspect, a 53-year-old transient white male, asleep under the bridge, and photographed him sleeping in his blanket. The officer has received many complaints of the suspect staying under the bridge, which is clearly posted with "No Trespassing" and "No Loitering" signs. The man was also photographed in front of the "No Trespassing" sign. He was warned by the officer not to stay under the bridge or he would be arrested. The suspect has mental problems, and SPD has received numerous complaints from residents who have seen him in their yards. Many residents are scared of him because of his size and mental health problems. He is often seen talking to himself. The officer has been in contact with the suspect many times in the last three years.

Pine Street Sidewalk. Pacific Place security called to report a mental male, later identified as the suspect, a homeless white male aged 32, yelling at people outside the Barnes and Noble store on 6th and Pike. Witnesses stated he was yelling, "I am a lethal weapon. My bag is a lethal weapon." He yelled this several times before walking westbound where officers contacted him. He was transported to the West Precinct where he was interviewed. After the interview officers decided there was no actual victim of the suspect's ranting. He was trespassed from Pacific Place, identified, and released.

Further analysis of encounters between the homeless and SPD officers published in *Real Change* allows us to better understand the circumstances that lead to the arrest of homeless persons for criminal trespass or trespass in the parks. These data differ from those presented before in that they include only persons described by SPD officers as homeless and often involve actual arrests, rather then just the issuance of admonishments or exclusion orders.

Of the 476 incidents involving transients published in the "Street Watch" column between January 2000 and June 2005,[17] over one-third (36.1 percent) resulted from investigations of criminal trespass or trespass in the parks. In other words, these data suggest that roughly one-third of all police encounters with transients that occurred in the West and East Precincts stem from trespass investigations. In just over a fourth of these cases—28.2 percent—the investigation was triggered by a civilian complaint. The remaining cases were prompted by an SPD "on view," or observation, of a person who appeared to be on property to which he or she lacked legal access or who appeared to be out of place. The following incidents are fairly representative of trespass investigations described in the "Street Watch" column.

Occidental Park. Officers on routine bicycle patrol of the Occidental Park area of Pioneer Square observed suspect sitting on the cement ledge of a flowerbed. They had prior knowledge that the suspect, a transient black male aged 45, was banned for a year from all Zone 4 parks under the "Trespass in the Parks" Seattle Municipal code. He was issued a new one-year ban, arrested, and booked into King County Jail for trespass.

22nd Ave. E, Abandoned Building. An officer working uniformed patrol was dispatched to a report of activity at an abandoned house on 22nd Ave. E. The report referenced several people sitting on the back porch, possibly smoking narcotics. Upon arrival the officer noticed two suspects, a transient black male aged 44 and a transient white female aged 37, exiting the property by moving aside the temporary fencing. He contacted both parties and detained them until other units arrived. When the other units showed up, the officer inspected the property that the suspects had just exited. He found the house abandoned with all the windows boarded up and several "No Trespassing" signs posted on the side of the building. He informed the suspects that they were under arrest for criminal trespass—they were subsequently booked into King County Jail.

Pike Place Market. Officers observed the suspect, a transient Native American male aged 44, on the second level of Pike Place Market. They were aware that he had been previously trespassed for one year, and they took him into custody. He was escorted to the Pike Place security office, identified, and released.

South Atlantic Bus Way. Officers responded to assist King County Metro for a sleeper complaint. The Metro worker stated that the suspect, a 41-year-old white male transient, has done this to him several times in the last month. He further stated that the suspect has been trespassed from all Metro buses. A routine name check showed this to be true and suspect stated that he lives on the buses. He was taken into custody and booked into King County Jail for trespassing.

Many of these incidents suggest that homeless people most typically experience banishment not because they are engaging in serious criminal behavior but because they are out of place: in violation of a "No Trespassing sign, on private property that is not normally open to the public, or, apparently most often, in a place that is normally open to the public but from which they have been banned. Indeed, roughly two-thirds of the trespass investigations published in *Real Change* involved people being present in such a contested or restricted space. In addition, analysis of the incidents published in *Real Change* indicates that although panhandling is, under most circumstances, not illegal,[18] trespass admonishments may be a response to requests for money.

> *Terry Ave.—St. James Cathedral.* The suspect, a transient male aged 45, is known to the church authorities and has been asked to leave the church premises several times for panhandling church patrons. He was observed loitering in the courtyard of the church, and as officers were aware of his previous trespass admonishment, he was arrested for criminal trespass and transported to King County Jail.

> *Dick's Drive-In on Broadway.* The officer observed a 39-year-old transient white male beneath the awning at Dick's. He has had previous dealings with the man at this location, and has trespassed him from the premises before for panhandling. The officer stopped his car, and the man noticed him and attempted to walk away. The officer ordered him to stop, and to return to the patrol car. The man said he'd been panhandling, and swore he would not trespass again. The officer has warned him on several occasions not to return to Dick's, but he always does. The man was arrested for trespassing, and was booked into King County Jail.

> *25th Avenue and East Cherry.* On November 24 the suspect, a 48-year-old black female, was warned about trespassing in the area and acknowledged that she understood the warning. On December 6 she returned to the area and entered a restaurant and began panhandling seated customers. The woman then fled the area once police arrived to the scene. After a short pursuit the responding officer arrested the woman and booked her into King County Jail for trespass.

Although primarily used to remove unwanted or disturbing people, trespass investigations also produce other kinds of arrests. This occurred in about one-third of the trespass incidents described in the "Street Watch" column. In most of these cases, the additional charge stemmed from the suspect's failure to appear for a previous court date, as was the case in this incident.

> *Elliot Ave. and Blanchard St., under the viaduct.* While on routine patrol in the area, police observed two individuals under the viaduct. This area is DOT property, and is clearly posted "No Trespassing." The

men were contacted on trespass violations, and identified. One man, a transient black male aged 35, was found to have an outstanding warrant, and he was arrested and booked into King County Jail. The other man was issued an oral warning and released.

In a smaller percentage (6.9 percent) of cases, the alleged trespassers were also arrested for possession of drugs or drug paraphernalia, or obstruction, as occurred in the following incidents.

> *Victor Steinbrueck Park.* An officer observed the suspect, a 29-year-old transient black male, in the park after closing. He was contacted and ID'd, and a drug warrant was turned up and he was arrested. A search prior to arrest recovered a small bag of suspected marijuana. The suspect was transferred to the precinct, where the contents of the small bag tested positive for drugs. He was booked into King County Jail.

> *Seattle Center Garage, 3rd Ave. N.* The suspect, a homeless white male age 22, was observed entering Seattle Center property at 3rd Ave. Officers were aware that the man had been previously trespassed from the property. They contacted the suspect, who was going through a garbage can. He refused a command to stay and quickly walked away. After a short foot chase he was taken into custody, transported to King County Jail, and booked with trespassing and obstruction.

These stories from *Real Change* further support the argument that banishment is used primarily to manage disorder. The ability to generate and enforce exclusions gives the police the power to closely monitor those people and places that generate widespread complaints from business owners and others worried about the presence of people perceived as disorderly. With this power, the police can intervene regularly in the lives of the banished to question and possibly arrest and search them. Rarely focused on serious crime, the police instead work primarily to enforce zones of exclusion and, in so doing, place pressure on the unwanted to relocate.

Conclusion

This chapter forms a part of our assessment of banishment. Our goal was to assess how banishment is practiced—against whom it is typically targeted and where and when it is invoked. Our data support several conclusions. First, the consequences of banishment fall disproportionately on Seattle's most vulnerable populations. The available evidence indicates that parks exclusion notices and trespass admonishments are frequently issued to people who lack permanent housing. Indeed, a third of all encounters between police officers and suspects identified as homeless begin with the investigation of an alleged trespass violation. Blacks and Native Americans, already disproportionately represented among the homeless, experience banishment at rates that are quite high relative to their representation in the Seattle population. Not surprisingly, banishment is disproportionately concentrated in downtown Seattle, where some of the city's poorest and most disadvantaged people mingle daily with professional workers, tourists, and increasing numbers of high-income residents. We also find that banishment orders, particularly trespass admonishments, are issued quite frequently in Seattle. It is important to remember that our data understate the extent to which spatial exclusion is employed in Seattle because they only include admonishments issued by the police. Although police records are incomplete, the available data indicate that parks exclusions and trespass admonishments are typically used to remove the unwanted and deal with situations that are better understood as nuisances than as dangerous.

The use of trespass law to deal with difficult, awkward, or troubling situations primarily reflects the lack of alternatives. In the absence of adequate low-income housing, shelter beds, drug and alcohol treatment programs, and inpatient health care facilities—and under pressure from city officials, business owners, and increasingly upscale urban residents—it is understandable that officers use banishment to try to "make the problem go away." Unfortunately, doing so has a host of other, unintended consequences, and does not, in fact, make the problem disappear. We use the following chapter to show that despite its inefficacy, the use of banishment is expanding. We also explore why this is the case, and assess the consequences of the increased use of banishment for the criminal justice system. Our analysis shows that responding to the people and problems increasingly framed as disorder with banishment generates a significant number of criminal cases each year and is thus a costly and, as we show in chapter 5, a highly ineffective way of addressing the problems generated by poverty and other forms of social disadvantage.

4

Banishment and the Criminal Justice System

With an economy built around "clean" corporations like Microsoft, Starbucks, Amazon.com, and Costco, a beautiful natural setting, and a robust tourist industry, Seattle is an iconic postindustrial city. It is associated with "green" environmental policy, and its stereotypical resident is a latte-swilling, granola-munching REI member. It is considered a desirable place, one that establishes trends worthy of emulation. Sadly, Seattle's embrace of novel social control techniques also appears to be an emulated practice. Certainly, the use of banishment is expanding within the city of Seattle at a notable rate, just as it is increasingly deployed in other metropolitan areas.

We use this chapter to address this growing popularity of banishment. Our first task it to demonstrate its expansion in Seattle over both time and space. Our analysis of police and court records shows that banishment is increasingly employed in the city. Our second task is to analyze why this practice is so popular. We draw on interviews with police and correctional officers, anticrime activists, community prosecutors, and defense attorneys to help explain banishment's appeal. The interview data indicate that the police and prosecutors face significant political pressure to "do something" to address disorder. One means to appease such pressure is to create and publicize mechanisms that enable banishment. Banishment further appeals to police and correctional officers because it significantly increases their power to monitor, search, and arrest those they encounter in public space. Banishment is also attractive to prosecutors, who can add exclusion orders as conditions of deferred sentences or as components of plea agreements. With this enhanced power, police and prosecutors can provide evidence that they are responsive to community concern about disorder. At the same time, anticrime activists are frequently encouraged to channel their concerns into support for practices that entail banishment. Moreover, defendants and their attorneys possess little capacity to contest the practices of banishment.

Banishment orders are sometimes touted by proponents as an alternative to criminal justice intervention. Yet the deployment of these new social control tools is best understood not as an alternative to criminal justice intervention but as a supplement to it. In fact, our analysis of court records indicates that the use of banishment generates a large number of criminal cases. By 2005, trespass cases were the third largest category of cases in the Seattle Municipal Court, accounting for 10 percent of the caseload. Processing these cases is, of course, quite costly. The use of spatial exclusion to reduce disorder thus consumes significant public resources that might be better spent on more sensible responses to poverty, such as low-income housing. These costs only increase as banishment is more widely practiced. We use the next section to document the growing use of banishment, as well as the expansion of the zones from which people are excluded.

Banishment's Expansion

As we noted, recent years witnessed growth in the number of people banished and in the number and size of the zones from which they were excluded. We begin our examination of these trends by looking first at off-limits orders.

The Growth of Off-Limits Orders

As we showed in chapter 2, people prosecuted for prostitution-related offenses typically receive a Stay Out of Areas of Prostitution (SOAP) order as a condition of a deferred sentence. Interviews with probation officers indicate that this has been the practice for some time. Because those convicted of prostitution almost inevitably "get SOAPed," the number of people with these orders likely mirrors the number of prostitution cases prosecuted each year. Seattle Municipal Court data indicate that since 1999, the average number of monthly prostitution cases filed has been fairly constant. Thus, it is likely that the number of people with SOAP orders has also remained relatively constant over time. By contrast, the rate of imposition of Stay Out of Drug Area (SODA) orders shows a marked increase. Moreover, because there are many more drug than prostitution cases, the number of people with SODA orders is probably much larger than the number of people with SOAP orders.

It is difficult to determine the precise number of people with SODA orders. Recall that these can be ordered by judges as part of a pretrial release or deferred sentence. They can also be imposed by correctional officers as a condition of supervision. Further complicating matters, the allocation of drug offenders to the municipal and superior courts has changed over time, as has the willingness of each of these courts to impose SODA orders.

Despite our inability to gauge the exact number of SODA orders issued annually, we are confident that they are an increasingly popular and widely used control mechanism. In 1991, shortly after the adoption of the drug traffic loitering ordinance that introduced SODA orders in the Seattle municipal courts, King County Prosecutor Norm Maleng announced that he would request that Superior Court judges also impose SODA orders on those convicted of felony drug crimes.[1] Because most drug crimes are felonies in Washington state, this development had the potential to impact a comparatively large number of people. According to researchers at the National Institute of Justice, these orders were commonly imposed not only on those convicted of felony drug offenses but also on defendants as a condition of pretrial release.[2] After falling out of use in the latter half of the 1990s, SODA orders are once again imposed by some King County Superior Court judges on those convicted of felony drug charges. In addition, acceptance of a SODA order is now an eligibility requirement for the King County Drug Court, which began operations in 1994.[3] According to many defense attorneys, King County prosecutors are increasingly asking judges to impose SODA orders on drug offenders released pending trial.[4]

On the municipal side, too, SODA orders are increasingly common. Historically, the issuance of these orders was limited by the fact that possession of any amount of any drug other than small amounts of marijuana is a felony offense under state law. In 2005, however, the King County prosecutor's office made a policy decision not to file felony charges against arrestees who possessed only residual amounts of narcotics with the understanding that these cases would be handled in municipal court instead.[5] According to his 2007 annual report, the city attorney began to "charge individuals arrested with trace residue of a controlled substance with the crime of Attempted Violation of the Uniform Controlled Substances Act (VUCSA)"—a gross misdemeanor offense.[6] At their first appearance, defendants would be offered a choice. One option was to agree to a deferred sentence coupled with a four-month SODA restriction. In this situation, compliance with the SODA order leads to dismissal of the case. The other option was to face charges for a felony VUCSA by the county prosecutor.[7] Not surprisingly, most of those faced with this choice opted for the deferred sentence. As a consequence, the average monthly number of drug cases filed in

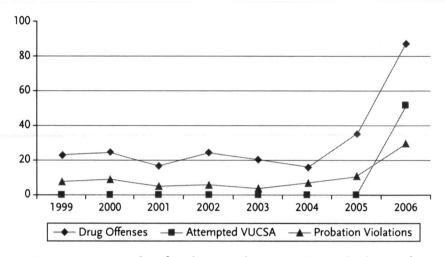

FIGURE 4.1. Average number of misdemeanor drug cases, attempted violations of the Uniform Controlled Substances Act, and probation violations filed monthly. *Source:* Seattle Municipal Court filing data were provided by Bob Scales, crime policy analyst, Seattle mayor's office.

the Seattle Municipal Court increased dramatically, from an average of approximately twenty a month prior to 2005 to nearly ninety per month in the first half of 2006.[8]

Predictably, the growth in SODA orders generated a growth in cases involving allegations of their violation.[9] When such violations occur, they commonly trigger a new charge, probation violation, in Municipal Court. They may also lead to the filing of the original felony charge in Superior Court. In short, because of the transfer of residue possession cases to the municipal court, the number of drug cases adjudicated in that setting grew significantly, as did the number of SODA violations.[10] The coincidence of these trends is clearly depicted in figure 4.1.

Data provided by the Department of Corrections (DOC) indicate that the number and proportion of felony drug offenders who receive SODA orders as a condition of their community supervision is also rising. According to these data, the proportion of King County felony drug offenders who had a "geographic boundary condition" increased from 7.1 percent in 2001 to 30.1 percent in 2005.[11] Although this category is slightly broader than SODA orders, DOC data analysts concluded that the geographic boundary condition is "a fairly good proxy for a SODA restriction."[12]

In short, SODAs are now widely imposed by the superior courts, municipal courts, and the DOC. At the same time, the SODA zones themselves are expanding. As the maps in figure 4.2 demonstrate, the portion of the city considered

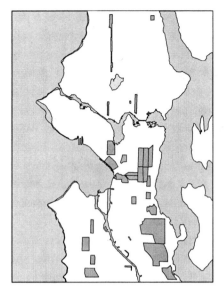 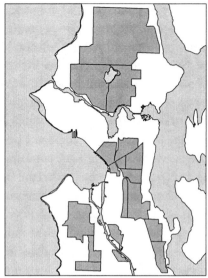

FIGURE 4.2. SODA zones, Seattle, 1998 (left) and 2005 (right). *Source*: City of Seattle.

a high drug trafficking area increased sharply between 1998 and 2005. Roughly half of the city's terrain now lies within a SODA zone. Many of these areas are places where few (if any) drug arrests occur. Thus, the considerable growth in SODA orders is coupled with the considerable spread of the zones in which they are enforced.

Like SODA orders, parks exclusion orders are issued with increasing frequency. During the first eleven months following the adoption of the parks exclusion ordinance, the Seattle Police Department (SPD) issued an average of 128 exclusions per month, for an estimated yearly total of 1,537.[13] Based on our four-month sample of parks exclusion notices, we estimate that the SPD issued 2,046 exclusion notices in 2005, an increase of 33 percent since the program's inception. The number and share of parks exclusion notices issued downtown rose even more sharply. In 1997–1998, 64.6 percent of all parks exclusion orders were issued downtown; in 2005, that figure rose to 90.5 percent. Unsurprisingly, the number of parks exclusion orders issued downtown increased significantly, from 1,024 in 1997–1998 to an estimated 1,851 in 2005. Thus, it appears that parks exclusion orders are issued with much greater frequency in the downtown area than before, perhaps as a result of pressure from business groups such as the Downtown Seattle Association.

Other important developments enhance the significance and impact of parks exclusion orders. First, the proportion of exclusion notices banning people from parks for an entire year has dramatically increased, from 4 percent to 34.6 percent. Second, the proportion of people who are excluded from only a single park is now quite small, just 8.8 percent.[14] In other words, the spatial consequences of a parks exclusion notice are increasingly significant; more than 90 percent of parks exclusion notices issued in 2005 banned people from a park zone (a group of geographically proximate parks) or from all city parks. In addition, city and parks officials created a new zone from which people may be banned. Parks Zone 13 includes twelve additional parks located in the Central District, historically home to Seattle's black population. Zone 13 includes twenty-four acres of recreational facilities and parks land from which people may be excluded. Moreover, the percentage of parks exclusion recipients who are of color has increased, from 41.2 percent in 1997–1998 to 54.2 percent in 2005.

In short, the available data indicate that parks exclusion orders today are issued more frequently than in the period immediately following the adoption of the parks exclusion ordinance. Their use has grown dramatically downtown. Parks exclusion order recipients are increasingly likely to be of color and to be banned from numerous city parks for longer periods of time. Given these trends, it is not surprising that the number of trespass in the parks arrests grew significantly in recent years. Two data sources provide evidence of this increase in "trespass in the parks" arrests. First, our own analysis of Seattle Municipal Court dockets indicates that the number of such arrests more than doubled from 2000 to 2005.[15] Similarly, data provided by the mayor's office indicate that the number of cases involving allegations of trespass in the parks filed with the Seattle Municipal Court nearly tripled from 1999 to 2005.[16] A similar pattern appears to characterize the use of trespass admonishments.

Trespass Admonishments

Because we possess only a four-month sample of trespass admonishments from 2005, it is difficult to establish directly that the use of trespass admonishments is increasing. Analysis of these records indicates that the SPD issued 3,175 trespass admonishments in four months of 2005, for an estimated yearly total of 9,525 admonishments. Although we do not know the number of admonishments issued in previous years, there are several reasons to suggest that their use is growing.

First, recent years witnessed marked growth in the number of trespass authorization forms signed by private property owners. These forms authorize the SPD to issue admonishments on privately owned properties normally open to the public. We obtained copies of all such forms from the SPD. Our analysis

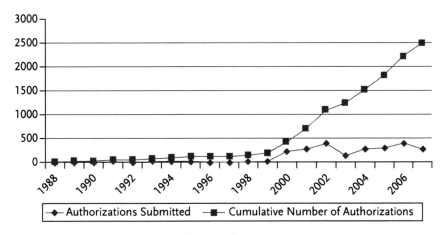

FIGURE 4.3. Growth of trespass enforcement authorization contracts signed; annual and cumulative numbers shown. *Source*: Trespass authorization forms, Seattle Police Department.

of these records indicates the growing popularity of the program since its inception in the late 1980s. Because these contracts stay in effect unless withdrawn by property owners, the cumulative number of trespass contracts on file has grown sharply (see figure 4.3). Due to the large number of extant contracts, the SPD's trespass authority is now quite broad. This enables officers to issue an increasing number of admonishments.

A second observation leads us to suspect an increased use of trespass admonishments: recent years show a marked increase in the number of trespass cases filed in the Municipal Court. Our analysis of court dockets indicates that the number of criminal trespass cases referred to the Seattle Municipal Court grew by 27 percent, from 1,528 in 2000 to 1,947 in 2005. Roughly 60 percent of these cases were ones in which criminal trespass was the sole charge.[17] Similarly, data provided by the mayor's office indicate that the number of trespass case filings rose by 40 percent between 1999 and 2005. Figure 4.4 depicts the rise in the number of criminal trespass and trespass in the parks cases filed since 1999.

Not all criminal trespass cases stem from violations of trespass admonishments, and many admonishments do not lead to arrest. Yet it is likely that the growth of admonishments made many of these trespass arrests possible. As noted previously, trespass cases (including criminal trespass and trespass in the parks) were the third largest category of cases filed in the Seattle Municipal Court in 2005 and constituted 10 percent of the court's caseload. That year, the SPD issued nearly 10,000 criminal trespass admonishments.

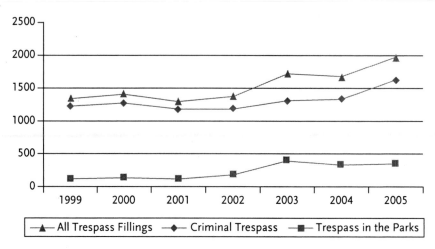

FIGURE 4.4. Annual criminal trespass and trespass in the parks case filings, 1999–2005. *Source*: Seattle Municipal Court filing data were provided by Bob Scales, crime policy analyst, Seattle mayor's office.

The creation of multiproperty trespass programs further underscores our belief that trespass admonishments are increasingly used. As noted previously, these programs group geographically proximate businesses together. Anyone banned from one of the participating businesses is banned from all of them, such as in the case of the West Precinct Parking Lot program, which includes 321 downtown parking lots.[18] The growth of these programs makes it that much harder for people to comply with admonishment orders and thus increases the likelihood that they will be arrested for trespass.

In short, numerous data sources lead us to conclude that the tools that entail banishment—particularly SODAs, parks exclusion notices, and trespass admonishments—are increasingly employed in Seattle and possess expanding spatial consequences. Next, we analyze the dynamics that help explain banishment's growing popularity.

Explaining Banishment's Expansion and Popularity

We have demonstrated that banishment is more common and the zones of exclusion are larger and more numerous. Here, we draw on interviews with police and correctional officers, citizen anticrime activists, and downtown business representatives to explain banishment's expansion and intensification.

Political Pressure

To a significant extent, the growing use of banishment reflects the inten-
sity of the political pressure to do something to address disorder. As noted
in chapter 1, the visible homeless increased notably beginning in the 1980s.
Because of the unemployment that accompanied deindustrialization, the nearly
complete withdrawal of the federal government in the provision of low-income
housing, and the expansion of gentrification, the number of people without
access to shelter rose significantly. As their numbers grew and their presence
became more obvious, the homeless attracted considerable concern.

Some of this concern was benevolent and was expressed most notably
through the construction of emergency shelter facilities. But some of this concern was focused more on the alleged negative impact of urban disorder. Such
rhetoric got a legitimating boost from the theory of broken windows, which
blamed the visible homeless and others for attracting more serious crime to
those neighborhoods where they clustered. As instances of public unsightli-
ness increased in a given place, the theory suggested, criminals would infer
that informal social control was anemic. They would then engage in crime
there because they lacked fear of apprehension.

A key implication of the broken windows philosophy was a redirection
of police energies. Rather than attempting to capture a major felony offender
after the commission of a crime, the police were advised to address low-level
offenses by the homeless and others who symbolized disorder. In this way,
the police would "fix broken windows" by clearing them from public space.
This argument, as we saw in chapter 1, helped motivate the growing number of civility codes passed in Seattle and other cities during the late 1980s
and through the 1990s. The key political advantage of these codes is that they
provided municipal governments with evidence that they were responding to
increasingly widespread concerns about crime and disorder.

Such political pressure to do something clearly underlay the move in Seattle toward yet more control of those considered disorderly. One key instigator
of such pressure is Seattle's Downtown Business Association, which has cited
public safety as one of its primary concerns for decades. This focus on safety
is understandable, given the downtown's reliance on shoppers and tourists.[19]
Frequently, the business community looks to the police to respond to concerns
about crime and disorder. This is seemingly sensible, given the preeminent
public role given the police as the primary defenders against crime.[20] Like other
groups concerned about crime, Seattle's downtown business community regularly expresses a desire for more officers able to exercise greater discretion and
actively resists efforts to reduce police presence.[21]

The creation of the Neighborhood Corrections Initiative (NCI) is one measure of the influence of the downtown business group. As described in chapter 2, the NCI combines SPD officers and Washington DOC officer-specialists in one patrol vehicle. Because the NCI arguably draws the DOC more toward a law-enforcement orientation and away from one focused on social work, it has faced some opposition within the organization. According to the longtime director of the NCI, Seattle's downtown business community was a key factor in persuading state-level officials to endorse the initiative.[22] Today, there is an NCI team in each of Seattle's five police precincts and two in the West Precinct, which is responsible for the downtown area.

Another manifestation of the downtown business community's concern about crime is its creation of a Metropolitan Improvement District (MID). The MID is a self-taxing organization, which provides services desired by downtown business owners. One of its most visible efforts is its Clean and Safe program. The program mobilizes employees, known as ambassadors, to both help clean the streets and monitor street-level behavior. According to a MID official, the ambassadors work to assist tourists and others who need help finding directions. They also notify anyone who is violating a law—such as a civility code—about the nature of their infraction. Although ambassadors possess no enforcement powers, they frequently summon the police.

In an interview, the MID official indicated a close working relationship between her organization and both the SPD and the Seattle city attorney's office; in fact, she described them as "sort of like family." In particular, she described ongoing communication with the assistant city attorney, who serves as the community prosecutor (or precinct liaison) in the West Precinct. As a consequence of these conversations, the MID official was well aware of the criminal trespass program—indeed, the MID office actively assisted businesses who sought to participate in it—as well as the SOAP and SODA restrictions. She strongly supported each of them. In her view, these programs work as "a wonderful tool for the police. They do not have to have probable cause to approach someone." The official also lamented a lack of both visible police presence and jail cells; the latter, she explained, were needed as a place to which to dispatch downtown miscreants.[23] Similar support for banishment practices emerged from members of other anticrime organizations, notably those focused on Aurora Avenue. As described in the previous chapter, Aurora Avenue was once Seattle's most heavily traveled north–south thoroughfare. Several motels sprung up along it to accommodate tourist traffic. The construction of an interstate highway about a mile to the east diminished Aurora's traffic and led to the gradual decline of the motels. Over time, those motels developed a reputation as sites for ongoing commerce in illicit drugs and sexual services. In recent years, while the motels continued to languish, the homes on side streets near Aurora became comparative bargains in the overheated Seattle housing market. Young couples, many with growing families, began to move into those neighborhoods, and many grew discontented with the illicit activity along Aurora Avenue. Some of them organized into a particularly vibrant anticrime organization, one that was able to work constructively with the mayor's office and the SPD. The group met regularly with police officials and even organized their own group to walk Aurora and surrounding streets in an effort to discourage criminal behavior.[24]

Activists in that group, and in another similar group focused on a more southerly section of Aurora, all spoke highly of the criminal trespass, SOAP/SODA, and NCI programs. Indeed, these activists were enthusiastic promoters of the expanded trespass program; they strongly endorsed any police efforts to pressure miscreants to avoid Aurora Avenue. One activist, when asked about the possibility of such efforts merely working to displace individuals to other locales, responded that the police simply need to extend their work into all locales. The police, she said, "need to hammer it apart." Another activist, when describing the SPD sergeant who organized the Aurora motels into a single criminal trespass program, praised that sergeant's work as "awesome."[25]

In short, whatever else the practices of banishment accomplish in Seattle, they do appear to provide evidence that the police are responding when anticrime organizations clamor for action. As the head of the NCI indicated, his program provides "the perception that something is happening." He was careful to note that such a perception was critical to ongoing support for the program, even as he expressed uncertainty about its overall impact on the crime dynamic in Seattle. Similarly, a former SPD officer noted the utility of the criminal trespass program and the power it gave to the police as a means to appear to respond to business owners' concerns about crime. As she noted, "People are constantly complaining, you've got business owners, I mean it looks bad if you've got bums all over the place, so you've got to scoot them along somehow, and trespass is an excellent way to do that."

That anticrime activists often support and advocate for banishment in large part reflects their close relationship to the community prosecutors and police who offered these tools as an answer to their problems. As anticrime groups organize, they are told that one of the most important things the police can do is to banish people from their neighborhood, and they are enlisted in the effort to expand the police's capacity to exclude the unwanted. Community prosecutors, for example, encourage anticrime activists to deliver letters to merchants advocating their involvement in trespass programs or write judges to encourage them to expand SODA zones.[26] Police officers also inform community activists of banishment's power and efficacy. Thus, police and prosecutors do not merely respond to political pressure to crack down on disorder, but they also shape the way that concerns about security are framed and channeled.[27] Police and prosecutors thus play a key role in creating the political pressure to which they subsequently feel compelled to respond.

Banishment and the Police

As the officer just quoted indicated, the power to banish is one that many officers welcome. It grants them increased authority to place pressure on those considered disorderly and disreputable. Certainly, the tools that entail banishment make it far easier for officers to conduct investigations and make arrests. As the number of possible bans increases, so do the odds that any individual who spends significant time in public space is burdened with one of them. This greater ease at arrest provides the police license to search and thus acquire evidence of more serious criminal activity. Even if the police choose not to make an arrest of a banned individual, they can use the threat of arrest to strongly encourage people to relocate. In sum, the territorial capacity of the police— their ability to place pressure on citizens to move from one place to another—is impressively enhanced by the tools that banishment grants them.[28]

The ease of arrest is illustrated vividly by the SOAP and SODA prohibitions. Each of these bans is aimed at those with an actual or alleged history of prostitution or drug offenses. Ordinarily, detecting an individual engaged in either of these activities is a challenge. The standard of probable cause for a legitimate arrest sets a fairly high bar for the police to surmount, at least in theory; officers must possess evidence of a clear promise or execution of a transaction involving the exchange of money for either sex or drugs. Often, to gather such evidence, the police will engage in undercover operations, wherein an officer poses as either a buyer or seller of sexual services or drugs. Once an exchange is promised between the police operative and the criminal suspect, a legitimate arrest is possible. But the time and resources the police must devote to secure these arrests is extensive; multiple officers are typically involved to prevent the suspect from eluding capture and to preserve officer safety.

Contrast this time- and labor-intensive effort with a SOAP or SODA arrest. For the latter, the police need merely spot someone who they either know or suspect possesses one of these restrictions. An arrest is made possible through the much more simple process of running a person's name through databases accessible from the in-car terminal. If such a search reveals the existence of a SOAP or SODA order (or a criminal trespass admonishment or parks exclusion order), an arrest is possible. It is hard to imagine an easier arrest. As one officer who works Aurora Avenue noted, it is "really hard" to make an arrest for prostitution without a SOAP order.[29]

Once arrested for a SOAP or SODA violation, an individual can legally be subjected to a full search, which may provide more evidence of criminal wrongdoing. This is another obvious advantage of lowering the bar for probable cause. As one city attorney noted, an arrest enables the police "to get in the pockets" of suspect individuals, a reality that several officers noted with strong approval. A former SPD officer noted the value of the year-long criminal trespass admonishment: "Then that gives you a year worth of, you know, being able to shake 'em, and pat 'em down."

In some locales, like Aurora Avenue, an arrest for a violation of a banishment order is a near certainty. Yet an arrest is not always required for the police to exert territorial power. Sometimes, officers merely threaten an arrest or otherwise communicate that they are casting a watchful eye. As one sergeant noted, "Some people have to be made uncomfortable. And, if we have to, we can make them move." She also noted that it is easy to communicate to individuals that the police are paying attention to them. "You can simply ask somebody if they are lost, or if they need help finding a business. They get the message."

The value of the criminal trespass program for the police was made quite clear by this sergeant, because she was largely responsible for its expansion along Aurora Avenue. One manifestation of this effort was the motel trespass program, which knits twenty-five motels together. If an individual is admonished from one motel, he or she is admonished from all of them. Beyond the motels, the sergeant succeeded in signing criminal trespass agreements with all but a handful of the other businesses on Aurora Avenue. She clearly valued the expansiveness of the criminal trespass effort. She suggested that for individuals prone to criminal activity, "There are not many more places on Aurora for them to go." As one Aurora-focused anticrime activist indicated, "It is easier to move a problem than eliminate it." For that reason, he, too, endorsed a robust criminal trespass effort.

Another way to illustrate how banishment broadens and strengthens the social control net is to witness their use by NCI units. Recall that the NCI brings together officers from the SPD with their counterparts from the Washington DOC. Given their respective databases and capabilities, the two boast an impressive combined power. The NCI began as something of an experiment in 1996, concocted by an SPD officer and a DOC employee who found themselves in frequent contact on the streets of Pioneer Square. According to the SPD officer involved in this early work, he and his DOC colleague realized that not only were they frequently dealing with the same individuals but their respective powers complemented each other well. In discussions during ride-alongs, police officers expressed admiration for the ability of the DOC officers to conduct searches of anyone who is DOC active for any reason. As one SPD officer said, while pointing to his DOC sidekick, "The power this guy has is awesome."

Given this power, it is perhaps not surprising that the SPD typically places one of its more aggressive officers in the NCI unit and concentrates the unit in areas of long-standing concern, such as Aurora Avenue. This enables the police to exert greater pressure to try to drive unwanted people from particular places. Each of the SPD officers involved with the NCI expressed strong approval of criminal trespass and SOAP/SODA restrictions, because they provided a ready excuse to question individuals and potentially arrest and search them. One NCI officer in the downtown area expressed particular fondness for SODA orders. He was especially pleased about a developing practice whereby prosecutors were willing to bypass bringing felony charges against an individual suspected of involvement in drug activity, in exchange for agreeing to a SODA order as a sentencing condition for a misdemeanor drug conviction. The SODA order, the officer noted, provided him and his colleagues with the continuing capacity to monitor many of those he encounters on the streets and to use the threat or actuality of arrest to convince them to relocate. As one officer said about police priorities, "Really, you just want to get them out of your area. That's all you really want."

Ride-alongs with NCI units reveal the frequency with which officers run checks on individuals who they suspect may possess one or another banishment order. Indeed, the centrality of using the computer-accessible databases to contemporary policing was obvious on one particular night. The Seattle police officer in the car was a veteran of several years. At one point during the ride-along, his in-car terminal ceased to function properly. "I'm dead," he noted. He turned to his passenger and expressed regret that his reliance on the computer was so complete. Early in his career, he said, he was much less dependent on the computer. But the malfunction revealed that he could no longer police in the fashion to which he had grown accustomed—running names or license plates through databases.

Of course, the police are not the only actors in the criminal process, nor are they the only ones involved in the deployment of banishment orders. Prosecuting attorneys and judges also play critical roles.

Banishment: The Role of Prosecutors and Judges

There is little question that the threat of banishment impressively enhances the territorial authority of the police. Yet the police do not act alone. Indeed, without the support of prosecutors and judges, banishment would not exist. In particular, several staff members in the Seattle city attorney's office endorsed the mechanisms used to enact banishment and provided explanations for how it is used. Key actors here are the precinct liaisons, who are assistant city attorneys whose offices are located within one of the SPD's precinct offices. Their job is to work closely with both the police and community members to address places that draw persistent complaints about alleged criminal activity. According to one precinct liaison, his job is to "use whatever potential tools are at our disposal," including some "nontraditional forms of problem solving." The tools he listed were numerous and included property abatement, seminars with motel owners to inform them of the regulations that constrain them, and contacts with mortgage companies to place pressure on owners of problem properties. SOAP and SODA orders, along with criminal trespass, earned voluble praise from this precinct liaison as tools he most relished seeing deployed. Especially attractive to him was the fact that a successful prosecution for a violation of either was a "slam dunk." Such cases, he said, were easy—all you needed was an officer's word that the individual was in a place from which he or she had been previously banned.

As this precinct liaison noted, any individual who was arrested was then subject to search. This capacity gave the police additional opportunity to find evidence of criminal activity and thus enable a potential charge for a more serious offense. Another liaison emphasized the advantages of "getting people into the system." This, she emphasized at a public meeting of a downtown-area organization, enables the police to make arrests. She encouraged down-town business owners to give names of people they found troublesome so the police "can see if the people who are causing problems are violating SODA orders."[30]

As we noted previously, SODA orders are increasing in Seattle, in part because of the rising popularity of attempted VUCSA charges. When defendants are offered a SODA order in lieu of a drug prosecution, they typically acquiesce. Several public defenders noted that the deal offered to defendants—face a charge or take a SODA order—is rarely a hard choice. One of them noted, "They're there in jail, looking at the possibility of a charge, or they could walk away with this deferred sentence, and so they take the deal 99 percent of the time." Yet the choice enables what the city attorney's office desires—ongoing surveillance of those who spend time on the city's streets.

SODA orders and other forms of banishment thus provide city attorneys with an opportunity to show that they are responding to citizen concerns about crime and disorder. This is enabled in part by the degree of cooperation between the police and the city attorney's office. As one assistant city attorney noted, it would be "shocking" if members of his office did not request that anyone charged with a prostitution or drug offense be given a SOAP or SODA order as a condition of release or sentencing. Any such request, he suggested, would invariably be granted by a judge, whose role is strongest in terms of imposing SOAP or SODA orders. Because judges determine sentences, it is up to their discretion whether to impose conditions of sentencing. The consistency with which judges in Seattle imposed SOAP and SODA orders was noted by several public defenders, as well as by city attorneys. Yet one public defender noted a striking discrepancy between the frequency with which judges imposed SOAP and SODA orders and their later unwillingness to meaningfully punish anyone for violating them. As he described a typical scenario:

> Oh yeah, if you get someone with prostitution, you know, they do their day in jail or whatever, and a couple of months later they come back before the courts because they were in an area of prostitution. Unless they have a new prostitution offense, the judge will kind of go, "Look, I'm serious, you have to stay out of there, I'm going to make you do another two days on work crew, and just stay out of there."

This reality undoubtedly contributes to the impression shared by several actors in the criminal justice system—police, prosecutors, defense attorneys, judges, and policy analysts—that many individuals perpetually cycle through the jail system as a result of violating SODA orders or other spatial exclusions. As one officer noted, he can arrest someone several times on just one SODA order. Indeed, our analysis of the impact on banishment suggests that it generates a significant impact on the criminal justice system. We turn to a consideration of these consequences.

Criminalizing Exclusion

Advocates of the new social control tools we highlight sometimes describe them as alternatives to arrest and incarceration. For example, as noted in chapter 2, proponents of the parks exclusion law argued that the denial of due process rights was justifiable because "under the ordinance individuals are excluded from a park, not arrested. Thus, due process is—and should be—less than for a criminal arrest."[31] As critics point out, this obscures the fact that due process is also required in civil proceedings, and these tools make possible arrests and criminal prosecutions that could not otherwise occur.

As we have showed, the number of criminal cases stemming from the practice of banishment in Seattle courts is increasing. These arrests and prosecutions are quite costly.

For example, in 2005, the SPD referred 1,947 criminal trespass arrests and 270 trespass in the parks arrests to the Seattle city attorney's office for review. Trespass was the sole complaint in the majority of these referrals. Over 90 percent of suspects identified in these referrals were booked into jail. These suspects served an average of 1.1 days in jail awaiting adjudication. City prosecutors opted to file charges in 67 percent of these cases. These figures suggest that 10,070 jail days were served as a result of the prosecution of these trespass cases. The costs of arresting, booking, prosecuting, defending, and jailing this many people clearly consumes significant public resources, resources that could be used in alternative—and arguably more productive—ways.

The incarceration of misdemeanor drug offenders who violate SODA orders is also costly. According to the Seattle city attorney's Office, 23.5 percent of those charged with attempted VUCSA in the municipal court between March 2006 and December 2007 were found to be in violation of their SODA order within that same time frame.[32] Some of them violated their SODA order multiple times. Together, these 192 violators generated 368 SODA (probation) violations. According to the city attorney, jailing these SODA violators cost the city approximately $1 million.[33] It is thus clear that the city of Seattle spends millions of dollars each year to jail and punish people who violate their banishment orders.

Conclusion

The data reviewed in this chapter lead us to conclude that banishment is growing in popularity and spatial extent in Seattle. This popularity stems from political pressure from a variety of groups—most particularly from downtown business organizations and other anticrime organizations—to address concerns about disorder. These tools certainly enable the police greater license to monitor and arrest, and prosecutors more opportunity to charge individuals for criminal offenses. At the same time, the legally hybrid nature of these tools and the weak rights protections they offer make it difficult for defendants and their attorneys to contest them.

Yet it is a costly endeavor. Even if the criminal offenses that banishment creates are minor, the costs of arrest, prosecution, and jailing are anything but small. Indeed, banishment costs Seattle many millions of dollars. In the context of severe budget crises and the projected need to build an additional city jail, these cases and costs deserve scrutiny.

Furthermore, the extensive fiscal resources devoted to banishment may well be wasted. That is because banishment provides no long-term solution to the perceived problem of disorder. Indeed, it arguably *enhances* that problem by rendering the lives of the excluded even more difficult and unstable. We come to this conclusion as a result of extensive interviews with the banished. These lie at the center of our discussion of the consequences of banishment, which is the focus of chapter 5.

5

Voices of the Banished

The visible manifestations of extreme poverty are often unappealing and, for some, frightening. It is therefore easy to understand why the desire to banish is sometimes strong, and why policies to enable it might be popular, even in an ostensibly progressive city like Seattle. Yet it also is necessary to consider what consequences flow from banishment. Banishment's short-term policy goal, it seems, is to force people to relocate. The long-term goal is to encourage them to desist from the various behaviors—such as sleeping in parks, consuming alcohol, or engaging in the drug or sex trades—that presumably lead the police to intervene in their lives in the first place.

Any assessment of whether these goals are being met and of the wider array of consequences of banishment requires understanding it from the perspective of its targets. In this chapter, we draw on interviews with the spatially excluded to explore the experience and effects of banishment. In doing so, we consider the validity of city officials' construction of spatial exclusion as a nonpunitive alternative to arrest and incarceration. We consider how banishment affects its targets and their ability to enjoy the rights associated with citizenship. As we demonstrate, the banished find many of these rights severely limited. These include the rights to enjoy spatial mobility, access necessary goods and services, and be free from searches and seizures based on a status rather than specific illegal behaviors.

We also assess whether the explicit policy goals that justify spatial exclusion are, in fact, achieved. The data needed to directly test whether the use of banishment reduces crime are unavailable. Nonetheless, the interview data we draw on here shed important light on this question. It enables us, for example, to ascertain if banishment results in relocation. We can also assess whether banishment orders have stabilizing or destabilizing effects on those who receive them, and whether they reduce or increase the likelihood of subsequent involvement in the criminal justice system. Our evidence suggests that banishment does not lead to relocation, stabilization, or reduced criminal justice involvement. For this reason, we are doubtful that it is an effective crime-fighting tool.

Our interviews also indicate that banishment is best understood as a punishment in and of itself. It functions as a pathway to criminal justice intervention, rather than an alternative to it. Furthermore, the policy goals underlying the use of tactics that entail banishment are not typically met. In particular, we find that banishment orders typically fail to relocate the banned. Of course, banishment uniformly fails to address the adverse circumstances that face the disadvantaged as they struggle to establish stable and productive lives. Even worse, it renders the lives of its targets more (rather than less) precarious.

That legal exclusion does not work even to relocate its targets reflects, most fundamentally, a misunderstanding about the meaning of place. Whereas city officials imagine the parks and neighborhoods from which people are banned largely in terms of the illicit opportunities those places afford, our respondents reported much more complex relationships to those areas. For many, these spaces are often the only place they felt themselves to be at home. Even those who lack permanent shelter possess strong attachments to particular places. Social networks, social services, and concerns for economic and physical security all tether the homeless and others considered disorderly to particular neighborhoods. The fact that services are often concentrated in those same areas made the exclusion order painfully ironic, and even nonsensical, to those we interviewed.

As a result of their deep attachment to and dependence on the spaces from which they were excluded, most of our respondents reported that they resisted their exclusion orders: most continued to frequent the places from which they had been banned. Yet their refusal to move led to a constant fear of detection and often to ongoing involvement with the criminal justice system. As a result, banishment appears to accomplish few of its intended effects, and has many adverse and apparently unintended effects. It is, then, a failure as a policy to reduce urban disorder.

We begin by outlining the goals associated with the use of banishment, then analyze why these goals are not achieved.

Justifying Exclusion

Banishment is typically justified in terms of two main goals. The first is to improve the quality of life in allegedly disorderly neighborhoods. By removing undesirable people from a particular locale, proponents argue, spatial exclusion improves the quality of life of other people who live and work there.[1] The second goal is to encourage the banished to desist from any deviant behaviors in which they may engage. Specifically, the threat of sanction, such as arrest or incarceration, is intended to deter the excluded from returning to the places that ostensibly offer temptation. Proponents of banishment contend that the separation of the disorderly from the spaces in which they get into trouble will facilitate their rehabilitation. This separation ideally helps them break the cycle of problematic behavior by limiting their capacity to reoffend.

Advocates offer additional arguments in favor of the new control mechanisms. In response to concerns about weakened due process rights associated with the new tactics, advocates emphasize banishment's ostensibly nonpunitive nature. For example, proponents of the parks exclusion ordinance insist that the diminution of due process rights it entails is appropriate because an exclusion order is not an arrest.[2] In addition, advocates stress that unlike arrest, exclusion from a park or park zone is a "relatively minor" sanction.[3]

These rationales rest on a set of questionable assumptions. For example, the idea that spatial exclusion enhances order assumes that the world is fairly neatly divided between the orderly and the clearly identifiable disorderly, with the latter serving solely as a vector of crime and diminished quality of life. Yet matters are more complicated than this social cartography allows. For example, in his well-known analysis of book and magazine vendors in New York City, Mitch Duneier argues that many of these street inhabitants committed what some would call disorderly acts, such as using drugs and spreading their wares on the sidewalk. But these same individuals also acted as agents of informal social control, sometimes preventing arguments from becoming violent. Moreover, the service they provided, selling recycled reading material, arguably enhanced the quality of life of some New York residents. In short, Duneier's subjects could not be characterized solely as "disorderly."[4]

Official claims about the laudatory effects of spatial exclusion also tend to ignore important empirical matters, including the vexing problem of displacement and the possibility that spatial exclusion may render the lives of the banished more (rather than less) precarious. That is because the locales from which people are banished offer much more than just temptation; they often offer jobs, services, or social connections people need. Thus, compliance with an exclusion order may mean loss of access to important and stabilizing resources.

Moreover, the viability of these policy arguments rests on the assumption that the banished comply with their exclusion orders. If the banished remain in places from which they are excluded, then the orderly inhabitants within zones of exclusion cannot benefit from their departure. By definition, if the banished frequently return to the spaces from which they have been excluded, none of banishment's intended rehabilitative effects are realized. The possibility of rehabilitation is further compromised if noncompliance leads the banished to cycle constantly through the courts and jails; this often results in the further destabilization of people's lives. In short, banishment's unintended consequences require consideration.

This leads us to two important questions.

1. Do people tend to comply with their exclusion orders, or do they resist these orders?
2. What consequences do both compliance and resistance have for the lives of the banished?

We draw on interviews with forty-one individuals who experienced banishment in Seattle to address these questions. We used the interviews to investigate how the banished respond to their exclusion orders and explore the consequences of this response. We also elicited our interviewees' thoughts and reflections on exclusion as a policy response to their presence and behavior. Their answers cast serious doubt on whether banishment can achieve its aims.

Interviewing the Banished

The interviewees were recruited through attorneys, social service providers, and by word of mouth. The interviews occurred between September 2006 and June 2007 and took place in locales such as coffee shops and park benches. They ranged from twenty to ninety minutes in length. The interviews were recorded, transcribed, and coded for analysis. Interviewees were paid $25 for their time.

Our sample included nearly equal numbers of men and women (twenty-one and twenty, respectively). The majority (twenty-three) of our interviewees are black; twelve are white, five are Native American, and one is Latino. Respondents ranged in age from twenty to fifty-four; the average age at the time of the interview was thirty-eight. A majority (thirty-three) were homeless at the time of their interview. Just over half (twenty-one) had experienced multiple forms of banishment. All told, twenty-four had been excluded from the parks, seventeen had been trespass admonished, seventeen had Stay Out of Drug Area (SODA) orders, and six had Stay Out of Areas of Prostitution (SOAP) orders. Our interviewees constitute a convenience sample. Because we cannot know the demographic composition and legal history of all of those excluded in Seattle, we cannot compare the characteristics of our sample with those of the banished population as a whole. However, it is possible that women, blacks, and possibly older people are somewhat overrepresented in our sample.

We used the interviews to learn more about the effects of banishment on our respondents' lives. The interviews were semi-structured: certain questions were asked of all interviewees, although our respondents were also able to introduce unique topics and issues. The coded transcripts were organized into three main topics: the reasons a person did or did not comply with his or her exclusion(s); the consequences of that person's banishment; and reflections on the legitimacy and efficacy of banishment as policy.

Truthfulness is a key methodological issue for researchers relying on interview data; how can we know whether to trust what our respondents are telling us? This question pertains not only to interviews with the socially marginal but also to interviews with police officers, attorneys, social service providers, and others. In the context of this chapter, we note several considerations that bolster our confidence in the validity of our findings and conclusions. First, many of our questions focused on the subjective experience of banishment. Although deceit remains a possibility, there is no higher authority on one's subjective experience than oneself.

However, some of our questions did focus on factual issues. For example, we were interested in whether people complied with or resisted their exclusion orders and what factors helped explain this response. We also asked questions about the events that precipitated the exclusion. For several reasons, we are confident that the answers we received to these and other factual questions are largely reliable. First, the responses we obtained were consistent with what we learned from other data sources. For example, our analysis of parks exclusion orders described in chapter 3 found that roughly 30 percent of these exclusions were triggered by alleged narcotics activity, 30 percent for possession of alcohol, and 30 percent for sleeping/camping. Of the twenty-four individuals we interviewed who had been excluded from city parks, a third fell into each of these three categories. Thus, the information provided in police records closely matched the information we obtained from our respondents.

In some cases we also checked people's accounts of their legal history against public information from the King County Jail registry. For instance, we were struck by the number of interviewees who reported having no criminal record and yet were being trespassed for nothing more than sleeping from parks, Department of Transportation property, piers, and other places. To determine the accuracy of these reports, we checked accounts against the jail registry, which lists each booking into King County Jail in the past year and the charges that precipitated the booking. In every case we checked, those who said they had no criminal record did not appear in the jail registry. We also checked the registry in a few cases when our interviewees' accounts strained credulity. For example, one person failed to arrive for his interview twice within a two-week period. In both cases, he called days later and explained that he had been arrested for trespass and was in jail during the scheduled time for the interview. Although we were initially dubious, his account was borne out by the jail registry. In short, the accounts of our interviewees were highly consistent with what we learned from other data sources.

Two additional factors further boost our confidence in the reliability of these data. First, we relied on the same indicators that are commonly used in everyday interaction to assess the reliability of the information with which we were supplied. That is, we considered the internal consistency of our respondent's accounts, as well as their demeanor. Most of our interviewees offered fairly consistent stories, convincingly explained any contradictions noted, and made eye contact throughout the interview, thereby bolstering our confidence. (This was not the case in two interviews, the results of which are not included here.)

In addition, many of our respondents freely admitted to engaging in illicit conduct. Those who had been SOAPed, for example, clearly identified themselves as "working girls." Others spoke candidly of their struggles with addiction. In short, most of our interviewees were quite open about their behavioral issues and problems. We suspect their candor stemmed from the fact that they were compensated for their time no matter what they said, and that we were likely perceived as friendly because we recruited participation through public defenders and social service providers.

In sum, although we were unable to verify all aspects of the individual accounts provided to us, we are confident that the interview data are largely reliable. The data were analyzed in several steps. First, we coded the interview transcriptions for main themes, concepts, and events. These were the themes that appeared frequently or seemed particularly salient to the interviewees. We then created memos that focused on key themes. We extracted representative excerpts from the interviews to illustrate and discuss these key themes. We also noted contrary or diverging comments; these allow us to highlight potential contradictions in informants' experiences or understandings.

We present the results of this analysis in four sections. First we explore whether people complied with their exclusion order and identify the factors that help explain this variation. The second section explores the experience and consequences of exclusion. The third section reviews the policy reflections offered by the banished. A conclusion summarizes our findings and considers theoretical and policy implications.

Understanding Compliance and Resistance

Only a third of those we interviewed indicated that they largely complied with even some of their exclusion orders. This finding, in and of itself, suggests that one of the official rationales for banishment is not met—the majority of the excluded do not leave the places that are thought to house opportunities for deviance.

For the minority that did comply, several factors were pertinent. First, many in this group likely found another place to live outside of their exclusion area. Second, the prospect of jail was especially terrifying and thereby helped compel compliance. This was especially true for those who had never been in carcerated. Said Claudia, a newly homeless African American woman who refused to return to Courthouse Park after her exclusion: "Thank God I didn't get arrested, I didn't come to Seattle to get pulled to jail. There is no way I'm goin' to jail." Pete, excluded from the parks for possessing an open container of alcohol, was similarly deterred: "No, I haven't been back to the parks since [being excluded]. Cuz, you know, I'm not looking for trouble and I'm not trying to go to jail."

In a few cases, the threat of going to jail led the banned to contemplate leaving town, as was the case for one homeless veteran: "I don't think they can put you in jail that long on some petty-ass misdemeanor shit I guess. But, uh, I don't appreciate goin' to jail and I sure as hell don't want to. So it might be best if I just go ahead and go down to San Diego for a while." In a few cases, fear of going to jail did not initially trigger compliance, but the repeated experience of incarceration was reported to have that effect: "When you're going to jail, you think, and you're doing it repeatedly, you know what I'm sayin', at one point you're gonna get tired, you'll get tired, and say, you know what, I'm done right there. And that's where I'm at right now."

In several instances, our interviewees complied with their exclusion order despite the fact that this meant the loss of a significant resources or opportunities. For example, one woman declined to participate in a job-training program because it required traveling through her SODA zone at night. Similarly, José, whose story was told in the introduction, complied with his exclusion from Casa Latina and lost access to day jobs as a result. Those who complied with their exclusion order, sometimes at great cost to themselves, did so largely to avoid going to jail.

In sum, about one-third of our respondents reported that they mostly complied with their exclusion orders. Those who found a place to stay outside of their exclusion area and who feared apprehension and jail were more likely to report complying with their exclusion order. More commonly, however, respondents said they remained in the locales from which they were banished. A number of factors help explain this. First, the prospect of going to jail, although widely considered unpleasant, was not sufficient to deter many:

> Well it [going to jail] affected me some, but uh, to be honest with you, you basically being a minority and being homeless, goin' to jail is something which, which is an ongoing policy. Like I say, it is the system which you kinda get used to.

> No, what can they do to you? At this point I can say they must be doing me a favor [by sending me to jail]. I don't care. I don't tell them that, but if they see that I'm homeless...nothing you could do to me. It's kinda pathetic. But what can they do? There's really nothing they can do.

The fact that the threat of jail was not a deterrent for many of our respondents speaks volumes about their existing circumstances, as well as the attractions offered by the places from which people had been banished. As Bob, a homeless veteran, explained:

> Well, nobody really wants to go to jail. I act like it doesn't matter to me, I let them think that. But I don't wanna go to jail, I'd rather be homeless anywhere than go to jail, you know what I mean? 'Cause you can't smoke. I don't wanna be told when to eat, what I gotta eat, can't do anything. And it's bad in there. You know, but I don't let it bother me too much. But I'm certainly not gonna leave the park, I like it there.

A few people explained their lack of compliance in terms of their perception that the likelihood of being detected was minimal: "A Metro thing, I've been caught drinking at a Metro stop. They told me I couldn't take the bus for like two months or whatever. How are they gonna know about it? Unless I screw up at a Metro stop again within that time, how they gonna know?"

In some such cases, respondents' belief that they would not be caught reflected their assumption that their exclusion order only applied if they were loitering or otherwise engaged in questionable behavior. In this case, Ernest had been trespassed from his god-daughter's apartment building:

He [the respondent's friend] had a daughter, and we was thinking
about that, you know, even though I was trespassed I wasn't thinking
about my trespass, I didn't see that at that point, like, okay, I'm
trespassing in this area, I didn't think it's like, don't, don't ever come
back. I'm thinking like, okay, I'm not going to be in here for that long,
I'm gonna come in my car and leave. You know what I'm saying? I'm
not going to be walking around and talking with everybody like I did in
the summer. It was like, in and out, I'm seeing my god-daughter, no
one else to see, I'm going to one building and one building only and
then leaving.

Thus, some reported not staying out of their exclusion zones because they
believed they would not get caught, especially if their presence was not problematic. But most explained their noncompliance in terms of the importance to
their well-being of the space from which they had been excluded. Many people
reported that parks and the other facilities housed in SODA zones were simply an essential dimension of their lives. Social contact was among the important amenities offered in parks and other exclusion zones. Darren, an African
American homeless man living with AIDS, felt strongly about this:

But uh, I go to parks where people be. People of all cultures and
colors. Not, not where, not just some open field. An open field,
that's creepy. Very creepy. . . . So the whole thing is just trying to find
a place to be that's safe and comfortable. Yeah, that's safe, that's
comfortable, that's out in the light, you know, with people around,
yeah. People of all cultures, you know.

Richard, a Native American man who had been arrested several times for
returning to a park known as a gathering spot for Native Americans, reported:
"All the natives like Victor Steinbrueck Park, you know, it's how we find each
other, or at least it used to be. And it's beautiful, it's got this great view, and
there's bathrooms there, and Debbie here, she used to bring us food once in
a while." In a follow-up phone conversation, Richard reported that he had just
been released from jail for the fifth time for trespass in the parks that year:
"They just can't kick me out of there. That's where my people are at."

This appreciation of the social contact and company afforded by parks and
other exclusion zones was also keenly felt by homeless veterans who worried
about their antisocial tendencies:

There's a park out there on Aurora and uh, you know, I can't stay in
the camp all the time. So I still sneak into the park and, uh, I dunno

what's gonna happen, this next time I mean. You know, 'cause I need
to be around other people sometimes. I can't stay in the camp alone
all the time, you know.

That's another thing about the parks, is you know that you go in there,
you have a thousand people around. You don't know one of them
and still sit there drinkin' beer. Have all the company you want but
don't have to talk to anybody in particular. And even though you may
not talk to them its good just to have somebody around, you know,
because I, uh, that's the worse thing I do, is that I isolate. And uh, so
I make it a point three, at least three times a week sometimes four,
to come out of the woods, just like so I could you know—like I said I
might not be social but I come to be around people.

For many, the fact that parks meant other people being around was crucial
to their sense of security:

I like to stay around in the parks, yeah I don't wanna you know go up
in a cubbyhole or somethin' you know, I don't . . . You don't feel safe.
Which it is not, safe.

I feel like, you know, if people are around, you know, you might, the
maniac might not catch you up, you know what I mean? 'Cause I been
in California where maniacs are, you know, people come and kill people,
harass people for nothing, just because they are homeless, you know
what I mean. So that's why I choose to be in a park around people.

You know, a whole lot of things could happen to you that wouldn't
happen to you if I was just sleepin' under my blankets out here at
Courthouse Park. Because there's a whole lot of people downtown,
walkin' around, plenty of police. But if I was to go to another
neighborhood where there's just dark quiet streets and someone
come along and just kick you in the head just because they happen to
be drunk and don't like homeless . . . I'm not with that.

Several interviewees told us that parks were simply the only place they felt they
could go:

You know, we really don't have no place to go because they kick us out
of there [the shelters] for a certain portion of the day and we get to go
back in at around 5:30 in the evening. So we really, really, really don't

have any place to go, but to that park, or to the fountains across the
street or to the other park, or whatever.

There's really nowhere you can go unless you got somebody and then
you can go somewhere. I mean I can go to Seattle Center, but what
can I do? The park is where, all the parks, even down
to the waterfront, is where you know, most homeless people
go. And, whatever they're doing, you know, it's just some place to be.

Finally, parks were seen by many as preferable compared to shelters as a
place to sleep for a variety of reasons. Darren, a homeless African-American
man living with AIDs, continued to avoid shelters even after being kicked out
of the parks for sleeping there:

You know, when you're in the shelters and when the shelters are
full they match you, match you up so close you touch together, you
know, this guy here, you right here, just like husband and wife...like
sardines kinda. You know with my immune system I, I can't—I am
afraid to catch a cold and—a cold for a regular person they just go get
Robitussin. But for me, you know, it's a big deal.

Others also appreciated the less crowded conditions and relative freedom
afforded by parks:

I just can't be smashed in with all them people. I mean, I can't even
share an apartment with one or two others. I just, it's just, ever since
the war, my PTSD makes it real hard to be around lots of people in a
small space like that.

Well, in the shelter, the women have head lice, it's dirty, it stinks. I
don't like the shelter. The park is better.

Living with a bunch of women is not the ticket. Okay? It's like...I
know we all have our little quirks and whatever, but man, I mean, we
have a bunch of women in this place, especially a bunch of women
from the street, they're out here all day long. You don't want to hear
that all day and all night long.

I've been to church shelters and stuff like that and I don't like all them.
All them rules, trying to maintain a job, they want you to do your house
chores and go and attend all these meetings. There's only like so many
hours in a day, I am not gonna get up at like five, six in the morning and

to do my chores before I run off to work. Work sometimes ten-, twelve-hour days and come back and have to attend a meeting and scrub your urinals, I'm not gonna do that. I'd rather sleep outside.

Those excluded from spaces other than parks also reported that the space from which they were excluded offered important opportunities for social contact. Ronald, an African American homeless man, found shelter and other needed services at the Downtown Emergency Services Center (DESC), located in the SODA zone from which he was banned. Because he stayed at DESC, Ronald was told by the judge that he could be outside in the area during the day as long as he was not loitering. Even with this allowance, he objected to the constraint his exclusion order imposed on his ability to maintain social relationships:

> They're sayin' I can't do that [socialize] anymore, but I'm gonna do it. I got to do it! I'm not gonna say, uh, "I can't talk to you, I got to get to the Lazarus center, I'm on a SODA." Nooooo. [Pauses, adopts a street voice] "Wassup, girl? Watch you doin'?" [laughter] That's it. You know, I'm goin' on with my life. I don't have a home, at least let me have some fun!

In sum, many of those we interviewed indicated that they did not comply with their exclusion orders because the spaces from which they were banned offered crucial opportunities for social contact and relationships. Many reported that they resisted their banishment order because they needed access to important services. In particular, both parks and SODA zones housed services that rendered compliance with an exclusion order impractical:

> They come over to 1st and Yesler, spread out the food, set up racks of clothes and you get a number and when they call your number pick out a few things. You know, they give out the hygiene kits. And it takes me out for all of that. Which I need, all of that. So no, I still go the parks.

> How can I stay outta here when I am homeless, I stay here at the shelter, I've got to use all, all of DESC, which is basically a couple of blocks, two or three blocks, and you tell me I can't be here?

> They got the clothing, they got the food, they got the medical attention right there, down here. Where am I gonna move?

> See that [complying with a SODA order] is kind of difficult for me because I use the public health area down there, I have a case worker down there. I go through there, also like right down Belltown, there's the DSHS office. I have to go to the DSHS office to complete my uh,

my work, to get my benefits and stuff....Uh, Chinatown, I had to go there to the Social Security office, cuz I'm applying for SSI....You know? So I had to walk through Chinatown. Um, the Central District, the CD area. My mother lives in the Central District, do you know what I'm saying? I can't stay out of these areas.

More generally, many of those we interviewed described a strong sense that the place from which they had been banished was home. This response was particularly common among those living with SODA orders:

I got to go there [to the SODA zone]—I don't know nothin' else! I know my way around, now, pretty good now the downtown area, I've been here now since 2002....But basically, this is me, this is home, this little downtown area, I don't know anything else.

But you got to realize, too, this is the only place I know...Good or bad, good or bad. It's the only place I know. I can get food, get housing, take a shower, brush my teeth, this place it provides for me, you know what I'm sayin', it provides for me, and then, even if I'm doing wrong, it still provides. Cuz if I mess up on my money, I can still go up to the park to eat. You know what I'm sayin'. So, you have to know that some people live here. This is home for us.

I came in 1990. The cab dropped me off on 2nd and Yesler. I been there ever since. Those four corners, that cycle. I don't know how to walk out of it....[The judge] said, "Oh, there are other places." I said, "Your Honor, I don't know how, understand? This is my home."

Them are the blocks that you walk around and keep your feet warm, or hustle, whether you panhandle, whether you wash windows or whatever it is. That's where you live. That's your home, downtown, I mean as far as being homeless, that's the only area you know. So, I mean, and a lot of times what they consider to be a dope area is not a dope area. You know it might be a place where a few smokers go smoke, but that's it. But it's your home, too.

In short, most of those we interviewed said they could not comply with their exclusion order. Those who did comply were more likely to have found a place to stay outside their exclusion zone and expressed intense fear of going to jail. For many others, though, the fear of going to jail was simply not enough to compel compliance. This was not because they particularly enjoyed jail, but rather that the locales from which they were excluded housed many important amenities, including social networks, contacts, and relationships; social services; a sense of safety and security; and a place they called home. For the banished, the places identified as high-drug and high-crime areas by city officials housed much more than opportunities for deviant behavior. It may seem a simple matter to agents of social control to force those who appear to be transient or disordered to relocate, but our respondents made plain that ties to place are not easily sundered.

Banishment's Consequences

Banishment generated many important consequences for our respondents, regardless of whether they complied with their exclusion order. The vast majority reported that banishment's effects were negative. Indeed, only five of the forty-one interviewees (12 percent) reported any positive effects. This small group of individuals reported that their exclusion order was working as intended: it provided an incentive to stay away from people and places that afforded opportunities for trouble. As William, a recipient of a SODA order, released from prison just days before, put it:

> Actually for me it [the SODA order] betters my situation. I guess it's strictly me because as times all happen, I'm tryin' to quit. This allows me not to be in that area anymore so therefore, I'm less likely to start usin', you know.... So when this was presented to me, it seemed like everything fell in place. Because I had an incentive to stay away from it, to get it over, to get on with my life.

Several others also reported that their exclusion order helped keep them out of trouble:

> Yeah, because it's like, it's a lot of drugs and stuff down there, so that it helps me not wanting to go down there, or I can't go down there. So it kind of helps me, and again I kinda like, sometimes want to go to the park, but they're kind of infested, so it's better for me not to go in there.

> It wasn't [a bad thing]. I just started focusing on other stuff. Whereas maybe if I hadn't gotten the ticket [exclusion order] I'd probably still be sitting in the park and smoking weed.

Some of those who reported that their exclusion order helped them also expressed some ambivalence about it. Marjorie, a former sex worker and recovering addict who was the recipient of several SOAP and SODA orders, put it this way:

> You know, so, it kind of, it can be helpful.... Depending on the, you know, which way of the road you're looking at. At least it keeps me on my toes, I'm out of it [the drug scene], and I'm not around those people, so it can be beneficial. But lookit, what if I'm staying clean and I'm doing good and they roll me into jail just for bein' in a SODA area and I go to jail and lose my job? Then it won't be so beneficial.

Vicky, also a recipient of several SODA orders over the years, expressed a similar sentiment:

> It, it, it has its good points, you understand that. I can't say that it's all a negative thing. Because it will give you time, set you aside, give you time to think, you want to keep going through this? You want to keep going to jail? But um, at the same time, it makes me duck and dodge even when I'm doin' good, and that's wrong.

A minority—12 percent—reported that their exclusion order had at least some positive effects by encouraging them to take stock of their lives and to stay out of trouble. The vast majority of our respondents reported that their exclusion orders had entirely negative consequences. The following exchange captures the prevailing sentiment well:

> INTERVIEWER   So do you think the SODA would ever affect your life, like in terms of, would it motivate you to stay out of trouble, get into treatment, or anything like that? Is there anything positive, anything good about it?
>
> CURT   Um...I, no. Nothin' at all.

One of the main complaints by respondents concerned constrained mobility. This complaint was registered both by those who complied with their exclusion order and those who did not. The consequences of impaired mobility ranged from relatively minor to very serious:

> Like for example, I can't go to any stores in the area that I live in, I have to go outside the area if I wanna go buy a bag of potatoes.

> I lost my wallet up there [in the SODA zone]. So therefore I can't get up there and get my wallet back, and uh the person who has been entrusted with my wallet stays up there so uh, and he doesn't have

a phone anyway for me to get in contact with. So I gotta go through the inconvenience of starting all over again, get the ID, Social Security card. And, uh, I got like a flagger's card, I dunno if I'll get that replaced. And my CPR certification, so I'm just going through a whole lot of changes with that.

Those who did not comply with their exclusion order reported that their days were full of "duckin' and dodgin'":

Oh, you duck and dodge a lot. Duck and dodge a lot.

I tried to be more careful, and dress with hoodies and hats and look like a little boy and shit like that. It was just a lot of ducking and dodging.

When I come out of the shelter, I got to duck my head and watch for them at all times.

Everything I do and I live downtown, so I just like, stand on guard. Just uh, you know, when you see the van, you get to running.

Ronald was one of several we interviewed who lived in a shelter in his SODA zone, and had been excluded from the parks:

I sneak all day long. I try to turn my head away [holding his hood over his head], try to see who's in the cop car to see him before he sees me, see if he knows you. If he knows me, I gotta make a move, maybe for a doorway or somethin'. Now, now, on this first arrest, for the SODA violation, DESC announced over the intercom, "They're feedin' in the park for anyone who wants to go over." Okay, first thing is, I'm trespassed from the park, so I got to go sneak in front of you [pointing at his friend], and I got to bribe somebody to let me up front so I could grab somethin' and get back out of the way. Then, I've got to be able to make back across 3rd Street, and get back up into DESC.

Many of our respondents also reported that their exclusion order limited their capacity to see family and maintain social contacts. This was especially painful for people when their capacity to connect with their family or people of the same cultural background was diminished. Recall Rhonda, who was unable to visit her mother as a result of her SODA order: "She was cryin'. She said, 'How could the judge do that?' And I told her that it's part of the system that they gave me. I know I just have to stay out [of the area] for four months. That's a long time to not see your mom." Others indicated an impaired capacity to maintain important social connections:

> When I got trespassed from out here…and I got trespassed from the Lake Washington [apartments], you know what I'm saying, it kind of clicked in my head, like, okay they don't want me here in this area. But this is my community, but I go to late night still, to this day, you know what I'm saying, I go to late night still, and I be hoopin' and playing dominoes and stuff. But now I can't be doin' that.

> [The trespass admonishment] stopped me from seeing my nephew every day like I wanted to, or every other day, or even every other week.

> I would say it's affected me, one, because most of the Hispanic people hang out at Casa Latina, so it's depriving me of people that, that I've gone to work with, from socializing with my own people!

> I used to bring dinners down to the park, you know, pot roast, stuff like that, for the Native men who won't eat if nobody feeds them. But I can't be doin' that no more.

Many of our respondents also reported that their exclusion order reduced their access to social services:

> And at Christmas you, I couldn't go in there and get nothin', no blankets, no food they was givin' out, nothing. You know what I'm saying? And that's not fair.

> Especially when I was trying to stay clean, it was really hard. When you're trying to stay clean and sober, you're trying to do things, get services, take care of things, but I wasn't supposed to be down there. It made it real hard.

> If they're feedin' in Courthouse Park, Occidental, I can't go. If they're over there feedin' at 1st and Yesler, I can't go.

In some cases, there were very severe consequences from the loss of social services. Bob, a homeless white veteran, was trespassed from the Veterans' Administration building after security found several clean needles in his backpack:

> They told me I can't go in any federal buildings now…it's a catch-22 I mean, so what are you telling me, that I can't go into the Veteran's

[Administration building]? Thing is, if I break a leg and I didn't have no ID, no hospital. What are you telling me, I can't get medical treatment at the Veterans?

For Curt, a longtime heroin addict, the possibility of being picked up by the Department of Corrections (DOC) when carrying used syringes to the needle exchange facility led him to go there less regularly, at serious risk to his health:

> And I told her [his probation officer], "Look there's no law against it [carrying clean needles], even though I'm on probation, even though I got a SODA, there's nothing to prohibit me from having clean syringes." And uh, you know, uh, she told me, "All right, I can't keep you from carrying the clean ones." But she said, "God help you if you have a dirty one." So sometimes, you know, if the [DOC] van is out, I'll just try to clean the needles I already got.

Ironically, Curt was back on heroin was a result of his recent exclusion from a methadone program:

> CURT   I got on methadone in 2004. I've been off about six months now. I got on it, uh, about three years before that out at, uh, Evergreen....And, uh, it actually gave me a life. I was, uh, you know, I was near death when I got on the program, and, um, I started having time to do things, I quit hanging out, I quit sellin' drugs, I quit stealin', I quit going to jail, I quit going to the hospital, you know.
>
> INTERVIEWER   Why did you stop going to the methadone clinic?
>
> CURT   Well they have a, a, because I was homeless and I never wanted to miss doses, so I kinda moved out that way, and what happened was, I got caught one or two times sleeping under their carport, you know, by staff. And then I got caught, you know, I would nod off when I read, so I got caught sleeping at the bus stops. You don't have to actually be on their property to be trespassed. So I can't get methadone anymore. I'm back on heroin now.

As Curt subsequently noted, his return to heroin use was quite costly to King County taxpayers:

> What gets me most now is I get infections [from injecting]. And I had one rage for a year and a half. And they used, you know, their little get-by measures, they don't want to spend no money, I had streaks up my arm and up my legs, and for them to not have hospitalized me would have been to say, "Go die." Once you've done it, you know and

you're in there, you're in the records, right, they're not going to deny you. They'll treat you like a real human being. I was in there twice, and in the last six months it cost about thirty grand.

Thus, banishment often works to reduce access to important social services. It can also diminish income-earning opportunities. Recall José, trespassed from Casa Latina: "Now I can't get regular work, so I gotta hustle." Others also reported losing a job or access to a job training program: "The main cost for me was, you know, I was going to do that program, that restaurant training program for homeless people, I was gonna do that, but after I got the SODA, I was too scared to go over to it, especially at night. You know, the cops would be all over me if they saw me walkin' around at night." Vic, a homeless veteran who made his living playing music at the Pike Place Market until he was trespassed for possession of alcohol, said that his exclusion imperiled his ability to make a living: "Oh man, I, I made my living at the Market. I've been there for almost thirty years so, uh, when I'm kicked out of the Market for a year, it really puts a kibosh on my, my ability to make money."

For some, the loss of work or income resulted from being jailed for violating an exclusion order. Because he was frequently jailed for being in his SODA area, Curt's Social Security checks were discontinued:

They, uh, basically they would use that [the SODA order], and they would either catch me with something, like syringes, or whatever and then they would take me in front of my PO [probation officer]...and I would end up in jail for a couple weeks to a month at a time. It affected my Social Security because after thirty days, they discontinue it, and you have to reapply. You know? So uh, you would get out and you don't have an income anymore, including food stamps, you have to go and start the whole process over and it takes months.

Marjorie lost a job as a result of being incarcerated for a SOAP violation:

MARJORIE   You know, you end up losing things. Like I lost a job because of being on SOAP, you know?

INTERVIEWER   How's that? What happened?

MARJORIE   Because I went into jail! And I stayed in there two weeks. So, because of that, they didn't want to hire me, or they didn't want to rehire me, cuz what if you go to jail again, because you're in this area.

Many said they felt far less secure as a result of their exclusion orders. This was especially common for homeless people trespassed from locales where they felt comparatively safe and for those excluded from the comparatively large

SODA zones. These zones of exclusion are described as scary and dangerous by many Seattleites, but are seen as safe and secure by the banished. In fact, for many we interviewed, neighborhoods that house fewer homeless people and people of color seem unsafe:

> I feel safe down here [in the Pioneer Square area]. Because there's a whole lot of people downtown, walkin' around, plenty of police. But if I was to go to another neighborhood where there's just dark quiet streets and someone come along and just kick you in the head just because they happen to be drunk and they don't like homeless...I'm not with that.

> Well yeah, because now I'm sleepin' in, you know, abnormal places, you know. Up there [at the park], like I said, everybody looks out for everybody. I wasn't worried about nothing. I am worried now. I am worried now.

> I don't like havin' to leave Chinatown. I don't, I don't like that. It's safer there than other areas. The people are a lot more peaceful.

For some, the sense of insecurity stemming from an exclusion order was so powerful that they had difficulty sleeping at all. Jose describes how he got through the previous night after being kicked out of the park in which he feels comfortable: "I just walked all night long. My eyes hurt right now. I'm not gonna lie down and have some crackhead think that maybe I got three dollars. No, I'll walk all night. Sometimes I'll walk over to that park called Freeway Park and I'll sleep over there, but that's not very safe. Mostly I walk." Darren also stayed up all night, lacking a place to sleep in which he felt comfortable: "Ah, sometimes I just wait until, I just be up all night and I just sleep during the day. I'm extremely tired."

The vast majority of our respondents complained about continual attention from police, even in places from which they were not banned. Julie, a homeless white woman, reported that she was harassed constantly after her exclusion from the parks:

> Once you have your name in the system that they just, it, they always gonna pick you up, you know, for something, and now it's like, but now they see me, I mean, they've run my name so many times. It used to be everyday, everyday, everyday. I'm just walking down the street and they say, "Hey, come here," you know? And I dunno if that's uh, you know if that's okay to do, but I mean, but they see I'm all clear and stuff but still every day it's, "Come here we're gonna run your name," you know?

Such complaints were common:

> And I just feel like they're watchin' me all the time, and stoppin' me all the time, even when I'm just pullin' in to Safeway…God! Oh, now I can't even drive to Safeway?

> I was being stopped by every, on sight, not by every cop, but by two or three different ones, and it just seemed like they, just wherever they saw me, whether I was staying at the mission, just wherever.…Once I seen a cop come through the alley and he seen me, he arrested me.

The fact that many felt unable to comply with their exclusion orders, combined with frequent police stops, meant that they cycled in and out of the courts and jail:

> And if those NCIs [Neighborhood Corrections Initiative vans] come on you, you're gone. You're goin' to jail. You know, you be back out in two, three, four days. And then you got to go back to court and take a chance on how many times this has happened, are you up to thirty days, forty-five days. Last time I got thirty.

> But um, I been arrested several…oh, maybe fifty times. It's overnight, then out the next day. It don't make sense.

> They um, they basically gave me the three days time served, gave me a year probation and told me I had to do eight hours of community service and also had to report to a probation officer. You know, it's just in and out, in and out.

This frequent flyer phenomenon was especially striking among the sex workers we interviewed. Tami, a young white woman who had recently quit the sex trade at the time of our interview, accumulated an estimated 160 cases during her career, a significant portion of which were due to violations of various exclusion orders. Marjorie similarly noted that enforcement of SOAP orders was intense:

> I told you about that experience when the bus door opened, the police officer seen me on the bus, he seen me on the bus. I was traveling through, going to where I lived right on Pacific Highway, out there by Larry's Market. I stayed in a trailer park over there. And so, um, I got off. I mean, once I got off the bus he was right behind the bus there, and stopped me. And took me right back to jail.…Cuz I had just got

out of jail that day for a SOAP violation, being in a SOAP zone, which
is where I was living. And, when I got out, and walked out of the bus,
here he is. I hang out forty-five minutes, I have enough time to get out
of that jail, walk into the store, get on the bus and go uptown...get off
that bus, and don't even make it across the street, and I'm gone, back
in jail. He just drove me back to Tukwila. Just drove me right back
down to the jailhouse.

Exclusion, many said, not only imposed material hardships but also triggered feelings of shame, anger, hurt, and resentment. Respondents found
offensive the symbolic message embedded in their exclusion order. Neil, kicked
out of various parks for sleeping or drinking, put it this way: "Just being
kicked out of a public place, it's kinda embarrassing. Not only embarrassing,
but I dunno, but yeah, being kicked out of society it's like you're just no longer
socially acceptable. Like you're not really a member of society." Claudia was
excluded from Courthouse Park for sleeping: "I felt offended, I was offended,
like I don't have any rights, like I don't matter or nothin'. And I was really
offended."

Many were particularly insulted because they believed that their exclusion
reflected a bias against the homeless, one rooted in stereotypes:

> [Sigh] It kind of upset me, because I feel that a lot of people categorize
> every person that's homeless as either on alcohol or drugs, and
> uneducated, and that's not true for everybody. You know, sometimes
> you just have a bad time, and that doesn't mean that you're a bad
> person, you know? Just because you're going through trials and
> tribulations.

> I don't think that was fair, you know? Cuz you know, everybody just
> look at you, when you're homeless, they just look at you like you're
> a thief and you're a liar, you use drugs and you sell drugs. And not
> everybody is like that when they're homeless.

For others, it was the fact that they were so frequently stopped by the police
that was especially irksome: "The way [the SODA] is being enforced and whatever, that it's more hurtful than not. Because it just brings up a lot of resentment, you know what I'm saying? It's them kind of hassles that we have to go
through all the time. Which, uh, gets you anger and whole lot of resentment."
For still others, it was offensive that they could not inhabit public space even if
they were doing nothing wrong: "I don't think, why do I have to leave a whole

neighborhood, you know, if everybody is walkin' down the street, why can't I walk down the street? I, I don't like that."

The fact that exclusion orders were so frequently experienced as offensive deepened the depression with which many struggled. Lanya, a twenty-two-year-old African American woman, was arrested for trespassing on the University of Washington campus. She put it this way:

> But it's just, like so much stuff like that going on, and it's hard to find a reason to live at all, even want to live. You know, I mean, why would anybody want to live if they have nowhere to sleep, if they are getting dragged out of the bushes by the cops, you know, and they have to go to jail and go to court. Because you can't go in this building, you can't go in that building. If they see you walking across the street, if they see you talking to a friend, you know what I'm saying, you're automatically arrested. And that, it takes my spirit away. It takes hope away. We're hopeless people, you understand, we're hopeless people…looking for hope.

In short, exclusion orders did not compel most of our respondents to relocate. Moreover, only for a small minority did an exclusion order generate a positive effect. Mere common were various negative consequences. These included impaired geographic mobility, diminished safety and security, loss of income and access to work, diminished access to social services, police harassment, and frequent entanglement in criminal justice institutions. For many, these material hardships were significantly exacerbated by the pain, hurt, shame, and anger triggered by banishment. Their accounts indicate that the use of banishment undermines the rights and capacities that are taken for granted by most citizens. Not surprisingly, respondents had much to say about banishment as a policy response to urban disorder.

Reflections on Banishment

Our respondents offered remarkably nuanced and thoughtful assessments of the use of banishment as a means of dealing with urban disorder. Despite the fact that many felt that their exclusion had solely negative consequences, some noted that their problematic behavior (to the extent that it existed) was in fact linked to the networks and opportunities afforded by particular places. Moreover, some of those we interviewed felt that their exclusion was at least partly justified. This was especially likely to be the case when they were adequately warned beforehand:

Yeah, I know you can't do that [drink in the park]. And smoke weed. I know you can't do that. Yeah, and it was less than a week later. That's why they gave me a year, before it was like thirty days. It was cool, they were giving me a deal there. A week later, caught me a week later at the park again. Doin' the same shit. It's my fault; I can't blame it on them. Yeah, I mean, it was my own stupidity. I was drunk when I did it, if I had been sober I wouldn't have done it.

Those who were excluded from the parks for narcotics activity were also likely to report that they saw their exclusion as legitimate:

I was doing wrong. I was doing wrong. And so, uh, my fault.

Let's see, what was I doin'…Ooh, man, this is hard. I was guilty. Guilty, guilty, guilty.

At first I was like, what for bud? I can understand if I was, you know, smokin' crack. There used to be a bench for where all the crack smokers went. I wasn't even over there, I was on the other side of the park, and it was like, man, just for like, for weed, of all things in the world. But you know, I guess it's because it's an illegal drug, you know what I'm saying, so I had to pay the consequences. I can see that.

Similarly, many of those who objected to their own exclusion saw the general effort to keep the area drug-free as legitimate:

But like I said, I was upset that he did that to me, but I'm not upset, you know what I'm saying, that he does that [enforces drug laws], because that's his job. He's just trying to keep the area safe and drug-free.

It makes a lot of sense. You know, the park, originally I think was for like people who work in those buildings and stuff like that, you know what I mean. I guess all the cracksters and whatever, alcoholics just took it over. But, at the same time, the other shelter is across the street from the park. So they have no place to go.

Curt, the heroin addict who lost access to methadone, also understood why he was excluded for sleeping in the adjacent parking lot and nodding off outside the building: "Well, it's for the greater good, you know, see a lot of drug dealing goes on, there's a lot of, uh, Benzo rollers, you know, bars and, when you're next to them with nothing going....They don't want a bunch of dope fiends hanging out, because when they do, they do silly stuff."

As these excerpts illustrate, many of our respondents saw exclusion as valid if triggered by narcotics activity. On the other hand, many non–drug using interviewees said they felt that the grounds for their exclusion were illegitimate. This was especially the case for those excluded from the parks for sleeping:

> I wouldn't consider it breaking the law, you know what I mean? Any other state—I've been in just a couple in Colorado and California, that's what the parks are for, you know. People sleep in the parks, you know. You're not drinking, you're not doing drugs, you're just sleeping.

> It's unnecessary. I mean, people, I understand, but we are not bothering anybody. It's not like we are harassing people, you know, causing chaos and you know, living in the streets wild and crazy. We mind our own business. And it's just, we go, we hang out, and we sleep for the night and leave first thing in the morning. We clean up after ourselves, you know, and we are gone.

Some who were kicked out of parks and other venues for drinking also questioned their exclusion:

> Well that's bullshit. I mean, what's up with this? I mean, when I was in California...you could drink down there and they don't really bug you. And San Diego's, uh, I'm tellin' ya they do not like homeless down there and they don't like people messin' around with parks but they tolerate it a helluva lot more than these people [in Seattle] do, not giving you access.

> It's bullshit you know for drinkin' a freakin' beer.

> You should be able to sit down. I can see not bein' able to sit on a bus stop drinkin', smokin' weed and crack. Which I don't do, 'cause you're around fellow people. But sittin' at a park, looking at the gorgeous view of Elliot Bay, you know, I mean to me it's sacrilegious not bein' able to drink!

Some also believed that their particular exclusion order violated the law and was therefore invalid. Sabrina was only in Seattle about a week when she reportedly had the following encounter:

Yeah, because I just got off of the bus and just got out of the hospital, and you know I wasn't feeling good, and where I had got off at, I had to go across the street to catch the bus to go out to my shelter. And before I could even cross the street, you know, the police just hit me up. Told me I couldn't come back for twenty-four hours. And I'm like, you know, what's going on? He said if he seen me within that area, anywhere from near where I was, and, um, between 3rd and James and Virginia, anywhere up that strip, that he was gonna arrest me for trespass. But he can't do that!

Frequently, our respondents said that both the imposition and enforcement of exclusion orders were often done in an unfair, arbitrary manner:

And if you're in that park [getting food] they can arrest you. A lot of cops won't, because they know you're there with a purpose. But the ones that don't like you for any personal reasons, um, they can arrest you, for being in the park.

Not so much the guy that was on the night shift, but the day shift guy, he will arrest me on sight.

You're sent to go see [the DOC officer], and she sometimes—if you are nice and she likes you, she might make a deal with you, not send you to jail, make you work it off [doing community service]. Depends if she likes you.

Others, particularly black youth we interviewed, believed that exclusion orders were imposed on those who did not show proper deference:

So, [the police officer] asked me, "What are you laughing at?" I told him, "I was laughin' at you." Okay, so that kinda pissed him off and uh, he told me, "Are you aware that this is no-trespassing area?" I go, "I didn't know, and I didn't even care 'cause I'm trying to get into an apartment." So he, uh, handcuffed me at the stairs, and arrested me for trespass. He was punishing me for being mouthy.

So, you know, I don't bite my tongue, and that's what he didn't like, that's why I got harassed a lot of times, and when [police officer] stopped me, he was like, just go ahead and trespass him, and they called a lot of other officers, and then my brother came outside my cousin's house, and he got trespassed, too.

I'm a mouthy person. If I feel that you're disrespecting me, I'm going to go out of my way to disrespect you. So, see, what are you, what are you doing wasting time running up on me for, [name of officer], I don't got no warrants, it's my birthday, I got an ID for you, here, you can have my ID, you can keep that one, I got copies. Oh, you're getting disrespectful, you're talking shit. Excuse my French, whatever. But um, then he's like, "Well how about I trespass you from around here." Da-da-da-da-da.

Others objected to what they perceived as race and class bias in the use of banishment. In fact, questions on this topic elicited some of the most impassioned responses:

Now, I have not, I have not drank in the [Pike Place] Market [since my exclusion], but I can go to any bar in the Market, I can sit down with the sloshy drunk guys next to me, you know, guys off the ships and the guys are you know, sailors off the boats and hey, I [feigns hiccup], I have [feigns hiccup] no problem with that guy. You know, they don't exclude him as he stumbles down the market and knocks over the veggie stand, you know. No, he's cool, or the fat guy with the big wallet who just got off the cruise ship from Alaska and he's still drunk when he gets off the ship. Yeah, see those guys, that's all right as long as you have money and you're dressed fine.

How does it make me feel? At that particular time, two years ago, I felt like a I was a noncitizen, I felt like I was racially profiled, I was an African American, and I believe the only reason why they stopped me was because they knew they could, and they could get away with it. And the repercussions of them doing what they did would be very, very much less if it was someone other than someone who was African American, or of a minority persuasion. So, it made me feel like a noncitizen.

It's definitely a class thing, there's no doubt about it. Now, how do you control the masses, huh? Most, most, of the, time, I work with Indians an awful lot here at Chief Seattle Club and many of them are indigent. Many of them have alcohol problems so they hang out in the parks, which is the only place on the streets you can go. They sit there and have a drink, 'cause that's the cheapest high they can get, to endure their meager existences and of course here comes a police, we want to clear 'em out because we're having those big ships come in from Alaska. You don't want those drunk Indians sitting on that park bench—that's just terrible. It's all right for the drunk Alaskans to

sit down there and puke, but it's not all right for the Indian guy. You
know.

I've seen tourist couples come here and they've got one of those
little cold packs you know, like those little red wine coolers and stuff,
but you know the whole six bottles. And, uh, I've also seen right here
where they got the concrete tables and stuff, I've seen them sit down
there and break a bottle of wine with a corkscrew and have some
wine with their lunches and stuff like that, and nobody bothers them.

In reflecting on the larger policy issues involved, respondents raised many
other concerns. The first of these had to do with the size of the exclusion zones,
particularly SODA zones:

There's too many, they have way too many. Everywhere! Have you ever
seen the SODAs? They're crazy! You may as well just say, well, I'm not
supposed to go out today!

Pretty soon, there's no where for you to go but in your house because
the SODA zones are all over Seattle.

Especially in this area here, they designated almost all of Madison
down to uh, whichever block that is, but they've got the whole central
area divided up into SODAs. You know, they range from one to six and
they have 'em downtown and, and they have 'em in, uh, Kinnear way
out by the Space Needle. They even got it down to as far as Lake City,
145th in Lake City. City's been chopped up. They say these are the areas
where the drugs are sold. Drugs are sold almost everywhere.

Well, yeah it [the SODA zone] is huge, it's all the way like Denny
Street—uh, from this side of Madison Street all the way back toward
the water, all the way toward the Seattle Center, down to Howell
Street, Denny Way, there's some other streets—it's huge.

No, you know I don't understand these zones...they're everywhere.
They try to tell you that you can't walk around, can't be in them, but
where can I go, I'm homeless, I got no place to go. They're everywhere.

Those banned from locales that were part of a trespass program complained about the spatial extent of their exclusion:

I mean, they [downtown parking lots] are everywhere. And I'm not
just talking about the ones on the surface...there's the underground

ones, they're on almost every corner that you take shortcuts through, like we just did. You know, and my feet aren't so good, so I take shortcuts.... It's too much.

On the back of the card, you know on the back of the card, it says when you sign this card, or if you don't sign this card, you trespassed from all these places on the back of the card. That's everywhere! You can't go to Sorry's, you can't go to Feathers, you can't go to Rainier Beach, you can't go to Bank of America, you can't go to the Moore place, you can't go to Safeway, you can't go nowhere!

The powers that banishment provided the police, many noted, worked to enable officers to make stops that might otherwise be unconstitutional. This was a nearly universally shared belief among our respondents:

Well just for the record, um, I say as I said earlier the whole setup of system is the, to keep people in the system and keep them available to harass them legally.

It's just another way of being able to harass us, you know, which, basically, make people move on.

Well see, this whole thing about the SODA is it allows the police officer the opportunity to arrest and stop you on the side.

I guess this SODA thing just giving them a license to stop whoever they want and uh, I guess and not violate a person's Fourth Amendment rights.

Ooh, plain and simple, so it's not only a tool for, for uh, policemen to use to put you down on paper, make sure they got somethin' against you, you know, first strike kinda thing.

They can stop you at any time. That's right, that's why they implemented this in the first place. And they do that.

Many indicated that they felt that the spatial and temporal boundaries around the exclusion zones were unclear. This ambiguity was, some said, exploited by officers:

No, you don't know where it [the SOAP zone] ends and where it begins, no you don't know. That can be anywhere they decide. Okay?

Even though the [SOAP] order says two blocks [on either side of Aurora Avenue], still, it's up to their discretion. And they tell you really four blocks, the police do themselves.

I'm like, SODA? What do you mean? What is that? [laughing] When I found out, at that, and he [the judge] didn't give me no map at first. He just said stay out of SODA two. And so, I didn't know what SODA was, and so I was in, I was in that area, so I was arrested, so I said, "Your Honor! I don't even know my boundaries." I still don't know the boundaries.

There was much confusion about exactly how SODA and SOAP orders worked. Some people were told by judges that they could be in the zone if they did not loiter, only to discover that they could be taken to jail simply for walking through the area:

He [the judge] said, ah well, the police know as long as you're not loitering, they don't have to mess with you. But that's not true! They do!

But, uh, uh, um, that's what confused me with the judge, you know what he told me? He said the police officers know, that as long as you're not loitering, they know you live there, they won't arrest you, see. It was a twister. But, your Honor, any time I was arrested, I was never loitering.

Others disagreed that their behavior constituted loitering:

A young lady, Charmagne, asked me if I could run up to Harborview with her. And I told her yeah, yeah, I'll run up there with you. So I cross the street thinkin' that she's right behind me and we're getting' ready to get on the bus. But when I looked back, she's crossed the streets, fat-mouthin' with one of her girlfriends or somethin', and I waved for her, come on, but DOC had rolled past me in the van and seen me, and I seen 'em turning around, and I know they're gonna arrest me. They pull right up and tell me, "We seen you hangin' around and things for the last two or three days,"' or something. And that's all it took. I was arrested. I didn't have anything on me, I wasn't standin' around dealin' dope or nothin'. None of that. I was standing there by myself, because she's across the street.

Still others complained that other judicially granted exceptions to their exclusion orders were not recognized by the police:

But I looked at the papers and it says from six in the morning until seven at night I can be here. But those are the times they keep arresting me! But it says I can be here [tapping the paper] from this time for the purpose of usin' the facilities at DESC or wherever, so how can you bust me?

[The judge] sent me to [a treatment program]. And it's supposed to open nine to four. They cannot bother me from nine to four. I'm entitled to be in that area, just from one corner to the next, from nine to four. And I was supposed to go there in thirty days, so I was on my way there, and I got arrested. Understand. The judge told me to go to this place. From nine to four. I'm on my way, I'm walking that direction. "Oh! SODA." And I went to jail. And so, umm, like I said, you never know.

Um, then I entered into drug court. Then they put me on SODA....And what confused me was, okay, I went to treatment, and they was going to give me housing. [Laughs] Guess where housing was? In the SODA zone! And so I stand before the judge, and I say, "Your Honor, every time I'm in that area, they're going to arrest me." So, the judge did, in fact, meet me halfway, because he gave me certain places I could be in like, go to the store, um, stuff like that. But I said, "Your Honor, the police doesn't listen to that! You know what I'm saying? All they know is I'm in a SODA zone. And now you're putting me in housing, you're giving me housing there, I'm confused." I was very confused, because, simply that, if the police see me, I'm gonna be by myself just standing there, and get arrested. I got arrested several times.

The interviewees frequently noted that even though the police had long sought to move them along, the exclusion orders simply facilitated these efforts. Many of these people suggested that the only real goal of banishment was to get them to go someplace else:

They used to tell me to get out of Pioneer Square, just leave, take my ass to Belltown. When you get up to Belltown they'll do the same thing. They're just passing the buck. Kicking us from one section to another section.

If I got citywide SOAPed in Seattle I would go to Tacoma. And so
when, once a year went by I would come back out here [to Seattle].
And by that time I was citywide SOAPed in Tacoma! You just travel
from area to area, like let's say I was SOAPed out of this area. So, I go
to Denny Park area. And then they SOAP you out of Denny Park area,
and then you go to Aurora. And then they SOAP you out of Aurora,
and then you go downtown. And then you're in downtown and you get
SOAPed out of that, then you can go to Tukwila. You know, and you
get caught in Tukwila, they citywide SOAP you pretty much. But then
you got [the city of] SeaTac. Then you got SeaTac.

As already noted, the goal of displacement is often not realized, simply
because people are too entrenched in particular places to move. But even when
it does occur, its consequences are not always beneficial. It can heighten the
adverse consequences of some people's behavior and subject them to greater
criminal justice sanction. Curt's experience provided the most dramatic example of this pattern. After being excluded from the methadone program, Curt
began using heroin regularly and returned to a life of property crime and drug
dealing. Yet many others also reported that their exclusion increased the likelihood that their behavior would harm themselves or others:

When you come into town, if I just gotta use the bathroom, you know
it's either that [go into the park] or go find a freakin' alley. And uh,
so it's puttin' me in a situation where uh, I got a ticket for urinating
in public downtown.... Now they can get you for sexual offense, too,
indecent exposure or somethin' like that. All because I can't go to the
park.

And they [the NCI team] say [adopting an official tone] "This is gonna
help you dry out for a couple of days," but what they're really doing
is pushing me further back. Cuz now I got to sneak, just to get a
sandwich. Or steal. They're makin' it worse.

Don't you see, the thing is, I go to the University District sometimes,
and I do the same thing, but over there I don't sell beer. But I'll go
over there and drink over there. So basically they're just pushing me
around.... Now, let's say you lived in the University District. You
don't want me in your neighborhood. Because I'm gonna piss on the
sidewalk. I'm gonna piss in the alleys. I'm gonna drink. And if I get
drunk enough, and you look at me wrong, I might tell you to go fuck
off. And so you don't want me there.... I'm not trying to excuse my

behavior. But if I am going to be doing what I do, you want me to do it here [gesturing toward DESC]. This is where you want me to do it. Because I am less of a threat here. Absolutely.

Recall José, who told us he began hustling after his exclusion from Casa Latina:

And when the people get out of the clubs, you know, the clubs down there in Pioneer Square, the bars, they're comin' out of the bars, and they're lit already, and they'll come up to you, "Hey man, what's goin' on," and they think they're all hip cuz they're talkin' to homeless people and I'm gonna make money off of 'em. If I can, I'm gonna get you for five bucks for one beer. Yeah, and because now I gotta hustle.

When Tami had to move out of her trailer, located in a SOAP zone, she returned to the streets:

Yep, and when I was eighteen, I found it [the trailer] you know, and I was so happy you know that I had my own place. And I probably could have started doing something better for myself, but my probation officer just put a big blank on it. Cuz I was going to go to school, I was gonna live there, I was gonna do things for myself, and she just put that big halt on it cuz it was in the SOAP zone. I didn't know where to go, so I just went back to the streets.

Several people highlighted the ironic fact that social services are concentrated in the downtown area from which many people are excluded:

When the city of Seattle decided to put services there they knew this was part of the game. You know? So I don't see why they're out there giving us a hard time. I mean, if I'm out there hitting somebody, yeah, if I'm out there selling dope, yeah. But if somebody's feeding at the park, uh, I can't go to the park and partake of the meal being offered? That's bullshit.

I mean, you don't put a bunch of mentally ill people in one place and expect them not to behave badly every now and then, or actually on a frequent basis. And then tell them they can't come to their shelter, or to see their case manager? Now you're going to arrest me for, for going where you put the services for me to get? You know, that doesn't make sense! It's crazy.

Those places that they're telling them that they cannot be, they're not moving. But they're asking the people to move. And I don't understand how that's gonna impact, really impact coordinating, or policing this, for the people who need those services, and they know, they know I can eat there, and I know if I can get in there and around the police I can eat. I'm going to do it, you know, and at all cost.

A frequent objection was that as a result of an exclusion order, simply being in a particular place could be treated as a criminal offense. For these respondents, the exclusion orders were simply too broad, and the failure to differentiate between criminal activity and mere presence was offensive:

Cuz you can't just assume somebody's doing something wrong... Uh, some people are doing the right thing, like going to the meal line. They got a meal line, out there, you know what I'm sayin', that people need to eat. And it's free.... And um, they see you in line, "Oh, you're on SODA, you're going to jail buddy." Um, it erases differences, if you're doing the right thing, or you're doing the wrong thing.

I agreed to that SODA area, it's fine. If I'm doing wrong. But if I'm trying to do the right thing, and, and, conducting myself in a manner... walking to the store, going to get some cigarettes, you know what I'm sayin', standing outside the building, smoking. Then I think that... SODAs are wrong.

But I mean, I can tolerate doing time if I do something wrong, I mean I understand there's consequences, but not when I'm not doing something wrong, and they understand the living conditions, that's different.

Finally, there was a frequent and strongly conveyed sense that banishment would not resolve either people's own issues or the general problem of disorder:

One officer told me, um, he arrested me one day, he arrested me on a Thursday, I got out on a Friday, I was back down here on a Friday. He said, "I'm not taking you to jail. I'm so fucking pissed off at the judge, because they never do nothing with y'all.... All they do is release y'all. I'm not even going to take you to jail. Send him a message." So, the courts, and the police officers, um, is not communicatin'. I mean, it's crazy. What you have [the SODA] for? You just, so they just arrest you one night. It doesn't make sense to me, I don't see the point.

Well, you know, you're more nervous, you're cautious inside that area, but it doesn't stop you from bein' there, I mean, that's where you at. I mean being an addict and being homeless especially, it don't make no difference.

And so, so um, they're not on drugs just because they like it. Because it's a very, very, very uh, uh, unhappy place. There's no peace. You know what I'm sayin', and everyone needs peace in their life. And so when you don't have it, you just keep doin' and doin' and doin'. And you're running, and running, and running, and you're chasing the illusion. You know what I'm sayin', scared that if you don't get a hit, you got to face reality, and um, so that's the place for an addict. And so everyone's there for a reason. Pushin' em around ain't gonna change that.

Conclusion

I don't like that we bother people. But they got to do somethin' else, cause I don't want them doggin' me up the way they are now. It don't change anything. I admit, something is really wrong, it's not working. I don't have the answer.

—Donald

Our interviews provide us with a unique opportunity explore the experience and consequences of banishment. As we demonstrated, compliance with banishment is difficult and therefore rare. A small percentage of our respondents, all of whom found a place to live outside of their exclusion zone and strongly feared going to jail, largely complied with their exclusion orders; five of these found that this helped them improve their lives. Even so, most of our interviewees reported that they did not comply with their exclusion orders, largely because they experienced the areas from which they were banished as essential to their physical and mental well-being. The fact that so many found in their exclusion zone meaningful social connections, important social services, and a place to call home reveals a problem at the core of the practice of banishment: a profound discrepancy between how officials understand "disorderly" areas and how those same places are experienced by the banished.

Officials appear to imagine these neighborhoods largely in terms of whether they house and tempt the deviant. For the banished, however, these places are often essential to their lives. These are not simply bounded areas on a map from which individuals can be relocated through the territorial capacity possessed by the police. They are, for many, places of deep historical connection and ongoing, vital social interaction. Like the rest of us, the homeless and other disadvantaged people are connected to place; they rely on predictable time-space patterns and social relationships to meet their daily needs. Because of these attachments, many of those we interviewed could not or would not quit the zones from which they were legally excluded. Yet their refusal to be relocated led to a constant fear of detection and often to regular involvement with the criminal justice system.

The richness of the places from which the excluded were banned also helps explain the fact that relocation can pose very real risks. Some of our respondents did attempt to comply with their spatial restrictions and suffered significant costs as a result. For example, many whose only offense was sleeping in parks at night felt compelled to move to other parts of the city where they felt more isolated and unsafe. Others lost access to work and training programs, family members and community support groups, public transportation, and even drug treatment programs. In these cases, the effect of the ban was not at all therapeutic but quite destructive.

Many of our respondents' objections stemmed not only from the practical effects of exclusion but also from its symbolic content. Being excluded was a powerful emotional experience for many, embodying their sense that they were no longer considered citizens, even fully human, by other residents of Seattle. In a variety of ways, then, banishment rendered the lives of some of Seattle's most vulnerable residents more difficult. Certainly, the material and symbolic harms triggered by exclusion orders often deprive the banished of many of the rights of citizenship associated with membership in a political community.

Our respondents also offered thoughtful reflections on the efficacy of banishment as a policy response to homelessness, addiction, and sex work. Although some noted—and regretted—that their behaviors sometimes adversely affected others, most were adamant that banishment did not address their underlying problems or reduce any harm some caused to themselves or others. Indeed, what seemed to be the obvious futility of this policy approach led many to conclude that the true purpose of these practices was simply to enhance police power, provide an end run around the Fourth Amendment, and "keep people in the system." This belief, combined with the perception that exclusions were based on race and class, intensified feelings of hurt, resentment, and anger and contributed to their sense that they were treated as noncitizens.

These findings support several conclusions. First, banishment as it is carried out in Seattle appears not to induce most of the banned to leave the neighborhoods from which they are excluded. Thus, we are not optimistic about the possibility that banishment will improve other residents' quality of life. Even if enforcement is intensified, we suspect that most people will relocate to adjacent areas, merely displacing disorder. Some proponents recommend the expansion of banishment in neighborhoods experiencing displacement. Yet this—along with the already dramatic expansion of SODA zones and trespass programs—raises the specter of a citywide banishment policy. This is a troubling specter to contemplate.

Second, whether or not our respondents complied with their exclusion orders, the vast majority of them reported that their exclusion orders had overwhelmingly negative effects on their lives. As a result, we believe there is compelling evidence that banishment as a policy tool enhances (rather than diminishes) instability among those who spend time in the streets and will therefore likely increase the behaviors that are often understood to constitute disorder.

Third, although defined as remedial and nonpunitive by city officials, spatial exclusions were experienced by our respondents as quite burdensome. Moreover, despite their civil nature, these exclusion orders deepened the entanglement of many in the criminal justice system. The argument that these exclusion orders are civil and nonpunitive is thus in marked tension with both the experiences of the banished and the court data presented in chapter 4. In short, the interview data indicate that banishment largely fails to achieve its stated goals of relocation and stabilization. By contrast, these data provide evidence that banishment does achieve a less frequently stated goal—allowing police officers greater discretion and authority when dealing with those deemed disorderly. In this sense, the deployment of banishment may be a policy failure but a political achievement.

Finally, listening to the voices of the banished highlights the need to go beyond the simplistic identification of complex and multifaceted people as the embodiment of disorder and move beyond the urge to exclude those whose presence disturbs us. As Leonard Feldman argues, the denial of citizenship rights to the homeless and other socially marginal urban residents both reflects and perpetuates their economic and cultural "misrecognition."[5] A more inclusive and proactive approach to the problems facing many of those deemed disorderly would not only more effectively address those issues but also avoid contributing to the stigmatization and marginalization of those deemed disorderly.

Toward this end, we explore policy alternatives in the following chapter.

6

Banishment Reconsidered

A sergeant from the Seattle Police Department makes the rounds through several downtown parks on a warm summer morning. He is accompanied by two staff members from the Downtown Emergency Services Center (DESC), which provides a variety of housing options and social services for low-income people. His hope is that DESC staff can help find suitable housing for any disadvantaged people they encounter.

All of the parks through which they traverse are located in the Pioneer Square neighborhood, a longtime gathering spot for the socially disadvantaged. Their first stop is Courthouse Park, which is colloquially referred to as Muscatel Meadow because it attracts chronic alcoholics and others who gather in public space downtown. The sergeant finds a new arrival, a man who says he just got off the train from St. Louis. The sergeant quickly introduces the man to a DESC staffer, who informs him of potential places he can sleep.

As the group walks from Courthouse Park, the sergeant takes note of a very small park, Prefontaine Place, just across the street. Set aside in earlier days as a space for a library, its minuscule size led the city in 1925 to build a park instead. It contains three large stone benches formed in a U around a fountain. The park memorializes Father Prefontaine, founder of the first Catholic church in the area.

Father Prefontaine would likely be distressed by the current status of his namesake park. Shut off long ago, the fountain now serves as a receptacle for trash and, given the odor, apparently also for urine. The benches primarily host the homeless, four of whom are present when the sergeant casts his gaze on the park. As the group nears 3rd Avenue and prepares to cross it toward Prefontaine Park, the sergeant stops. He sweeps his left arm toward the park, turns to his companions, and says, "Whose responsibility is this?"

It is an excellent question. That the sergeant even raises it indicates that he shares our concern with excessive reliance on the criminal justice system to address a social problem like homelessness. Banishment promises a quick fix to the concerns many express about disorder in its various manifestations. It mobilizes and enhances the territorial power of the police to try to convince undesirables to relocate. It uses civil law to stretch the reach of the criminal law apparatus, such that many who gather in Seattle's public spaces, especially downtown, are perpetually stuck in the web of surveillance and control.

It is a fundamentally flawed endeavor. For multiple reasons, the criminal justice system—buttressed by civil sanctions or not—is an inadequate and inappropriate venue for addressing the dynamics that generate social disadvantage: poverty and joblessness, chemical addiction and mental illness, government inattention and a frayed social safety net, insufficient public housing and overheated gentrification. Banishment does not address these underlying problems. Furthermore, it is costly, prone to expansion, and insufficiently open to challenge by those it targets. In the words of an assistant city attorney in Seattle, "The criminal justice system is a lousy place to solve a social problem."

The previous chapters should make obvious why we see banishment as an inappropriate and ineffective response to urban social ills. As a creative synthesis of various legal sanctions, as an effort to restore police discretion and authority, and as a political response to public concerns about urban disorder worsened by growing inequality, banishment is a novel and impressive accomplishment. It is also a remarkable expansion of the social control net, an extraordinary tightening and widening of the capacity to surveil and arrest. Although civil and criminal law have all been mobilized in efforts to stamp out urban vice, their fusion in the new social control practices analyzed here appears to be a novel means of enhancing the power of criminal law and those who enforce it.

However much benefit it provides to the police as a mechanism for making otherwise unwarranted stops and as evidence that they are doing something about disorder, it should not be embraced. In many ways, banishment represents a return to nineteenth-century policing, in which officers enjoyed broad discretion and engaged in ambitious projects of moral regulation. As we demonstrated in chapter 3, it is targeted primarily at socially marginalized individuals, whose lives are already characterized by multiple forms of disadvantage. As we showed in chapter 4, it is extremely expensive; the costs of arresting and jailing the banished are significant and rising steadily. And, as we explained in chapter 5, it is counterproductive. Banishment only increases the marginalization of the disadvantaged and does nothing to address the challenges that make their lives so difficult.

Fortunately, the pluralistic political climate in Seattle and the prospect of extreme budget shortfalls provide space for challenging banishment's popularity. Recall that some of these measures, notably parks exclusions orders, faced stiff opposition when first proposed. Even if these challenges were unsuccessful, they revealed the presence of alternative framings of disorder within the Seattle polity.

This alternate discourse takes expression in three prominent forms, which we review and assess in this chapter. One involves attacking the legal bases on which banishment is constructed. Several public defenders we interviewed identified a range of possible challenges they would like to advance, given an opportunity to do so. Such efforts are to be applauded, not least because they remind us that the banished are, after all, rights-bearing individuals. Yet for various reasons, it is unlikely that recourse to the courts will, in and of itself, result in a significant diminution of banishment's use.

A second alternative, one practiced to a considerable extent in Seattle, is the use of so-called therapeutic courts. Here, the goal is to direct the socially marginalized not toward jail but toward various forms of social services. The logic is sensible. If a person's criminal behavior is in significant part generated by mental illness, lack of housing, and/or some form of addiction, it is better to address those underlying conditions. Jail stays are likely to only exacerbate such afflictions and thus are counterproductive. As a humane alternative to more incarceration, therapeutic courts are clearly preferable. But their location within the criminal justice system creates numerous problems, not least of which is to reinforce (perhaps unwittingly) the practices of exclusion we critique. For this reason, we are unable to celebrate therapeutic courts as a meaningful alternative to banishment.

The third option we review, one that combines elements from both the harm reduction and the housing first movements, is rather more promising. The harm reduction model posits that it is not possible to entirely eradicate undesirable behaviors such as drug use and public alcohol consumption. Therefore, even as we try to address those behaviors, we also need to work to reduce the harm they cause—to both those engaged in them and society as a whole. The housing first model holds that individuals must possess steady and secure housing before they can address any other problems that may (or may not) beset them.

In other words, the problem of homelessness must be addressed prior to any other social service intervention aimed at improving the situation of the socially marginalized.

These two philosophies come together in a Seattle program worthy of emulation, 1811 Eastlake. Chronic alcoholics are provided housing here, and they are allowed to drink. Although this latter component is controversial, it is preferable to allowing alcoholics to remain on the streets, where they will face regular trips to jail and the emergency room. It is cheaper and more humane to provide supported housing. The provision of housing for those who require it and do not need additional social services is less expensive still.

Implicit in the construction of places like 1811 Eastlake is a spirit of compassion and inclusiveness. Rather than castigating the downtrodden as unwanted and seeing their problems are entirely self-generated, harm reduction and housing first advocates recognize a shared sense of connection to the less fortunate. This spirit of inclusiveness, generosity, and shared responsibility contrasts noticeably with the impulse to ostracize that characterizes banishment. These more inclusive tendencies, we hope, can gain more political traction in the years to come and provide a more robust antidote to the desire to banish. Because banishment is both expensive and ineffective, alternative approaches to social disadvantage deserve serious consideration.

Contesting Banishment

The problems associated with social disadvantage are often unattractive. The sight of disheveled and mentally unstable people is not pleasant, and the impulse toward avoidance is understandably common. The detritus associated with sexual commerce and drug use—used condoms, dirty needles—are both unsightly and unhygienic. It is thus easy to empathize with a business owner in Seattle's Pioneer Square neighborhood, or a parent who lives near Aurora Avenue, when they express interest in seeing their neighborhood improved. They understandably fear for the health of their business if customers are wary of visiting their neighborhood; they may prefer that their teenage daughters not be propositioned by a john while walking along the street.

Given the territorial power they possess, the police are an obvious instrument to deploy to help clean up a neighborhood of unwanted people. The police can use their coercive power to threaten or actuate an arrest or otherwise convince someone to relocate. It is thus unsurprising that the police figure large in efforts to reduce disorder. Banishment as practiced in Seattle unleashes the discretionary authority of the police to place pressure on unwanted individuals to convince them to relocate. Banishment works to help achieve what one Seattle judge referred to as "damage control." As the judge explained, "You want to minimize the effect that disorder has on people, whether it be the victims or the neighborhood—and the neighborhood is a victim—or others that this may affect. And so sometimes we have to impose sentences just for that purpose alone. We don't get to some of the underlying things. So, many times the exclusions are just damage control." In similar fashion, a public defense attorney described banishment as a "brilliant strategy," because it enables the police "to appear to be doing something in response to community pressure. They can take immediate action in response to a perceived problem with virtually no constraint."

We are not persuaded that damage control and enhanced public relations efforts are sufficient justification for banishment, in Seattle or elsewhere. We used previous chapters to substantiate this claim by describing and assessing banishment as it is deployed in Seattle. We emphasize the Seattle case because we know it well and because we see the city as an unfortunate possible harbinger of the future in other cities. Indeed, many of the practices we assess here already are in place across the United States and, increasingly, across the globe.

The problem with banishment, at root, is that it mobilizes the criminal justice system in a wrongheaded way. The criminal process essentially casts the state in opposition to an accused individual and mobilizes the threat or reality of punishment to deter wrongdoing. Unfortunately, social problems are not individual matters. As we noted in chapter 1, the sudden rise of homelessness in the 1980s was not a result of individual choice. Instead, it was caused by economic change and government withdrawal from the provision of public housing. It simplifies matter grotesquely to suggest that individuals "choose" homelessness and can leave it behind if threatened with jailing. An emphasis on individualism is, of course, regnant throughout American culture. This may be inspiring when we celebrate particularly notable individual success stories, but it is repugnant when it is used to justify practices like banishment.

It is little surprise, then, that banishment does not really change matters on the ground all that much. As we showed in chapter 5, the homeless are like the rest of us in their need to stay attached to particular places. None of us can get our basic needs met without reliable time-space patterns that bring us in contact with the goods, services, and social connections we require. As a consequence, the banished commonly resist compliance with their exclusions; their requirement to stay in place is simply too great. Yet the failure of banishment oftentimes leads, rather perversely, to its expansion. If one takes the zoning logic of banishment seriously, then the spatial extent of exclusion only increases. Why would one business *not* sign a criminal trespass contract when others on the block are doing likewise? Why would one neighborhood *not* seek a Stay Out of Drug Area (SODA) designation when adjacent areas possess one?

The web of social control not only widens across space but intensifies in its ability to keep an individual ensnared. The homeless and others in public space face the increasing likelihood of bearing multiple spatial exclusions, such that they face the nearly perpetual threat of arrest and jail. This creates what one Seattle judge described as a "continuing cycle of crimes of criminal trespass" and the ongoing flow of the same individuals through her courtroom.

The expansion of zones of exclusion and the increased rates of arrest they generate helps multiply the fiscal costs that taxpayers must bear. Our analysis in chapter 4 made obvious the extensive burden Seattleites implicitly embrace when they ask the police to clean up allegedly disorderly places. As appealing as it may be to turn to the criminal justice system as a quick fix to clear out unwanted people it is a costly move. This embrace of criminalization is by now quite common in American politics and underlies the position of the United States as the world's most incarceration-happy country.[1] Yet this places the criminal justice system in the position of being, in the words of one Seattle government official, "the last safety net." This is regrettable.

Also regrettable is that banishment is practiced in Seattle in a way that resists contestation by its targets. Those who are banned possess limited or no means to challenge the bases of their banishment. This violates the spirit—if perhaps not always the letter—of the U.S. Constitution and its guarantees of due process. When community members are unable to contest government policies that place them under surveillance and arrest, they are, in effect, something less than full citizens. Of course, when they are broadly defined as disorder, their status as rights-bearers is implicitly denigrated. Moreover, the impossibility of contestation means that there is no check on the overreach of police power—to the detriment of all of us.

Finally, the embrace of banishment has restored a form of policing that is fundamentally incompatible with democratic policing. As Ian Loader argues, democratic police institutions pursue crime control in a way that recognizes "the legitimate claims of all individuals and groups affected by police actions and affirms their sense of *belonging* to a democratic political community."[2] The routine activities of police institutions communicate important and consequential messages about who does and does not belong. Insofar as banishment is now common practice in Seattle and elsewhere, the police are pursuing safety and security in arguably undemocratic ways.

Yet we need not accept banishment, we need not forget that the homeless remain members of the political community even if they lack shelter.[3] Indeed, one form of resisting banishment seeks to address the issue of constitutionality by challenging the legal foundations on which banishment is constructed. We turn now to a consideration of the logic and viability of this means of contesting banishment.

Criminal Courts as a Means to Contest Banishment

From their position as advocates for the banished, defense attorneys find much to deplore with social control as presently practiced in Seattle. Unsurprisingly, they register many of the same complaints about the creation and enforcement of zones of exclusion that were directed at loitering and vagrancy statutes in the 1960s and 1970s. They argue that banishment provides the police far too much capacity to exercise power arbitrarily and far too few mechanisms to contest that power.

As we found in chapter 2, targets of SODA or Stay Out of Areas of Prostitution (SOAP) orders, parks exclusion orders, or criminal trespass admonishments are endowed with limited means to challenge their exclusions. SODA/SOAP orders are levied by judges and correctional officers, both of whom enjoy significant discretion in sentencing or regulating those they supervise. Parks exclusion orders are created in the field by the police or park officers and can be challenged only in an administrative hearing overseen by parks officials; substantive barriers to challenging these orders are significant. Until arrest and prosecution, criminal trespass admonishments cannot be contested by recipients, absent the proactive filing of a civil rights challenge.

Trespass admonishments most rankle public defenders, because they enable significant state action without due process. As one defender argued, "A state actor can't come and just ban you from a place and there's nothing you can do about it. But that's the situation [with trespass admonishments]." The counterargument, of course, is that a police officer who delivers an admonishment is acting at the implicit request of the property owner; this is what the trespass authorization form makes legally permissible. Furthermore, the admonishment provides a citizen with the opportunity to avoid arrest. It functions, in effect, as a warning; if you wish to stay out of jail, stay away from this property in the future.

Yet there are complex issues here. One concerns the spatial extent of trespass zones. As we noted in chapter 2, the Seattle police created several trespass programs that combine multiple properties. It is one thing, noted a public defender, for the police to say that they are merely acting at the behest of a single property owner when issuing a trespass admonishment. But, he said, "As they broaden them out and they start excluding people from whole neighborhoods, it starts to look a lot more like government action, because no individual owner could accomplish anything like that."

In addition, defense attorneys point to the problematic lack of constraints on an officer's decision to admonish. These decisions are made in the field and are governed by no independent authority. Indeed, in the majority of cases in our sample of trespass admonishment forms, the officer in question provided no justification for the decision to exclude. The vagueness of the rules governing the police and the lack of due process safeguards for the admonished thus make criminal trespass a suspect enterprise to many members of the defense bar. As one defense attorney complained, "We say by giving the police officers the ability to just decide who's legitimate or not legitimate in a place, they're essentially law makers out there acting on whatever arbitrary instinct they have."

Whatever merits these legal arguments possess, they are rarely granted an audience in court, a reality that further frustrates defense attorneys. There are multiple reasons why broad challenges to the legal authority on which banishment is based are hard to raise. For starters, any such challenge requires a defense attorney dedicated and energetic enough to write legal briefs substantiating larger constitutional issues. Underpaid and overworked public defenders are not uniformly inclined to devote this level of commitment to their work. Even those who do possess such motivation cannot typically succeed. That is in part because their clients, who almost universally face short jail stays, may not wish to endure the long process a substantive legal challenge entails. Multiple hearings, ongoing continuances, and other complexities attendant to the appeals process are difficult for many defendants to navigate. When prosecutors are willing to offer a plea bargain that seems attractive, many defendants pursue this path of least resistance.

This illustrates the role prosecutors can play in thwarting legal challenges to banishment or other state practices. As mentioned, one is to dangle an attractive plea arrangement that entices a defendant to drop the challenge. Another is for the prosecutor to simply drop the charges against a more pugilistic defendant. This makes the case disappear, and with it the potential challenge to the legal basis that underlies it. Furthermore, even when a challenge does succeed at a lower court level, it does not change law. An appellate court ruling is required to create binding precedent. These courts, by definition, act only on appeals. In this situation, the prosecution would need to appeal a defense-friendly ruling, a risk they may be unwilling to take for fear of creating a precedent unfavorable to their interests.

Thus, there are significant structural impediments that interfere with the use of the criminal courts to impede the project of banishment. For their part, the defense attorneys we interviewed were hardly sanguine about what they could accomplish within the courtroom. Even as they chafe at what they perceive to be the injustices of banishment, they are clear-eyed about its goals; as one said, the point is "to make people legitimately arrestable for loitering, which is not normally a legitimate arrestable crime." This places continuing pressure on undesirables to relocate and fear the watchful eye of the police perpetually. Said one public defender, "He can get taken away tomorrow and he knows that. So, you know, the court process is really pretty irrelevant to the fundamentals." As another public defender noted, the practice of law is a "cat-and-mouse game," whereby each side perpetually looks for ambiguities in the law to exploit. He argued, "It's kind of like an arms race or the relationship between bacteria and antibiotics; the bacteria keeps evolving to be resistant to the antibiotics and the antibiotics keep getting better in response to the new strains of bacteria." Focused as they are on clients who are enmeshed in the legal system, attorneys must continue to play this game and thus cannot typically directly address the wider structural factors that make disorder an issue in the first place. One attorney explained, "And I guess I feel like my job as a lawyer is just to make it hard for them each and every time....I mean my job is that guy and that's how I see it."

This does not prevent many of the defense attorneys we interviewed from bemoaning the limited reach of the courts in addressing the problems they believe attend to banishment. Even the victories they might win can seem to ring hollow, given the wider injustices banishment perpetrates. Said one, "The due process argument is really fun to argue legally, but basically what it does is to say that deprivation's okay as long as you provide process, which is fundamentally not what I think. I mean, I think it's improper to exclude people from public places, period."

We share this attorney's concern with the impulse to exclude, just as we share her concern about whether the criminal courts are the best venue for challenging banishment.[4] Interestingly, courts are often touted as an appropriate place for redressing many of the social ills experienced by the disadvantaged. This occurs in so-called therapeutic courts, ones that seek to assess the conditions that may underlie a given criminal defendant's behavior, such as mental illness or chemical addiction. We now turn to an evaluation of therapeutic courts as a possible alternative to banishment.

Reducing Disorder through Therapeutic Courts

In recent years, many jurisdictions across the United States created "therapeutic" or "problem-solving" courts.[5] The logic is straightforward. If criminal behavior is significantly caused by some underlying pathology, then public safety might be better guaranteed through nontraditional means. In other words, the threat or actuality of incarceration may not, for many individuals, deter criminal behavior but merely increase its likelihood. Incarceration may, for example, intensify mental illness and thereby fuel rates of recidivism for those so afflicted.[6] Given this, it makes sense for courts to serve as a gateway not to jail but to the services needed to improve mental health or reduce chemical dependency. This might thereby decrease the frequency of much criminal behavior.

The therapeutic justice movement takes various forms, such as drug courts, mental health courts, and community courts. Although they differ in their particulars and vary from jurisdiction to jurisdiction, these courts are commonly organized around a core set of principles. One, as suggested, is an emphasis on treatment. Rather than primarily wielding the threat of incarceration to compel compliance to the criminal law, the court tries to connect a defendant with relevant service providers and address the underlying issues. The approach is defendant-based rather than case-based: courtroom encounters are used to work with the defendant to craft a care plan and monitor compliance with that plan.[7]

This requires a second key characteristic of problem-solving courts: that they mobilize a team approach, whereby all the actors—including judges and attorneys—deliberately seek to minimize the adversarial nature of the courtroom.[8] Instead, courtroom actors consciously work together to craft individualized approaches to each defendant. To accomplish this, many problem-solving courts require defendants to surrender many of the due process rights they ordinarily possess. The team approach also means that court personnel are paying attention less to precise legal procedure and more to social science evidence about what treatment options are best suited to a given individual.[9]

A third characteristic of therapeutic courts is that their docket is kept sequestered from other branches of the criminal court structure. This enables an individual defendant to remain within the jurisdiction of the therapeutic court and experience ongoing continuity with that court. It also enables the defendant's progress—or lack thereof—to be monitored at regular intervals by the same court personnel.[10] The development of a specialized court also helps provide its staff with the expertise necessary to determine effective treatment plans.[11]

At both the municipal and superior court levels, Seattle and King County are active participants in the therapeutic court movement. At the time of this writing, a drug court, a community court, and a mental health court are all in operation in downtown Seattle. King County's Drug Diversion Court was created in 1994 and was the twelfth drug court implemented in the United States. Approximately 550 defendants currently participate in the program. In many ways, it is quite progressive. For example, successful "graduates" of the program acquire no criminal record. Recently, the King County prosecutor's office modified the eligibility requirements to allow those arrested for drug delivery (rather than drug possession) to participate in the program under certain conditions. The city of Seattle operates the mental health and community courts, which, other than making a guilty plea a condition of eligibility, are founded on similar principles and seek to link eligible misdemeanants with needed services.

The popularity of these problem-solving courts reflects an embrace both of their underlying logic—that treatment and services are more effective and humane than incarceration—and recognition of some cold fiscal realities. The King County Jail possesses the second-largest concentration of mentally ill individuals in the state of Washington.[12] Given the cost of incarcerating these individuals, it makes considerable fiscal sense to search for more effective and affordable alternatives.

There are, at first glance, strong reasons to support therapeutic courts. For starters, treatment for drug addiction and mental illness is more effective than jail in reducing recidivism.[13] That is because, unsurprisingly, treatment appears to work better to address the underlying issues with which many criminal offenders struggle.[14] In the case of mental health court, Seattle's example suggests that therapeutic courts can link people reasonably well with the services they need and thereby help reduce recidivism.[15]

That said, there is still no evidence that either the King County Drug Diversion Court or the Seattle Community Court reduce recidivism. Indeed, the first evaluation of the Community Court found that it increased rather than reduced recidivism.[16] More generally, there is considerable debate regarding the efficacy of therapeutic courts in reducing the likelihood that defendants will reoffend.[17] Thus, although treatment is clearly more effective than incarceration, it is unclear whether the provision of treatment through therapeutic courts is the most effective way to provide treatment and to improve people's lives.

Therapeutic courts do appear to make fiscal sense—at least in the short term and when compared with the alternative of incarceration. Treatment options, including supportive housing, are significantly cheaper than jailing.[18] For example, although Seattle's Community Court does not appear to reduce recidivism, it did reduce the number of jail days served by program participants, and thereby lowered costs.[19] (Of course, it is possible to impose shorter jail stays without developing a therapeutic court.) The excessive reliance on incarceration in recent decades is generating expenses that are progressively harder for many jurisdictions to handle, and Seattle and King County are no exceptions. These fiscal burdens help explain the growing popularity of problem-solving courts.

There are aspects of these courts that prevent us from seeing them as a compelling alternative to banishment. As mentioned previously, considerable debate still swirls around the efficacy of these courts in reducing recidivism. In addition, although the provision of treatment through the courts may be less expensive than incarceration, it is considerably more expensive than providing drug treatment and other needed services *in the community*.[20] According to the Substance Abuse and Mental Health Services Administration's *National Treatment Improvement Evaluation Study*, drug treatment in the community cost an average of $2,941 in 1994 (equivalent to $4,065 in 2007 dollars). By contrast, the Washington State Institute for Public Policy reports that the cost of Washington state drug court in 2003 was $11,227 per participant (equivalent to $12,634 in 2007 dollars). It thus appears that providing drug treatment through the courts costs about three times more than providing it in the community, *before* someone is arrested.[21] It makes sense to avail people of treatment before they get into trouble with the law, particularly because this is far more cost-effective.

Other concerns have more to do with what happens within therapeutic court. As noted, defendants are typically required to submit a guilty plea and surrender any due process rights they ordinarily possess within the courtroom. This may make sense to buttress the teamwork approach said to characterize problem-solving courts. But it calls into question whether, in the process, these legal arenas continue to function as intended. In therapeutic courts, neither judges nor attorneys play their usual roles; they trade concerns for process, legality, and legal accountability for concerns about desirable therapeutic outcomes. Candace McCoy makes this point well: "Problem-solving courts are not courts. They are not concerned with due process or adjudicating guilt, either by plea or trial. They are correctional agencies, and as such might be an excellent new model of correctional agency. But as post-adjudicative bodies, they must be called what they really are, and it is *not* courts."[22] As James Nolan argues, this courtroom transformation requires that judges, trained as lawyers, act primarily as social workers, a role for which they are not as well prepared.[23]

It is also worth considering the landscape of service provision on which therapeutic courts rely. There are several issues here. One concerns whether the necessary level of provision of those services can be assumed to exist. Therapeutic courts generally rely on treatment providers that they cannot control and whose future well-being they cannot presume. Furthermore, these various providers often operate quite autonomously, a reality that creates considerable coordination challenges.[24] Of course, we should consider why it is that someone may need to be arrested to get treatment. Indeed, in many jurisdictions, a trip to therapeutic court essentially means a chance to skip ahead in line for access to scarce social services.[25] The total number of treatment slots is generally not increased as a result of the adoption of drug or other therapeutic courts. To the extent that this is the case, the courts primarily serve to place program participants at the top of waiting lists, pushing others further down. Any improvements in community health and safety would, by definition, be slim to none.

Finally, we have concerns about how much therapeutic courts can impact other components of the criminal justice system, most notably the police. Because banishment is now well established in Seattle—as we showed in chapter 3, it is a common means of contact between the police and the homeless—it is easy to presume that individuals will face the continuing threat of arrest, regardless of their treatment plan. We are therefore concerned that banishment will continue to fuel a steady flow of entrants into the criminal process and the ongoing entrapment of the destitute in the state social control net. For example, the Seattle Community Court reduced jail costs by $221,000 in its first nineteen months of operation.[26] Yet this figure is dwarfed by the additional million dollars the city spent to jail SODA violators in a single year.[27] Banishment's expansion thus continually undermines the rehabilitative and fiscal goals of therapeutic courts.

The humanitarian impulse that underlies therapeutic courts stands in sharp contrast to the impulse to ostracize that fuels the practice of banishment. As much as this should be applauded, the practices of therapy and of criminal justice are not easily reconciled, no matter how innovative a given problem-solving court may be. We therefore believe that the best alternative to banishment lies outside the criminal justice system. Most broadly, we believe that the reduction of inequality and the restoration of the social welfare net are central to any effort to meaningfully address urban disorder. Less broadly, we find greater promise in a combination of two distinct but complementary approaches—harm reduction and housing first—to which we now turn.

Harm Reduction and Housing First

At its basic level, the criminal justice process pits the state against a person it alleges violated the criminal law. The process is meant to determine whether the individual is guilty of a legally defined crime and, if so, determine an appropriate punishment. Although punishment can serve multiple social functions, one of its main goals is to deter. If the pain of punishment is sufficient, then an offender should desist from future infractions. If someone is caught, say, injecting illegal drugs, then a stint in prison should persuade that person to kick the habit.

One of our core arguments is that it is a flawed endeavor to use the criminal justice system to address the manifestations of social disadvantage. This is especially obvious when one considers behaviors such as injection drug use or chronic alcoholism. As much as we might hope that the threat of punishment would hasten the cessation of these behaviors, this is wishful thinking in a vast number of cases.

The harm reduction philosophy accepts this reality. A central principle of harm reduction is the recognition that some people will always engage behaviors that are risky, such as drug use and sexual commerce. Although we can and should attempt to reduce these behaviors, no society has ever eradicated all unwanted forms of deviance. From this perspective, "abstinence cannot be the only goal of [drug] policy, or of treatment providers."[28] From here, it is just a short step toward recognizing that social policy might do better not to seek to eradicate such behavior altogether but to lessen its negative consequences. Harm reduction practitioners accept the need to assess each individual's particular circumstances and recognize that the path toward abstinence may often be long, and sometimes nonexistent.[29]

In addition, harm reduction advocates distinguish between primary and secondary harms associated with deviant behavior. Primary harms are those caused by the behavior itself, such as liver damage caused by excessive alcohol consumption. Secondary harms are those that flow from the policy response to the behavior in question. For example, an injection drug user who contracts HIV because clean syringes are not made available has suffered a secondary—and quite avoidable—harm. Similarly, the adverse consequences that flow from the incarceration of an addict are considered by harm reduction advocates to be both secondary and avoidable.

Thus, from a harm reduction point of view, the active intervention of the criminal justice system is often counterproductive and a source of damage. If policed aggressively, activities such as drug use and sexual commerce may be pushed into more and more dangerous places. This may leave those who engage in those behaviors even more vulnerable to physical assault.[30] Drug users may inject more quickly, or in darker locales, or with dirty needles, thereby endangering themselves and others.[31] A drug user who is convicted, incarcerated, and loses her ability to secure work and housing as a result of her conviction is more likely to relapse. Thus, criminal justice intervention can *increase* the harms attendant to risky behaviors.

Harm reduction advocates therefore argue that forms of risky behavior should be defined primarily as matters not of criminal justice but of public health.[32] In many cases, punishment is an inappropriate response to these behaviors. Instead, the priority should be the provision of health care and social services to help reduce overall levels of harm. It makes more sense, for example, not to incarcerate people for injecting drugs but to provide a safe site where they can do so while simultaneously establishing the trusting relationships that are necessary for effective treatment. This way, they can avoid needlessly endangering themselves or disturbing others; users can reduce the potential harm they might cause to themselves, such as through an overdose, or to others, through the spread of infectious diseases. At a safe injection site and similar venues, care providers can begin the process of establishing trusting relationships with users that might eventually make abstinence a plausible outcome.[33]

Of course, many who abuse drugs, engage in sexual commerce, or otherwise behave in risky and socially disapproved fashion also suffer from poverty and homelessness. For precisely this reason, they attract police attention in the first place and thus stand vulnerable to banishment. If homeless, they typically face the prospect of either sleeping on the street or in one of various emergency shelters. For most, neither option is especially attractive. Life on the street is often uncomfortable and sometimes dangerous. Shelters can be noisy, crowded, and unhygienic. In addition, many shelters place demands on their residents, such as work requirements or abstinence from drugs or alcohol. As already noted, abstinence is not an option for some. Furthermore, shelters are typically only emergency housing options; life in one is hardly a ticket to permanent housing.

The Housing First approach, first articulated in the early 1990s by Dr. Sam Tsemberis, a New York University psychologist, stresses the importance of permanent housing.[34] For some of those who find themselves banished, the lack of stable housing is the sole problem. Others also require social services. Without permanent housing, individuals are less likely to respond favorably to any social service intervention designed to propel them toward independent living. From this perspective, housing is a basic need, one that deserves to be met regardless of any troublesome behavior, such as alcohol or drug use. In the best-case scenario, permanent housing is accompanied by strong social services where they are needed, all geared toward helping individuals and families attain stability.

Housing First is attracting considerable attention in contemporary American policy. It is now embraced by the U.S. Department of Housing and Urban Development and is a centerpiece of many cities' ten-year plans to end homelessness.[35]

Although harm reduction and Housing First are distinct, they are highly complementary. Each approach accepts the need to view disadvantaged individuals in broad perspective, to see clearly the wide array of challenges they may face. Each recognizes the need to develop comprehensive plans to help people achieve greater degrees of stability. Each accepts that eradication of all unwanted behaviors is unlikely, but nonetheless posits that significant harms may be reduced. Each also recognizes the possible negative impact of criminal justice intervention. Most fundamentally, each perspective recognizes that improving the quality of life of all urban residents requires improving the lives of the most disadvantaged.

One specific place where these two philosophies meet in an exemplary fashion is in a building on the northeast edge of downtown Seattle, 1811 Eastlake. Run by the DESC, which oversees a wide array of shelter for disadvantaged people in Seattle, 1811 is so-called wet housing. Here, especially chronic alcoholics are given subsidized housing. Contrary to typical practice, they are allowed to drink there. This is for the very sensible reason that long-term, chronic alcoholics are most likely going to continue to drink. Rather than make housing contingent on an impossible demand—that they stop drinking—it is better to provide a more realistic option.

The alternative to wet housing, of course, is to allow poor, chronic alcoholics to live largely on the streets, from which they will face regular trips to jail or the emergency room—often both. It is not only more humane to offer them a place in wet housing but significantly cheaper; jails and emergency rooms are far more expensive places to house people than is supportive housing. Unsurprisingly, the residents are healthier, and some reduce their drinking substantially over time.[36] That, in large part, is due to the fact that they no longer must sleep outside, where they often feel a need for chemical assistance to cope. Also, at 1811 Eastlake, residents possess ready access to staff who can assist them with various forms of treatment. Of course, providing housing to those who do not require drug or alcohol treatment would also be an effective and ultimately cost-effective alternative.

It may seem ironic that some of key supporters of banishment practices, such as the Downtown Business Association, also support projects like 1811 Eastlake. According to the head of DESC, this is largely for fiscal reasons. As he notes, business people recognize a cost-effective plan when they see one. Robust support for 1811 Eastlake also comes from the former director of the King County Jail. He recognizes the harm it can cause many people to jail them, as well as the high cost to the public purse. As he noted in an interview, supported housing like 1811 Eastlake is both morally and fiscally a more sensible policy than jailing.

When the director of a jail is willing to declare publicly the need to send people elsewhere, perhaps the rest of us should pay close attention. For their part, police may not necessarily need or want to send disorderly people to jail. However, when they receive complaints about transients sleeping in a park or public inebriates bothering pedestrians, they may need to transport them to another locale. Said one former police officer, "Yeah, I mean, if there was like [another] place that you could take everybody, I mean more cops would be happy to do that, rather than take them to a jail. Because to take them to jail, and then getting the criminal justice system involved, is a big pain in the ass." As she noted later in the interview, "People think that the cops love arresting people. But it's not true. What [we] want is lack of problems."

Banishing Banishment

Yet we have problems. It is deeply unfortunate that extreme poverty is so widespread in American cities and that its manifestations are visible on too many urban streets. Nationally, approximately three and half million people experience homelessness each year; nearly a million are homeless on any given day.[37] In some cases, extreme poverty is accompanied by other problems, such as mental or physical illness or addiction. Neighborhoods like Seattle's Pioneer Square are not always comfortable to traverse, as some of those who spend time on the streets occasionally engage in erratic or unsettling behavior.

It is even more unfortunate that we so readily turn to the police when we see such "disorder" on display. Even if the police can mobilize their power to cajole or coerce people to relocate, they are ultimately irrelevant to any effort to meaningfully address social disadvantage. To endow them with the power to banish and enforce zones of exclusion in an ongoing fashion may provide an illusion of order, to borrow Bernard Harcourt's apt phrase.[38] But it is only an illusion. The banished are likely to return. After all, were else are they to go?

1811 Eastlake is one place where some of them can go. Sadly, it only houses seventy-five people and tailors itself to a narrow if underserved population, chronic alcoholics. Many such facilities—with and without supportive services—are needed if we wish to address urban poverty and its challenges in any thoroughgoing fashion. Without more affordable housing; better access to treatment, health care, and other forms of social service; and more available low-skill and adequately paid jobs, disorder will not notably abate. As a Seattle judge noted in an interview, "I am tired of the criminal justice system being blamed for, and asked to deal with, without resources, the failure in our social service system." We need to try something different.

We particularly need to do something different given the evidence we assembled about the practice of banishment. Poor people of color are the most likely to garner police attention. Furthermore, many individuals are ensnared in the web of social control merely for being present in public space. This is too low a threshold for criminal justice intervention. The tradition in the United States of robust civil liberties, if nothing else, is endangered in the process.

Sadly, reasoned discussions of civil liberties, governmental budgets, and policy efficacy are often rendered impossible when the charged topics of order and security enter the discourse.[39] The key political challenge, then, is to replace the fear-inducing language of "disorder and decline"[40] with a more capacious, just, and inclusive public discourse. Such a discourse would recognize several realities: that extreme inequality adversely impacts us all, that poverty stems from structural dynamics that extend well beyond the lone denizen of the street, that security means something more than protection for middle-class whites from the discomforts of urban life, that justice includes the proposition that everyone enjoy a minimal quality of life, and that tolerance of diversity is integral to democracy. Such a political appeal would aim not at fear and castigation but at the human capacity for empathy and respect.

Whether scholars in another twenty-five years will write a story about a more or less punitive city will depend on which of these appeals resonates more strongly in the political contests to come. It will also, of course, depend on our willingness to make hard choices regarding the generation and reallocation of scarce public resources. Banishment may well continue apace in Seattle and elsewhere, yet it will accomplish little more than increased costs and needless heartache. Seattle, and those cities that increasingly adopt similar social control practices, can be better places than that.

Notes

These stories were collected through interviews and reflect the point of view and experience of our respondents. Although we are unable to verify many of the facts of their individual cases, their stories are entirely plausible given the elasticity and breadth of the legal tools they involve.

1. Ordinance 115171 prohibits drug traffic loitering, which is defined as remaining in a public place and intentionally soliciting, inducing, enticing, or procuring another to engage in illegal drug activity. Conviction does not require any evidence that a drug transaction occurred (such as recovered narcotics) but rests on an officer's testimony that he or she observed the suspect engage in behaviors that are believed to manifest the *intent* to commit a drug crime. Similar statues exist in other municipalities, such as Tacoma, Washington (TMC 8.72), and Oakland, California (OMC 9.58.020), and in such states as Louisiana (RS 40:981.4).

2. According to her attorney, Rhonda's conviction was subsequently overturned on appeal due to insufficient evidence.

3. Seattle Ordinance 111727, formally titled the Parks Enhanced Code Enforcement Ordinance, authorized administrative suspension of park use by individuals who violate laws and rules in the parks.

4. In Seattle, the University of Washington recently banned someone from the campus indefinitely (*State of Washington v. Michael Thomas*, No. C06975UW).

5. James Fallows, "Saving Salmon, or Seattle," *Atlantic Monthly*, 286 (2000): 20–24.

6. The term "social control" refers generally to the process by which social order is maintained, but it has been defined in a number of ways.

We define it here more narrowly to refer to the process by which actors undertake concerted efforts to manage or regulate deviant behavior. This definition closely parallels that of Stanley Cohen (*Visions of Social Control*, Cambridge: Polity Press, 1985) and Donald Black (*The Behaviour of Law*, New York: Academic Press, 1976), and can be differentiated from approaches that are so broad as to equate social control with socialization. For extended discussions of the debate around these various conceptions, see Martin Innes, *Understanding Social Control: Deviance, Crime and Social Order* (New York: McGraw Hill International, 2003).

7. See www.nyc.gov/html/nycha/html/residents/trespass.shtml.

8. See www.bostonhousing.org/pdfs/Trespassing%20Draft%20Policy.pdf.

9. Don Mitchell, "Property Rights, the First Amendment, and Judicial Anti-Urbanism: The Strange Case of *Hicks v. Virginia*," *Urban Geography* 26, no. 7 (2005): 565–586. See also dls.state.va.us/pubs/briefs/brief31.htm.

10. Elena Goldstein, "Kept Out: Responding to Public Housing No-Trespass Policies," *Harvard Civil Rights-Civil Liberties Journal* 38 (2003); Mitchell, "Property Rights, the First Amendment, and Judicial Anti-Urbanism."

11. Ibid.

12. *People v. Carter*, 169 Misc.2d 230, 234 (Kings City, 1996).

13. Jaime Adame, "Operation Safe Housing," *Gotham Gazette*, August 17, 2004; Goldstein, "Kept Out."

14. See New York County District Attorney's Office, Trespass Affidavit and Narcotics Eviction Programs, available at manhattanda.org/officebrochures/TAP-NEP. pdf.

15. Adame, "Operation Safe Housing"; Manny Fernandez, "Barred from Public Housing, Even to See Family," *New York Times*, October 1, 2007, A1; New York City, "Mayor Michael R. Bloomberg Announces Operation Safe Housing," June 24, 2004; Cara Tabachnick, "Jump in Trespassing Arrests Draws Anger," *Newsday*, April 10, 2007; Rocco Parascandola, "Trespass Arrests under Attack," *Newsday*, April 13, 2007.

16. Peter M. Flanagan, "Trespass-Zoning: Ensuring Neighborhoods a Safer Future by Excluding Those with a Criminal Past," *Notre Dame Law Review* 79 (2003): 327–379; Gordon Hill, "The Use of Pre-Existing Exclusionary Zones as Probationary Conditions for Prostitution Offenses: A Call for the Sincere Application of Heightened Scrutiny," *Seattle University Law Review* 28 (2005); Sandra Moser, "Anti-Prostitution Zones: Justifications for Abolition," *Journal of Criminal Law & Criminology* 91 (summer 2001): 1101; Lisa Sanchez, "Enclosure Acts and Exclusionary Practices: Neighborhood Associations, Community Police, and the Expulsion of the Sexual Outlaw," chapter 6 in *Between Law and Culture: Relocating Legal Studies*, edited by David Theo Goldberg, Michael Musheno, and Lisa C. Bower (Minneapolis: University of Minnesota Press, 1997).

17. American Prosecutors Research Institute, *Unwelcome Guests: A Community Prosecution Approach to Street level Drug Dealing and Prostitution* (2004); Sanchez, "Enclosure Acts and Exclusionary Practices"; Abby Sewell, "How Well Do Drug-Free' Zones Really Work?" *Portland Alliance*, November 2005. As Sewell notes, in Portland, exclusion orders stay on a person's record even in the absence of conviction. Other

Oregon municipalities appear to be following suit. See www.cascade-locks.or.us/
leftmenus/ordinances/ord354.pdf. A similar ordinance was in effect in Cincinnati,
Ohio, from 1996 to 2000 but was overturned in the Sixth Circuit. These spatial
restrictions are now imposed on those convicted as a condition of probation in
Cincinnati (Associated Press, "High Court Refuses to Review Cincinnati's Anti-
Trespass Law," April 29, 2002).

18. For a critical appraisal of the increased use of no-contact orders, see Jeannie
Suk, "Criminal Law Comes Home," *Yale Law Journal* 116, no. 2 (2006): 2–70. For
an empirical assessment of the growth and effects of juvenile curfews, see Kenneth
Adams, "The Effectiveness of Juvenile Curfews at Crime Prevention," *Annals of the
American Academy of Political and Social Science* 587 (2003): 136–159.

19. The use of nuisance statutes, civil injunctions, and abatement proceedings
in the war on disorder is not new. Nuisance abatement statutes were an important
part of nineteenth and twentieth centuries in campaigns against prostitution and
vice. Indeed, some historians suggest that injunctions against brothels and houses
of prostitution, in combination with the enforcement of criminal prohibitions
against vagrancy, loitering, and prostitution, ultimately sealed the fate of many
Progressive era red-light districts. See William J. Novak, *The People's Welfare: Law
and Regulation in Nineteenth Century America* (Chapel Hill: University of North
Carolina Press, 1996), 165–166. See also Charles S. Ascher and James M. Wolf,
" 'Red Light' Injunction and Abatement Acts," *Columbia Law Review* 20 (1920):
605–608; Robert McCurdy, "The Use of the Injunction to Destroy Commercialized
Prostitution in Chicago," *Journal of Criminal Law* 19 (1929): 513–517. With
the development of gang injunctions, however, nuisance laws now place civil
restrictions on the movement of people as well as on the uses of property.
Moreover, the legal hybridity of the gang injunctions and other legal tools described
here does appear to be novel.

20. Edward L. Allan, *Civil Gang Abatement: The Effectiveness and Implications of
Policing by Injunction* (New York: LFB Scholarly Publications, 2004); Gary Stewart,
"Black Codes and Broken Windows: The Legacy of Racial Hegemony in Anti-Gang
Civil Injunctions," *Yale Law Journal* 107, no. 7 (May 1998): 2249–2280.

21. Like the new control mechanisms now deployed in Seattle, civil
gang injunctions raise a number of constitutional issues. Like civil trespass
admonishments and parks exclusions, these gang injunctions proscribe otherwise
legal behaviors (such as associating with others and being in public spaces). They
also create personal criminal codes that attach to particular individuals as a result
of that person's alleged status as a gang member. Finally, gang injunctions offer
very little in the way of due process protections. In particular, only a preponderance
of evidence is required to sustain a determination that the injunction has
been violated; the accused does not enjoy the right to legal representation; and
challenging the constitutionality of the law that makes it a crime for the accused
to engage in otherwise legal behavior is quite difficult. See Christopher S. Yoo,
"The Constitutionality of Enjoining Street Gangs as Public Nuisances," *Northwest
University Law Review* 89 (1994): 212. Stewart, "Black Codes and Broken Windows";
Matthew Mickle Werdegar, "Enjoining the Constitution: The Use of Public Nuisance

Abatement Injunctions against Urban Street Gangs," *Stanford Law Review* 51, no. 2 (January 1999): 409–448.

22. On the United Kingdom, see Adam Crawford, "From the Shopping Mall to the Street Corner: Dynamics of Exclusion in the Governance of Public Space," presented to the World University Network, University of Leeds, June 2008; Adam Crawford and Stuart Lister, *The Use and Impact of Dispersal Orders* (Bristol: Polity Press, 2007; Andrew Millie, "Anti-Social Behaviour, Behavioural Expectations and an Urban Aesthetic," *British Journal of Criminology* 48 (2008): 379–394; Elizabeth Burney, *Making People Behave: Anti-Social Behaviour, Politics, and Policy* (Cullompton: Willan, 2005) and *Crime and Banishment: Nuisance and Exclusion in Social Housing* (Winchester: Waterside Press, 1999); John Flint and Judy Nixon, "Governing Neighbours: Anti-Social Behaviour Orders and New Forms of Regulating Conduct in the UK," *Urban Studies* 43 (2006): 939–956; Mike Raco, "Remaking Place and Securitizing Space: Urban Regeneration and the Strategies, Tactics and Practices of Policing in the UK," *Urban Studies* 40 (2003): 1869–1887; Peter Ramsay, "The Theory of Vulnerable Autonomy and the Legitimacy of the Civil Prevention Order," Law, Society and Economy Working Papers, 1/2008. On Germany, see Bernd Belina, "From Disciplining to Dislocation: Area Bans in Recent Urban Policing in Germany," *European Urban and Regional Studies* 14 (2007): 321–336; Jurgen von Mahs, "The Sociospatial Exclusion of Single Homeless People in Berlin and Los Angeles," *American Behavioral Scientist* 48 (2005): 928–960.

23. Crawford, "From the Shopping Mall to the Street Corner."

24. See Michael F. Armstrong, "Banishment: Cruel and Unusual Punishment," *University of Pennsylvania Law Review* 111, no. 6 (April 1963): 758–786; Matthew D. Borrelli, "Banishment: The Constitutional and Public Policy Arguments against this Revived Ancient Punishment," 36 *Suffolk University Law Review* 470 (2002–2003); William Garth Snider, "Banishment: The History of Its Use and a Proposal for Its Abolition under the First Amendment," 24 *Northeast Journal on Criminal and Civil Confinement* 455 (summer 1998).

25. Ibid.

26. Of course, migrants without papers are often banished; this process is referred to as deportation.

27. Armstrong, "Banishment: Cruel and Unusual Punishment."

28. The more complete legal definition is as follows: banishment is the "expulsion, or deportation by the political authority on the ground of expediency; punishment by forced exile, either for years or for life; a punishment inflicted on criminals, by compelling them to quit a city, place or country, for a specified period of time, or for life." 8 C.J.S. *Banishment* § 593 (1930). See also Black, *Law Dictionary* 183 (4th ed., 1951).

29. Snider, "Banishment: The History of Its Use."

30. Ibid.

31. The legal definition of *banishment* similarly underscores the role of political authorities in effecting banishment orders (see note 28). Similarly, the *American Heritage Dictionary*'s first definition of *banishment* is this: "To force to leave a country or place by *official decree*" (emphasis added).

32. Elsewhere, we argue that these conclusions are largely consistent with Stanley Cohen's dystopian account of the net-widening impact of efforts to reform criminal justice practices and institutions. See Katherine Beckett and Steve Herbert, "The Punitive City Revisited: The Transformation of Urban Social Control," pp. 106–122 in *After the War on Crime: Race, Democracy, and a New Reconstruction*, edited by Mary Louise Frampton, Ian Haney Lopez, and Jonathan Simon (New York: New York University Press, 2008); Cohen, *Visions of Social Control*.

33. Howard S. Becker, *Outsiders: Studies in the Sociology of Deviance* (New York: Free Press, 1963).

34. Zygmunt Bauman, "Social Issues of Law and Order," *British Journal of Criminology* 40 (2000): 205–221, 208.

35. Alan Hunt, *Governing Morals: A Social History of Moral Regulation* (Cambridge: Cambridge University Press, 1999). See also Jeffrey S. Adler, "A Historical Analysis of the Law of Vagrancy," *Criminology* 27, no. 2 (1989): 209–229; Novak, *The People's Welfare*.

36. A. L. Beier, *Masterless Men: The Vagrancy Problem in England 1560–1640* (New York: Methuen, 1985); Leonard C. Feldman, *Citizens without Shelter: Homelessness, Democracy and Political Exclusion* (Ithaca, N.Y.: Cornell University Press, 2004).

37. Ibid. See also William Chambliss, "A Sociological Analysis of the Law of Vagrancy," *Social Problems* 12, no. 1 (1964): 67–77.

38. Beier, *Masterless Men*, 12; Chambliss, "A Sociological Analysis."

39. Stewart, "Black Codes and Broken Windows." See also Christopher R. Adamson, "Punishment after Slavery," *Social Problems* 30, no. 5 (June 1983): 493–507.

40. Adamson, "Punishment after Slavery."

41. Novak, *The People's Welfare*, 150. See also Jeffrey S. Adler, "A Historical Analysis of the Law of Vagrancy," *Criminology* 27, no. 2 (1989): 209–229; V. A. Leonard, *Survey of the Seattle Police Department* (Seattle, Wash., 1945).

42. Greg Lange, "Police Arrest Vagrants," *Seattle Times*, January 4, 1901, 7.

43. Armstrong, "Banishment: Cruel and Unusual Punishment"; Caleb Foote, "Vagrancy-Type Law and Its Administration," *University of Pennsylvania Law Review* 104 (1956): 603.

44. Ascher and Wolf, " 'Red Light' Injunction and Abatement Acts"; McCurdy, "The Use of the Injunction."

45. Ahmed A. White, "A Different Kind of Labor Law: Vagrancy Law and the Regulation of Harvest Labor, 1913–1924," *University of Colorado Law Review* 75 (2004): 667.

46. Dorothy Roberts, "Race, Vagueness, and the Social Meaning of Order-Maintenance Policing," *Journal of Criminal Law and Criminology* 89 (1999): 775–836; Stewart, "Black Codes and Broken Windows"; Robin Yeamans, "Constitutional Attacks on Vagrancy Laws," *Stanford Law Review* 20 (1968): 782–793.

47. Quoted in Stewart, "Black Codes and Broken Windows," 2259.

48. Feldman argues that there is another difference as well. Whereas vagrancy laws were primarily concerned with idleness, the civility laws may reflect increased concern about those who fail to consume. Feldman, *Citizens without Shelter*.

49. Greg A. Greenberg and Robert A. Rosenheck, "Jail Incarceration, Homelessness, and Mental Health: A National Study," *Psychiatric Services* 59, no. 2 (February 2008): 170–177.

50. Fifty-five percent of the defendants in the Seattle Municipal Court system are identified as homeless. Thomas Carr, "Seattle Community Court," *Seattle City Attorney's Liaison Links*, spring 2006, www.cityofseattle.net/law/precinct_liaisons/newsletters/LiaisonLinkSpring06.pdf.

51. Maria Foscarinis, "Downward Spiral: Homelessness and Its Criminalization," *Yale Law and Policy Review* 14 (1996): 1–63; Bernard Harcourt, *The Illusion of Order: The False Promise of Broken Windows Policing* (Cambridge, Mass.: Harvard University Press, 2001); Don Mitchell, *The Right to the City: Social Justice and the Fight for Public Space* (New York: Guilford, 2003); National Coalition on Homelessness, *A Dream Denied: The Criminalization of Homelessness in U.S. Cities* (January 2006).

52. No-contact orders are also increasingly deployed in Seattle. According to Seattle Municipal Court data, the average monthly number of cases involving violation of a no-contact order rose from forty-seven in 1999 to sixty-eight in the first half of 2006. Bob Scales, crime policy analyst, Seattle Mayor's Office.

53. The new tools are also far more widely used than traditional civility laws in Seattle. In 2005, for example, an average of 167 trespass cases were filed in Seattle Municipal Court per month. By contrast, there were an average of eleven failure-to-sign-infraction cases, ten pedestrian interference cases, and two disorderly conduct cases filed per month. Bob Scales, crime policy analyst, Seattle Mayor's Office.

54. We do not wish to diminish the problems associated with the civility codes. In particular, because they criminalize many behaviors common to those who spend much time outdoors, the civility codes fall heavily on those who lack regular shelter. These ordinances also provide the police with an important set of order maintenance tools; they enable officers to make stops and conduct searches that they otherwise would not have legal authority to make. See Foscarinis, "Downward Spiral"; Harcourt, *The Illusion of Order*; Mitchell, *The Right to the City*; National Coalition on Homelessness, *A Dream Denied*. Still, it appears to us that the new legal tools have even broader utility and applicability and may prove more resistant to legal challenge.

55. Feldman, *Citizens without Shelter*.

56. See Steve Herbert, *Policing Space: Territoriality and the Los Angeles Police Department* (Minneapolis: University of Minnesota Press, 1997).

57. Feldman, *Citizens without Shelter*.

58. We review more theoretical matters in Katherine Beckett and Steve Herbert, "Dealing with Disorder: Social Control in the Post-Industrial City," *Theoretical Criminology* 12 (2008): 5–30.

59. See Elijah Anderson, *Streetwise: Race, Class and Change in an Urban Community.* (Chicago: University of Chicago Press, 1990); Lyn Lofland, *A World of Strangers: Order and Action in Urban Public Space* (New York: Basic Books, 1973); Sally Engle Merry, *Urban Danger: Life in a Neighborhood of Strangers* (Philadelphia: Temple University Press, 1981).

60. Feldman, *Citizens without Shelter*.

61. See, for example, Anis Bawarshi et al., "Media Analysis of Homeless Encampment Sweeps," 2008, faculty.washington.edu/stygall/ homelessmediacoveragegroup.

62. Psychologists Lasana T. Harris and Susan T. Fiske found that the homeless and addicted are most likely to be seen as low in competence and to elicit low levels of warmth. As a result, exposure to images of apparently homeless or addicted individuals elicited a neurological pattern consistent with disgust and to therefore be subject to extreme dehumanization. See Lasana T. Harris and Susan T. Fiske, "Dehumanizing the Lowest of the Low: Neuroimaging Responses to Extreme Out-Groups," *Psychological Science* 17, 10 (2006): 847–854.

63. Andreas coined this phrase to describe U.S. efforts to restrict immigration by enhancing border enforcement and interdiction efforts. See Peter Andreas, *Border Games: Policing the U.S.-Mexico Divide* (Ithaca, N.Y.: Cornell University Press, 2001).

CHAPTER 1

1. On Pioneer Square, see Mildred Andrews, *Pioneer Square: Seattle's Oldest Neighborhood* (Seattle: University of Washington Press, 2005); Murray Morgan, *Skid Road: An Informal Portrait of Seattle* (Seattle: University of Washington Press, 1982). For a history of single resident occupancy hotels, see Paul Groth, *Living Downtown: The History of Residential Hotels in the United States* (Berkeley: University of California Press, 1994).

2. See Andrews, *Pioneer Square*.

3. See especially James Spradley, *You Owe Yourself a Drunk: An Ethnography of Urban Nomads* (Boston: Little Brown, 1970). See also Morgan, *Skid Road*. Occasionally, persons charged with vagrancy were given the option of leaving town in lieu of jail time, but this appears to have been a sporadic rather than systematic practice.

4. Western Regional Advocacy Project, *Without Housing: Decades of Federal Housing Cutbacks, Massive Homelessness and Policy Failures* (San Francisco: Western Regional Advocacy Project, 2006), wraphome.org/wh/index.php.

5. See Martha Burt, "Causes of the Growth of Homelessness During the 1980's," *Housing Policy Debate* 2 (1991): 3.

6. B. D. Levy and J. J. O'Connell, "Health Care for Homeless Persons," *New England Journal of Medicine* 350 (2004): 2329–2332.

7. B. G. Link, E. Susser A. Stueve, et al., "Lifetime and Five-Year Prevalence of homelessness in the United States," *American Journal of Public Health* 84 (1994): 1907–1912.

8. S. L. Isaacs and J. R. Knickman, eds., *To Improve Health and Health Care*, vol. 7 (San Francisco: Jossey-Bass, 2004), 199.

9. K. Hopper and N. G. Milburn, "Homelessness among African Americans: A Historical and Contemporary Perspective," pp. 123–131 in *Homeless in America*, edited by J. Baumohl (Phoenix: Oryx, 1996).

10. Seattle/King County Coalition on Homelessness, *2008 One Night Count of People Who are Homeless in King County, Washington*, 2008, www.homelessinfo. org/2008ONC.pdf.

11. C. N. Dolbeare, I. B. Saraf, and S. Crowley, *Changing Priorities: The Federal Budget and Housing Assistance, 1976–2005* (Washington, D.C.: National Low Income Housing Coalition, 2004), www.nlihc.org/doc/cp04.pdf.

12. There are a wide range of analyses of this economic shift and its relationship to poverty and affordable housing availability. See, among others,: Gregg Barak, *Gimme Shelter: A Social History of Homelessness in Contemporary America* (Westport, Conn.: Praeger, 1992); David Harvey, *The Condition of Postmodernity: An Enquiry into the Origins of Cultural Change* (Oxford: Blackwell, 1991); and Jennifer Wolch and Michael Dear, *Landscapes of Despair: From Deinstitutionalization to Homelessness* (Princeton, N.J.: Princeton University Press, 1987).

13. Wolch and Dear, *Landscapes of Despair*.

14. The federal minimum wage remained at $3.35 an hour between 1980 and 1990. Consequently, the real value of the minimum wage fell by about 30 percent over the decade. See Martina Morris and Bruce Western, "Inequality at the Close of the Twentieth Century," *Annual Review of Sociology* 25 (1999): 623–652. See also Martha Burt, *Over the Edge: The Growth of Homelessness in the 1980s* (New York: Russell Sage Foundation, 1992).

15. Bennett Harrison, *The Great U-Turn: Corporate Restructuring and the Polarizing of America* (New York: Basic Books, 1988). See also Martin Carnoy, *The New Global Economy in the Information Age: Reflections on Our Changing World* (University Park: Pennsylvania State University Press, 1993); Morris and Western, "Inequality at the Close of the Twentieth Century"; and Kathryn M. Neckerman and Florencia Torche, "Inequality: Causes and Consequences," *Annual Review of Sociology* 33 (2007): 335–357.

16. Mary Gregory, Wiemer Salverda, and Stephen Brazen, *Labour Market Inequalities: Problems and Policies of Low-Wage Employment in International Perspective* (Oxford: Oxford University Press, 2000).

17. Wolch and Dear, *Landscapes of Despair*, 33.

18. Burt, *Over the Edge*.

19. Phuong Cat Le and D. Parvaz, "Census 2000: Seattle's Rich Areas Get Richer," *Seattle Post-Intelligencer*, September 17, 2002.

20. For a wonderful introduction to gentrification, see Loretta Lees, Tom Slater, and Elvin Wyly, *Gentrification* (New York: Routledge, 2008). See also Jason Hackworth, *The Neoliberal City: Governance, Ideology, and Development in American Urbanism* (Ithaca, N.Y.: Cornell University Press, 2007); Neil Smith, *The New Urban Frontier: Gentrification and the Revanchist City* (New York: Routledge, 1996); and Elvin Wyly and Daniel Hammel, "Islands of Decay in Seas of Renewal: Urban Policy and the Resurgence of Gentrification," *Housing Policy Debate* 10 (1999): 711–771.

21. Jennifer Wolch and Michael Dear, *Malign Neglect: Homelessness in an American City* (San Francisco: Jossey-Bass, 1993).

22. Joint Center for Housing Studies of Harvard University, *The State of the Nation's Housing 2003* (Cambridge, Mass.: Harvard University Press, 2004).

23. James Wright and Julie Lam, "Homelessness and the Low-Income Housing Supply," *Social Policy* 17 (1999): 48–53.

24. Coll Thrush, *Native Seattle: Histories from the Crossing-Over Place* (Seattle: University of Washington Press, 2007).

25. See Timothy Gibson, *Securing the Spectacular City: The Politics of Revitalization and Homelessness in Downtown Seattle* (Lanham, Md.: Lexington Books, 2004); Hackworth, *The Neoliberal City*. For an analysis of gentrification in Seattle, see Chandler Felt, "Seattle's Rich Areas Get Richer; Gentrification Widens 'Neighborhood Gap,' Census Shows," *Seattle Times* September 17, 2002, A1.

26. Seattle Displacement Coalition, *The Continuing Loss of Affordable Housing in Downtown Seattle*, www.zipcon.net/~jvf4119/downtownhousing.htm.

27. City of Seattle, Department of Design, Construction and Land Use, *Monitoring Our Progress: Seattle's Comprehensive Plan* (March 2003), 32.

28. See Gary Blasi, "Policing Our Way out of Homelessness? The First Year of the Safer Cities Initiative on Skid Row" (2007), www.sfgov.org/site/uploadedfiles/mocj/CommInvlv_News/blasi_study.pdf

29. Seattle/King County Coalition on Homelessness, *2007 One Night Count of People Who Are Homeless in King County, WA*, www.homelessinfo.org/ONCreportv2.pdf.

30. For overviews of neoliberalism and its effects, see Neil Brenner and Nik Theodore, *Spaces of Neoliberalism* (Oxford: Blackwell, 2002); David Harvey, *A Brief History of Neoliberalism* (New York: Oxford University Press, 2005); Steve Herbert, "The Trapdoor of Community," *Annals of the Association of American Geographers* 95, no. 4 (2005): 850–865; Wendy Larner, "Neo-Liberalism: Policy, Ideology, Governmentality," *Studies in Political Economy* 63 (2000): 5–25; and Jamie Peck and Adam Tickell, "Neoliberalizing Space," *Antipode* 34 (2002): 380–404.

31. Wolch and Dear, *Malign Neglect*.

32. Western Regional Advocacy Project, *Without Housing*.

33. U.S. government support for low-income housing trails far behind its counterparts in Europe. In England and France, for instance, publicly owned or financed housing accounts for more than 40 percent of the housing market. In the United States, it accounts for 1 percent. See Loic Wacquant, *Urban Outcasts: A Comparative Sociology of Advanced Marginality* (Cambridge: Polity Press, 2008).

34. John Gilderbloom and Richard Applebaum, *Rethinking Rental Housing* (Philadelphia: Temple University Press, 1988); National Low Income Housing Coalition, *The Crisis in America's Housing: Confronting Myths and Promoting a Balanced Housing Policy* (Washington, D.C.: National Low Income Housing Coalition, 2005), www.nlihc.org/doc/housingmyths.pdf.

35. Western Regional Advocacy Project, *Without Housing*.

36. See Maria Foscarinis, "The Federal Response: The Stewart McKinney Homeless Assistance Act," pp. 160–171 in *Homelessness in America*, edited by J. Baumohl (Phoenix: Oryx Press, 1996); Wesley Gabbard, Bryan Ford, and James May, "The Stewart B. McKinney Homeless Assistance Act: A Historical Overview," *Journal of Social Distress and the Homeless* 15 (2006): 99–116.

37. Western Regional Advocacy Project, *Without Housing*.

38. Dolbeare, Saraf, and Crowley, *Changing Priorities*.

39. Congress of the United States, *Meeting Our Nation's Housing Challenges*, Report of the Bipartisan Millennial Housing Commission (Washington, D.C.: U.S. Government Printing Office, 2002).

40. Burt, *Over the Edge*.

41. Gibson, *Securing the Spectacular City*.

42. Port of Seattle, Seaport Statistics: Cruise Passengers, www.portseattle.org/seaport/statistics/cruisepassengers.shtml. See also Kery Murakami, "Seattle Tourist Boom! Record Numbers of Visitors Pouring In," *Seattle Post-Intelligencer*, July 25, 2006.

43. See Susan Christopherson, "The Fortress City: Privatized Spaces, Consumer Citizenship," pp. 409–427 in *Post-Fordism: A Reader*, edited by Ash Amin (London: Blackwell, 1994); Don Mitchell, "The Annihilation of Space by Law: The Roots and Implications of Anti-Homeless Laws," *Antipode* 29 (1997): 303–335; Smith, *The New Urban Frontier*.

44. Burt, *Over the Edge*.

45. Ibid.

46. Dear and Wolch, *Landscapes of Despair*.

47. H. Richard Lamb, "The Deinstitutionalization of the Mentally Ill," *Hospital and Community Psychiatry* 35 (1984): 899–907; H. Richard Lamb and Linda Weinberger, "Persons with Severe Mental Illness in Jails and Prisons: A Review," *Psychiatric Services* 49 (1998): 483–492.

48. Andrew T. Scull, *Decarceration: Community Treatment and the Deviant* (Englewood, N.J.: Prentice Hall, 1977).

49. Ibid.; Wolch and Dear, *Malign Neglect*.

50. Burt, *Over the Edge*, 120.

51. Bruce Western, *Punishment and Inequality* (New York: Russell Sage, 2006).

52. Nearly all of the increase in incarceration rates is a consequence of policy shifts rather than an increase in crime rates. Katherine Beckett, *Making Crime Pay: Law and Order in Contemporary American Politics* (New York: Oxford University Press, 1997); Western, *Punishment and Inequality*.

53. On the causes and consequences of the politicization of crime, see James Austin and John Irwin, *It's about Time: America's Imprisonment Binge* (Belmont, Calif.: Wadsworth, 2000); Beckett, *Making Crime Pay*; David Garland, *The Culture of Control* (Chicago: University of Chicago Press, 2001); Jonathan Simon, *Governing through Crime: How the War on Crime Transformed American Democracy and Created a Culture of Fear* (New York: Oxford University Press, 2007); Michael Tonry, *Thinking about Crime: Sense and Sensibility in American Penal Culture* (Oxford: Oxford University Press, 2004); Loic Wacquant, "The New 'Peculiar Institution': On the Prison as Surrogate Ghetto," *Theoretical Criminology* 4, no. 3 (2000): 377–389; and Western, *Punishment and Inequality*.

54. Katherine Beckett and Theodore Sasson, *The Politics of Injustice*, 2nd ed. (Beverly Hills, Calif.: Sage, 2004).

55. In the two decades following 1980, the national black drug arrest rate increased from roughly 650 to 2,907 per 100,000 population, whereas the national white drug arrest rate increased from approximately 350 to 463 per 100,000 persons (Beckett and Sasson, *The Politics of Injustice*). Latinos are now as likely as blacks to be incarcerated in state prison for drug offenses. For a discussion of the impact of the war on drugs on racial disparities in incarceration, see Alfred Blumstein, "Racial Disproportionality of US Prison Populations Revisited," *University of Colorado Law*

Review 64 (1993): 751–773; Troy Duster, "Pattern, Purpose and Race in the Drug War," pp. 260–287 in *Crack in America: Demon Drugs and Social Justice*, edited by Craig Reinarman and Harry G. Levine (Berkeley: University of California Press, 1997); and Michael Tonry, *Malign Neglect: Race, Crime, and Punishment in America* (New York: Oxford University Press).

56. Marc Mauer and Ryan S. King, *A 25-Year Quagmire: The "War on Drugs" and its Impact on American Society* (Washington, D.C.: Sentencing Project, 2007).

57. Ryan S. King and Marc Mauer, *Distorted Priorities: Drug Offenders in State Prisons* (Washington, D.C.: Sentencing Project, 2002).

58. James Q. Wilson and George F. Kelling, "The Police and Neighborhood Safety," *Atlantic Monthly*, May 1982, 28–38.

59. The popularity of the broken windows theory lies in sharp contrast to the empirical evidence to support it. Several studies of the relationship between disorder today and crime tomorrow suggest only a weak connection, if any. See Bernard Harcourt, *The Illusion of Order: The False Promise of Broken Windows Policing* (Cambridge, Mass.: Harvard University Press, 2001); Robert Sampson and Stephen Raudenbush, "Systematic Social Observation of Public Spaces: A New Look at Disorder in Urban Neighborhoods," *American Journal of Sociology* 105 (1999): 603–665; and Ralph Taylor, *Breaking away from Broken Windows* (Boulder, Colo.: Westview Press, 2000).

60. Wilson and Kelling, "Broken Windows," 32.

61. William Chambliss, "A Sociological Analysis of the Law of Vagrancy," *Social Problems* 12, no. 1 (1964): 67–77; Markus Dirk Dubber, *The Police Power: Patriarchy and the Foundations of American Government* (New York: Columbia University Press, 2005); and Gary Stewart, "Black Codes and Broken Windows: The Legacy of Racial Hegemony in Anti-Gang Civil Injunctions," *Yale Law Journal* 107, no. 7 (1998): 2249–2280.

62. William J. Novak, *The People's Welfare: Law and Regulation in Nineteenth Century America* (Chapel Hill: University of North Carolina Press, 1996).

63. Benjamin Bowling, "The Rise and Fall of New York Murder: Zero Tolerance or Crack's Decline?" *British Journal of Criminology* 39, no. 4 (1999): 531–554; Richard Curtis, "The Improbable Transformation of Inner-City Neighborhoods: Crime, Violence and Youth in the 1990s," *Journal of Criminal Law and Criminology* 88, no. 4 (1997): 1233–1277; John E. Eck and Edward R. Maguire, "Have Changes in Policing Reduced Violent Crime? An Assessment of the Evidence," chapter 7 in *The Crime Drop in America*, edited by Alfred Blumstein and Joel Wallman (Cambridge: Cambridge University Press, 2000); Judith Greene, "Zero Tolerance: A Case Study of Police Policies and Practices in New York City," *Crime and Delinquency* 45 (1999): 171–182; Harcourt, *The Illusion of Order*; Bernard E. Harcourt and Jens Ludwig, "Broken Windows: New Evidence from New York City and a Five-City Social Experiment," *University of Chicago Law Review* 73 (2006): 271; Bruce D. Johnson, Andrew Golub, and Eloise Dunlap, "The Rise and Decline of Hard Drugs, Drug Markets, and Violence in Inner City New York," chapter 6 in *The Crime Drop in America*, edited by Alfred Blumstein and Joel Wallman (Cambridge: Cambridge University Press, 2000); and Andrew Karman, *New York Murder Mystery: The True*

Story of the Crime Crash in New York City (New York: New York University Press, 2000).

64. Peter Manning, "Theorizing Policing: The Drama and Myth of Crime Control in the NYPD," *Theoretical Criminology* 5 (2001): 315–344. On the export of zero tolerance, see Katharyne Mitchell and Katherine Beckett, "Securing the Global City: Crime, Consulting, Risk and Ratings in the Production of Urban Space," *Global Legal Studies* 15, no.1 (2008): 75–99; Cathy Schneider and Paul E. Amar, "The Rise of Crime, Disorder and Authoritarian Policing: An Introductory Essay," *NACLA Report on the Americas* 37, no. 2 (2003): 12–15; Neil Smith, "Global Social Cleansing: Postliberal Revanchism and the Export of Zero Tolerance," *Social Justice* 28, no. 3 (2001): 68–75. Loic Wacquant, "Toward a Dictatorship over the Poor? Notes on the Penalization of Poverty in Brazil," *Punishment and Society* 5, no. 2 (2003): 197–205.

65. Elsewhere, we argue that the political-economic perspective provides a compelling account of the attractions of intensified urban social control efforts to urban developers and officials. We also argue, however, that recognition of the law's constitutive power is crucial for comprehending the particular form the new techniques have taken. By emphasizing law's unintended and contradictory effects, the constitutive perspective enables us to appreciate how the Supreme Court's invalidation of the traditional vagrancy and loitering laws fueled and shaped the quest for legal alternatives to them. See Katherine Beckett and Steve Herbert, "Dealing with Disorder: Social Control in the Post-Industrial City," *Theoretical Criminology* 12, no. 8 (2008): 5–30.

66. Western Regional Advocacy Project, *Without Housing*.

CHAPTER 2

1. This petition, and the correspondence from which these quotations were taken, are located in the Seattle city archives' records of vagrancy law in Seattle. Copies are also on file with the authors.

2. George L. Kelling and Catherine M. Coles, *Fixing Broken Windows: Restoring Order and Reducing Crime in Our Communities* (New York: Free Press, 1996), 69; see also Robert C. Ellickson, "Controlling Chronic Misconduct in City Spaces: Of Panhandlers, Skid Rows, and Public-Space Zoning," *Yale Law Journal* 105, no. 5 (1996): 1165–1214.

3. Seattle Police Department memo, dated December 1, 1988, available in the Seattle city archives; a copy is also on file with the authors.

4. Seattle Police Department memo, dated April 30, 1991, available in the Seattle city archives; a copy is also on file with the authors.

5. Timothy Gibson, *Securing the Spectacular City: The Politics of Revitalization and Homelessness in Downtown Seattle* (Lanham, Md.: Lexington Books, 2004); Leonard Feldman, *Citizens without Shelter: Homelessness, Democracy and Political Exclusion* (Ithaca, N.Y.: Cornell University Press, 2004).

6. Kelling and Coles, *Fixing Broken Windows*, 51.

7. As Feldman points out, this is a misnomer; using the civility law to create security for some citizens renders the lives of others less civil and secure. Feldman, *Citizens without Shelter*, 54.

8. Maria Foscarinis, "Downward Spiral: Homelessness and its Criminalization," *Yale Law & Policy Review* 14 (1996): 1–69; Bernard Harcourt, *The Illusion of Order: The False Promise of Broken Windows Policing* (Cambridge, Mass.: Harvard University Press, 2001); Don Mitchell, *The Right to the City: Social Justice and the Fight for Public Space* (New York: Guilford, 2003); National Coalition for the Homeless, *A Dream Denied: The Criminalization of Homelessness in U.S. Cities* (January 2006).

9. New York State Penal Code § 240.35. See also Fernanda Santos, "From Jail, a Panhandler Fights New York's Loitering Law as a Violation of Free Speech," *New York Times*, May 30, 2007.

10. National Coalition for the Homeless, *A Dream Denied*, 40.

11. Kelling and Coles, *Fixing Broken Windows*.

12. Ibid.

13. Steve Brandt, "Lurking Law under Scrutiny," *Minneapolis Star Tribune*, May 21, 2008.

14. The city of Chicago's efforts to adopt an ordinance prohibiting loitering by perceived gang members have been particularly controversial. See Albert Alschuler and Steven J. Schulhofer, "Antiquated Procedures or Bedrock Rights?: A Response to Professors Meares and Kahan," *University of Chicago Legal Forum* (1998): 215; Tracey L. Meares and Dan M. Kahan, "The Wages of Antiquated Procedural Thinking: A Critique of *Chicago v. Morales*," *University of Chicago Legal Forum* (1998): 197; and Dorothy Roberts, "Race, Vagueness, and the Social Meaning of Order-Maintenance Policing," *Journal of Criminal Law and Criminology* 89 (1999): 775–836. Although some of loitering-with-intent laws, including the Chicago ordinance, have been rejected by the courts, many others have been upheld (Kelling and Coles, *Fixing Broken Windows*, 58–60).

15. Kelling and Coles, *Fixing Broken Windows*, 58–60; Diana R. Gordon, *The Return of the Dangerous Classes: Drug Prohibition and Policy Politics* (New York: Norton, 1994), chapter 7.

16. Seattle Police Department Intra-Department Communication from Chief F. C. Ramon to Mayor J. D. Braman, dated September 13, 1968. Available at the Seattle municipal archives and on file with the authors.

17. In particular, the release of the film *Streetwise* in 1984 featuring the lives of Seattle's 600–800 street children—many of whom survived by engaging in prostitution—galvanized concern about adults who procured the sexual services of children.

18. 113 Wn.2d 850 1989.

19. Ibid., 855.

20. Ibid., 857.

21. Ibid., 858.

22. Letter regarding the proposed drug loitering ordinance dated April 26, 1990, from City Attorney Mark Sidran to Norman B. Rice, mayor, and Jane Noland, chair of the Seattle City Council's Public Safety and Environment Committee.

23. Gordon, *The Return of the Dangerous Classes*, chapter 7; William Lyons, *The Politics of Community Policing: Rearranging the Power to Punish* (Ann Arbor: University of Michigan Press, 1999).

24. In his analysis of the politics of the local crime issue, Lyons argues that despite the activism of many south-end residents and organizations, only the South Precinct Crime Prevention Council was able to garner the attention of city authorities. Residents and organizations that emphasized other issues or non–police-oriented solutions to public safety problems were, Lyons argues, largely ignored by city officials. Lyons, *The Politics of Community Policing*.

25. The ordinance also specified the circumstances an officer may legally consider as manifestations of the intent to engage in illegal drug activity. These include being seen in possession of drug paraphernalia (other than clean needles obtained from a needle exchange facility); being considered to be a known drug trafficker; repeatedly beckoning to, stopping, or attempting to stop passersby; repeatedly stopping or attempting to stop motor vehicles; circling an area in a motor vehicle and repeatedly beckoning to, contacting, or attempting to stop pedestrians; being the subject of a SODA order; or having been evicted as a result of illegal drug activity. However, according to the law, none of these circumstances constitute drug traffic loitering or intent in and of themselves. It is not clear exactly how many of these conditions must prevail for intent to be established. The racially disparate impact of the law garnered center stage when, in 1992, the American Civil Liberties Union released a report analyzing drug traffic loitering arrest data. The report indicated that nearly three-fourths of those arrested for drug traffic loitering were people of color, despite the fact that roughly 70 percent of the Seattle population is white. The implication of the analysis was clear: the law was being used to harass people of color, most of whom, subsequent events suggested, had not violated the law. Opponents launched an initiative to repeal the drug traffic loitering ordinance. Ultimately, the proposal to repeal was narrowly defeated in a vote of 5 to 4 in 1992.

26. Confidential City Attorney's Office memo regarding the Drug Loitering Ordinance dated May 1, 1990; emphasis added. Available in the Seattle city archive and on file with the authors.

27. As one journalist wrote, "Calling anti-trespass laws 'a rather inartful way of dealing with the drug problem', Sidran said the new proposal is an attempt to move way from what we're doing now, which is bending existing ordinances…in a way I think all of us would prefer not to do" (Kerry Godes, "Drug-Loitering Law to get Public Hearing," *Seattle Post-Intelligencer*, May 23, 1990: B1; see also Briefing paper on Drug Traffic Loitering Ordinance, Mark H. Sidran, Seattle City Attorney, February 3, 1992, available at the Seattle municipal archive and on file with the authors).

28. Gordon, *The Return of the Dangerous Classes*, chapter 7.

29. Ibid.; Lyons, *The Politics of Community Policing*.

30. Robert T. Nelson, "Council Passes Drug-Loitering Law Amid Boos," *Seattle Times*, June 26, 1990, B3.

31. Nelson, "Council Passes Drug-Loitering Law Amid Boos." Several council members made their support of the legislation contingent on the addition of a requirement that the police monitor the law's enforcement and keep statistics about those arrested and that the law be subject to sunset review in two years.

32. Theoretically, SODA orders could have been imposed on other misdemeanor drug offenders, namely, those charged with possession of small amounts of marijuana or paraphernalia only. A comparatively small number of such cases were filed, however. Thus the adoption of the drug traffic loitering ordinance enabled the more widespread use of SODAs in the municipal courts.

33. Lisa Schellinger, "Drug War Now Has Borders," *Seattle Post-Intelligencer*, December 12, 1990.

34. Peter M. Flanagan, "Trespass-Zoning: Ensuring Neighborhoods a Safer Future by Excluding Those with a Criminal Past," *Notre Dame Law Review* 79 (2003): 327; Gordon Hill, "The Use of Pre-Existing Exclusionary Zones as Probationary Conditions for Prostitution Offenses: A Call for the Sincere Application of Heightened Scrutiny," *Seattle University Law Review* 28 (2005): 173; and Lisa Sanchez, "Enclosure Acts and Exclusionary Practices: Neighborhood Associations, Community Police, and the Expulsion of the Sexual Outlaw," chapter 6 in *Between Law and Culture: Relocating Legal Studies*, edited by David Theo Goldberg, Michael Musheno, and Lisa C. Bower (Minneapolis: University of Minnesota Press, 1997). In Anaheim, California (and other municipalities), city officials tried an alternative approach, banning anyone with a prior drug conviction from all city parks.

35. In Seattle, the standardization and expansion of these off-limits orders was facilitated by state legislative action. In 1989, Washington state authorized municipalities to designate areas with high levels of drug activity as PADT (Protected Against Drug Trafficking) areas and to limit some people's right to be in these zones. Under this law, judges may issue these off-limits orders to "known drug traffickers" or tenants who were evicted for allowing drug trafficking to occur on their premises. RCW 10.66 defines "known drug traffickers" as a person who has been convicted of any drug offense in any state and is subsequently arrested for a drug offense involving the manufacture, distribution, or possession with intent to distribute a controlled substance.

36. In Portland, Oregon, orders to remain outside "drug-free zones" and "prostitution-free zones" may be imposed by police officers at the time of arrest. These orders remain in effect even if the banished person is not convicted of a drug offense. Violation of these orders is a criminal offense (trespass). A similar law was in effect in Cincinnati, Ohio, from 1996 to 2000, but was overturned in the Sixth Circuit; these spatial restrictions are now imposed on those convicted as a condition of probation in Cincinnati. Associated Press, "High Court Refuses to Review Cincinnati's Anti-Trespass Law," April 29, 2002. In Portland, exclusion orders stay on a person's record even in the absence of conviction. Abby Sewell, "How Well Do Drug-Free' Zones Really Work?" *Portland Alliance*, November 2005.

37. Barbara Boland and Kerry Murphy Healey, *Prosecutorial Responses to Heavy Caseloads* (Washington, D.C.: National Institute of Justice, 1993).

38. Flanagan, "Trespass-Zoning."

39. Hill, "The Use of Pre-Existing Exclusionary Zones," 173.

40. See also Sandra Moser, "Anti-Prostitution Zones: Justifications for Abolition," *Journal of Criminal Law & Criminology* 91 (summer 2001): 1101; Hill, "The Use of Pre-Existing Exclusionary Zones."

41. According to the probation officer who told us this, the SOAP order increases sex workers' "awareness of the potential consequences of continuing to engage in sex work." She also pointed out that a violation of the SOAP order could lead to the imposition of the full sentence for the original prostitution charge and increased the likelihood that sex workers would be rearrested. When asked if she thought this was a positive or a negative thing, she declined to answer. When asked if SOAP orders facilitated rehabilitation, she replied, "Hell, no."

42. Tim Cresswell, *In Place/Out of Place: Geography, Ideology and Transgression* (Minneapolis: University of Minnesota Press, 1996).

43. American Prosecutors Research Institute (APRI), "Unwelcome Guests: A Community Prosecution Approach to Street Level Drug Dealing and Prostitution," 2004, 1.

44. The formal title of the Seattle ordinance is the Parks Enhanced Code Enforcement Ordinance (SMC 18.12.278).

45. In the archival materials, we found records of fifty-four letters urging that the law be repealed entirely, seven urging its amendment, and forty-four arguing for its retention. However, a survey of 226 people registered to vote in Seattle found that nearly two-thirds of those surveyed favored retaining the ordinance. Moreover, many of the letters urging retention came from well-established business associations and community groups.

46. *Seattle Post-Intelligencer*, May 26, 1999, A10.

47. Seattle Police Department, "Summary of 6/16/98 SPD Parks Exclusion Special Report."

48. John Sheehan Gerard, "Seattle Parks Banishment Ordinance: Second Analysis and Report," ACLU, Seattle, 1998, available at www.aclu-wa.org/Publication/banishment_ordinance.html.

49. Personal communication, Larry Campbell, Director, Seattle City Parks Security, June 6, 2007.

50. Letter from Assistant Chief Harv Ferguson to Councilmember Nick Licata re: "Proposed Amendment to Parks Exclusion Ordinance," September 29, 1998, available at the Seattle city archive.

51. Letter to Seattle city council members from Lisa Daugaard, staff attorney. Defender Association, May 17, 1999. On file in the Seattle city archive.

52. For a partial list of other Washington state municipalities that have similar laws, see www.mrsc.org/Subjects/Parks/adminpg.aspx#Enforce. Parks exclusion ordinances also operate in several municipalities in Oregon, including Portland and Gresham. Although these laws have been subject to a number of successful challenges, modified versions of them remain on the books. In Portland, those alleged to have violated park rules may be excluded by police officers, parks officials, and private security officers. Those who return to the park in violation of an exclusion order may be arrested for trespass, a misdemeanor offense punishable by up to a year in jail. In 2004, two plaintiffs successfully challenged Portland's park exclusion ordinance in U.S. District Court (*Yeakle and Sheffer v. City of Portland*, Civil no. 02-1447 HA). In response to Judge Haggerty's determination that the law was overly broad and failed to provide adequate opportunities for appeal, the city tweaked the ordinance

such that any exclusion order is stayed pending appeal and those excluded may only be excluded from the particular park in which the alleged violation occurred. In response to the judge's determination that the thirty-day exclusion for any and all violations was insufficiently tailored, the ordinance now allows for 30-, 90-, and 180-day exclusions for first, second, and third violations, respectively. According to Ed Johnson, counsel for the plaintiffs in the *Yeakle* case, "good decisions" such as the ruling in the *Yeakle* case have had only a limited impact on the law itself.

53. It is arguable, however, that this is neither necessary nor sufficient to ensure the validity of a trespass arrest. See *State of Washington v. Blair* (827 P.2d 356).

54. Flanagan, "Trespass-Zoning"; Don Mitchell, "Property Rights, the First Amendment, and Judicial Anti-Urbanism: The Strange Case of *Hicks v. Virginia.*" *Urban Geography* 26, no. 7 (2005): 565–586.

55. Danielle Zielinski, "No Trespass: A Public Housing Solution and Problem," available at docket.medill.northwestrn.edu/archives/000131print.php.

56. Elena Goldstein, "Kept Out: Responding to Public Housing No-Trespass Policies," *Harvard Civil Rights-Civil Liberties Journal* 38 (2003); Mitchell, "Property Rights, the First Amendment, and Judicial Anti-Urbanism."

57. Manny Fernandez, "Barred from Public Housing, Even to See Family," *New York Times*, October 1, 2007, A1.

58. Jaime Adame, "Operation Safe Housing," *Gotham Gazette*, August 17, 2004; Fernandez, "Barred from Public Housing"; New York City, "Mayor Michael R. Bloomberg Announces Operation Safe Housing," June 24, 2004; Cara Tabachnick, "Jump in Trespassing Arrests Draws Anger," *Newsday*, April 10, 2007; Rocco Parascandola, "Trespass Arrests under Attack," *Newsday*, April 13, 2007.

59. See Zielinski, "No Trespass."

60. Goldstein, "Kept Out," 216.

61. Data illustrating this are presented in chapter 3.

62. In Hawaii, for example, the ACLU alleges that Act 50, which authorizes police officers to issue trespass admonishments from public places for nonspecified reasons, has been used in a discriminatory fashion. See ACLU of Hawaii Foundation, "Complaint for Declaratory and Injunctive Relief," available at www.acluhawaii.org/downloads/news/squatbrief.pdf.

63. David Birkland, "Loitering Law Is Resulting in 'Crack' Down," *Seattle Times*, September 18, 1987, E3.

64. The leader of the Seattle Neighborhood Group also claims a prominent role in creating the more robust trespass initiative in Seattle. In an interview, she cited her group's close work with the police to address issues at a Seattle Laundromat, where alleged drug sales were occurring in the parking lot with poor visibility. This made it nearly impossible for the police to witness sales, she said, so trespass became an alternate means to arrest those suspected of involvement in the drug trade.

65. Other authorities, including metro transit police, public housing authorities, and public library staff, also have the right to exclude alleged rule breakers.

66. This conjecture is based on the finding that the SPD issued over 3,000 such admonishments in four months of 2005.

67. Tamara Soukup, "Parking Lot Trespass Program," Seattle City Attorney's *Liaison Links*, spring 2005.

68. *The Center v. Lingle*, No. 04-537 KSC (D. Haw. 2004); see also National Coalition for the Homeless, *A Dream Denied*, 82.

69. In *City of Bremerton v. Widell* (2002), *Thompson v. Ashe* (2001), and *Daniel v. City of Tampa* (1994), the Washington State Supreme Court, Sixth Circuit Court of Appeals, and Eleventh Circuit Court of Appeals, respectively, upheld various trespass programs. However, the courts struck down such programs in a number of other cases, including *Vasquez v. Housing Authority of the City of El Paso* (2001, Fifth Circuit Court of Appeals), *Minnesota v. Holliday* (1998), and *Diggs v. Housing Authority of the City of Frederick* (1999). See Zielinski, "No Trespass." In Taylor, Texas, a resident recently sued the Taylor Housing Authority in the federal courts over its trespass policy. The policy she challenged did not specify the behaviors that could trigger exclusion, did not provide an opportunity to appeal an exclusion order, and did not place time constraints on any exclusions issued. See Austin's Tenants' Council, "Suit Results in Changes to Criminal Trespass Policy," *Housing Rights Advocate* 20 (fall 2001): 1–2.

70. In this case, the defendant was arrested for trespassing when delivering diapers to his daughter; he did not receive formal notification of his banishment until after his second such arrest (see Mitchell, "Property Rights, the First Amendment, and Judicial Anti-Urbanism"). Despite the Supreme Court's unanimous ruling, the use of trespass programs in public housing facilities remains controversial.

71. Center for Civic Innovation at the Manhattan Institute, *Broken Windows Probation: The Next Step in Fighting Crime* (1999), 5.

72. Ibid., 7.

73. Kent Reichert, *Police-Probation Partnerships: Boston's Operation Night Light*, 2, available at www.sas.upenn.edu/jerrylee/programs/fjc/paper_mar02.pdf.

74. Dale Parent and Brad Snyder, "Police-Corrections Partnerships," Issues and Practices in Criminal Justice series, National Institute of Justice, 1999.

75. As was discussed in the introduction, many cities have adopted other new social control tools that involve spatial exclusion and, like the innovations described here, are not based solely on criminal law. These include gang injunctions, based on the law of public nuisance, juvenile curfews, and no-contact orders. Civil gang injunctions mobilize the civil power of the injunction to address what is typically thought of as a crime problem. For example, prosecutors and other officials in many of these municipalities and counties have requested that judges use their injunctive power to prohibit alleged gang members from, among other things, being within a specified target area. In many cases, judges have complied with these requests and issued these civil injunctions. As in the case of trespass exclusions, violations of these civil orders are a criminal offense. Like civil trespass admonishments and parks exclusions, they proscribe otherwise legal behaviors (such as associating with others and being in public spaces). They also create "personal criminal codes" that attach to particular individuals as a result of that individual's alleged status as a gang member. Finally, gang injunctions offer very little in the way of due process protections. See Edward L. Allan, *Civil Gang Abatement: The Effectiveness and Implications of*

Policing by Injunction (New York: LFB Scholarly Pubications, 2004); Matthew Mickle Werdegar, "Enjoining the Constitution: The Use of Public Nuisance Abatement Injunctions against Urban Street Gangs," *Stanford Law Review* 51, no. 2 (January 1999): 409–448; Gary Stewart, "Black Codes and Broken Windows: The Legacy of Racial Hegemony in Anti-Gang Civil Injunctions," *Yale Law Journal* 107, no. 7 (May 1998): 2249–2280; Christopher S. Yoo, "The Constitutionality of Enjoining Street Gangs as Public Nuisances," *Northwest University Law Review* 89 (1994): 212. Analysts point out that no-contact orders share many of these same characteristics. See Jeannie Suk, "Criminal Law Comes Home," *Yale Law Journal* 116, no. 2 (2006): 2–70.

76. On police territoriality, see Steve Herbert, *Policing Space: Territoriality and the Los Angeles Police Department* (Minneapolis: University of Minnesota Press, 1997).

77. The claim that broken windows policing (also called "zero-tolerance policing" by some) was responsible for New York City's decline in crime has been well refuted by a number of authors. See, for example, Judith Greene, "Zero Tolerance: A Case Study of Police Policies and Practices in New York City," *Crime & Delinquency* 45 (1999): 171–182; Bernard Harcourt, *The Illusion of Order: The False Promise of Broken Windows Policing* (Cambridge, Mass.: Harvard University Press, 2001); Andrew Karman, *New York Murder Mystery: The True Story of the Crime Crash in New York City* (New York: New York University Press, 2006); and Franklin Zimring, *The Great American Crime Decline* (New York: Oxford University Press, 2007).

78. There is one important exception to that generalization: the philosophy that undergirds the many "therapeutic" courts that have emerged in many cities in recent years. These courts admit classes of defendants thought to be in need of particular social services, especially treatment. Although therapeutic courts recognize the need to address underlying causes, their capacity to do so is jeopardized by their inability to meaningfully address the structural conditions that fuel the problems they seek to address (such as massive declines in the availability of low-income housing). It is also limited by the fact that the spatial exclusions now routinely imposed on the disorderly continually generate new crimes and criminal cases that require adjudication and remediation[o]. We assess therapeutic courts in more depth in chapter 6.

79. Mitchell, *The Right to the City*. Many analysts have pointed out that the rights and obligations associated with citizenship are increasingly negotiated in "global cities." See Engin Fahri Isin, *Democracy, Citizenship, and the Global City: Rights, Democracy and Place* (New York: Routledge, 2000); and Saskia Sassen, *The Global City* (Princeton, N.J.: Princeton University Press, 2002).

80. Mary M. Cheh, "Constitutional Limits on Using Civil Remedies to Achieve Criminal Law Objectives," *Hastings Law Journal* 42 (1991): 1325–1348.

81. Katherine Beckett, *Making Crime Pay: Law and Order in Contemporary American Politics* (Oxford: Oxford University Press, 1997).

82. Gordon, *The Return of the Dangerous Classes*; Roberts, "Race, Vagueness, and the Social Meaning of Order-Maintenance Policing"; Sanchez 1997.

83. Meares and Kahan, "The Wages of Antiquated Procedural Thinking."

84. Roberts, "Race, Vagueness, and the Social Meaning of Order-Maintenance Policing".

85. Matthew D. Borrelli, "Banishment: The Constitutional and Public Policy Arguments against this Revived Ancient Punishment," *Suffolk University Law Review* 36 (2002–2003): 470.

86. Feldman, *Citizens without Shelter;* Foscarinis, "Downward Spiral"; Harcourt, *The Illusion of Order;* Mitchell, *The Right to the City;* National Coalition for the Homeless, *A Dream Denied.*

CHAPTER 3

1. In response to a public disclosure act request for these records, the SPD informed us, "Locating and providing access to [the requested] records is considerably more difficult [than providing the admonishment records] because of the SPD's computer system. Records are entered into the system by the name of the individual and by the incident number.... As the system is currently programmed, we cannot perform a word search of computer records to locate incidents according to the nature of the suspected or charged offense."

2. See www.realchangenews.org/about.html.

3. See www.realchangenews.org.

4. Seattle Parks Exclusion Notice 05-506847.

5. Seattle Parks Exclusion Notice 05-499671.

6. Seattle Parks Exclusion Notice 05-484944.

7. According the Seattle Municipal Court's summary of the Community Court's first nineteen months of operation, 42 percent of the cases involved charges of theft, 17 percent involved trespass charges, and 12 percent involved prostitution cases. "Seattle Community Court: Nineteen Months in Review," report prepared for the Downtown Seattle Association/Metropolitan Improvement District, December 12, 2006.

8. More generally, 55 percent of the defendants in the Seattle Municipal Court system are considered homeless. Thomas Carr, "Seattle Community Court," *Seattle City Attorney's Liaison Links,* spring 2006, www.cityofseattle.net/law/precinct_liaisons/newsletters/LiaisonLinkSpring06.pdf. Although not all trespass arrests result from admonishments, it is likely that the majority do.

9. Although these data show people of color are overrepresented among the excluded relative to the general population, it is not possible to determine whether persons of diverse racial backgrounds are more or less likely to be excluded/admonished for the same behaviors.

10. Katherine Beckett, *Race and Drug Law Enforcement in Seattle,* report prepared for the ACLU Drug Law Reform Project and the Defender Association, September 9, 2008.

11. King County Committee to End Homelessness, "A Roof over Every Bed in King County: Our Community's Ten Year Plan to End Homelessness," p. 1.

12. Evidence of the importance of criminal trespass also comes from the recent honoring of a Seattle police officer by the Rainier Chamber of Commerce. Among the officer's accomplishments was his issuance of seventy-five criminal trespass admonishments. See www.seattle.gov/police/precincts/South/Recognition.htm.

13. Paul Dorpat, "Seattle Neighborhoods: First Hill—Thumbnail History," HistoryLink.org, March 14, 2001, accessed January 4, 2006; Adam Hyla, "Yesler Terrace: Future in Question," *Real Change*, March 23–29, 2005, p. 4.

14. Although we did not conduct systematic interviews with hotel or other property owners, it is our sense that some willingly and happily shared their trespass authority with the police, whereas others were pressured to do so. Indeed, one community prosecutor reported being willing to call in the health inspectors and "use every tool at his disposal" to pressure property owners to sign a trespass authorization agreement.

15. A former SPD officer told us that the county public hospital discouraged officers from bringing mentally ill people there and encouraged them to use the Emergency Psychiatric Services (EPS) facility instead. However, because they are required to submit significant paperwork for each case they brought to the EPS, this option had been rendered less attractive to officers, who, according to this respondent, "are always going to be attracted to the no-paperwork option."

16. Seattle Municipal Courts, "Mental Health Court Results: A One Year Snapshot," www.seattle.gov/courts/comjust/mhresults.htm.

17. The column is available online at the *Real Change* Web site. In a few cases, the column did not appear in the weekly paper, or a particular edition of the paper was unavailable online. Our analysis includes all entries included in the online version of the newspaper and published between January 2000 and June 2005.

18. Panhandling is protected by the First Amendment except under certain circumstances, for example, in confined spaces with a captive audience.

CHAPTER 4

1. Julie Emery, "Drug-Infested Areas Off-Limits to Offenders," *Seattle Times*, September 16, 1991, B5; Barbara Boland and Karen Murphy-Healey, *Prosecutorial Response to Heavy Drug Caseloads: Comprehensive Problem-Reduction Strategies* (National Institute of Justice, DIANE Publishing, 1994).

2. Boland and Healey, *Prosecutorial Responses to Heavy Caseloads*.

3. See *Eligibility Requirements*, King County Drug Diversion Court Services, www.metrokc.gov/kcscc/drugcourt/eligible.doc 8/28/2008.

4. A supervisor of one of several nonprofit legal organizations defending indigent defendants in King County Superior Court told us that when lawyers in her office object to these requests, their objections are sustained by judges, and SODA orders are not imposed on defendants released pretrial. However, it is not clear whether defense lawyers from other organizations also object to these requests.

5. Thomas A. Carr, Seattle City Attorney, *2007 Annual Report*, 14–15, www. seattle.gov/law/docs/AnnualReport2007.pdf.

6. Ibid. See also Tamera Soukup, "Attempted Possession of Narcotics," Seattle City Attorney's *Liaison Links*, spring 2006.

7. There is some question about the new crime that the program created "attempted VUCSA." Several defense attorneys and one municipal judge described the charge as a "legal fiction" and dismissed its legitimacy.

8. Seattle Municipal Court filing data provided by Bob Scales, crime policy analyst, Seattle Mayor's Office.

9. At a public safety meeting held in January 2007, a community prosecutor for the West Precinct reported that the Seattle Municipal Court had between 380 and 500 people on SODA restrictions, most of whom reside in the downtown area. She also reported that the Seattle city attorney's office was working with King County prosecutors to encourage them to more consistently request SODA orders as a condition of pretrial release and that Juvenile Court would begin imposing SODA orders soon.

10. Violations of criminal no-contact orders issued by the municipal court also generate a significant and increasing number of criminal cases. Indeed, the average number of no-contact order violation cases filed monthly rose from 46.9 in 1999 to 67.7 in the first half of 2006. Seattle Municipal Court filing data provided by Bob Scales, crime policy analyst, Seattle Mayor's Office.

11. In part, the increased proportion of supervisees with geographic boundary conditions reflects the fact that the number of drug offenders on community supervision decreased as a result of the adoption of state law ESSB 5990. This law specified that offenders with only monetary obligations (Legal Financial Obligations) would no longer be kept under DOC supervision. Still, the absolute number of King County drug offenders with geographic boundary restrictions (i.e. SODA orders) more than doubled in this four year period, from 694 to 1557. Washington State DOC data provided by Keri-Anne Jetzer, Research Analyst, Washington State Department of Corrections, Budget Resource Management.

12. Keri-Anne Jetzer, Research Analyst, Washington State Department of Corrections, Budget Resource Management.

13. John Sheehan Gerard, *Seattle Parks Banishment Ordinance: Second Analysis & Report*, ACLU of Washington, August 1998.

14. Unfortunately, neither the ACLU nor the SPD reports on the implementation of the parks exclusion ordinance included this measure. We therefore cannot compare our estimate for 2005 with data from 1997–1998.

15. In 84 percent of these cases, trespass in the parks was the sole charge. Analysis of court records further indicates that the number of cases referred to the court by the SPD rose from 110 in 2000 to 270 in 2005. The number of referrals that involved only allegations that the arrestee trespassed in the parks also rose significantly in this period, from 93 to 228.

16. Specifically, data provided by staff at the mayor's office indicate that the number of cases involving trespass in the parks filed with the court rose from 114 in 1999 to 342 in 2005.

17. If we only count cases in which criminal trespass is the sole charge, the number of trespass case filings rose from 940 in 2000 to 1,142 in 2005.

18. Tamara Soukup, "Parking Lot Trespass Program," Seattle City Attorney's *Liaison Links*, spring 2005.

19. Seattle's downtown business community might be especially concerned about public safety issues because more than 50 percent of the money spent downtown comes from outside the area. See Todd Bishop and Christine Frey,

"Resurgent Downtown Still Faces Challenges," *Seattle Post-Intelligencer*, February 10, 2003. Timothy Gibson, in his historical account of downtown redevelopment in Seattle in the 1990s, does a masterful job of explicating the emphasis on public safety. He provocatively uses the phrase "projects of reassurance" to describe efforts to rid downtown of urban undesirables and thus keep shoppers and tourists feeling comfortable. Timothy Gibson, *Securing the Spectacular City: The Politics of Revitalization and Homelessness in Downtown Seattle* (Lexington, Ky.: Lexington Books, 2003).

20. See Robert Fogleson, *Big-City Police* (Cambridge, Mass.: Harvard University Press, 1977); Samuel Walker, *A Critical History of Police Reform* (Lexington, Ky.: Lexington Books, 1977).

21. Jennifer Sullivan, "Police to Increase Patrols Downtown," *Seattle Times*, August 17, 2007; Robert Marshall Wells, "Up Town—For One End of Downtown Seattle, 1998 Was a Glittering Triumph. For the Other End, the Hard Work Has Just Begun," *Seattle Times*, January 24, 1999; Dick Lily, "Mayor's Plan to Reduce Police Force Draws Fire—Downtown Group Opposes Plan," *Seattle Times*, May 11, 1991; Sharon Pian Chan, "Downtown Struggling with Safety Perceptions," *Seattle Times*, April 27, 2006; Polly Lane, "Downtown Merchants Want Action on Crime," *Seattle Times*, April 23, 1993; Michael Barber, "Battle Street Crime Harder, City Urged," *Seattle Times*, August 27, 1986.

22. Interview with Jim McKinnis, Washington State Department of Corrections.

23. From this official's perspective, the homeless and other symbols of disorder— some of which she described as "feral"—impair the reputation of downtown as a safe and comfortable place to spend time. As a result, she endorses efforts to find other locales to which individuals can be dispatched during the day.

24. Both a police captain and a police sergeant cited the group as particularly influential in placing pressure on the mayor's office to free up resources to enable increased police patrols on Aurora Avenue. These resources were used primarily to provide overtime pay to allow officers to work extra shifts.

25. The head of the Seattle Neighborhood Group, a city-wide anticrime organization, claimed significant credit in spearheading the criminal trespass program.

26. See, for example, Ellen O'Neill-Stephens, senior deputy prosecuting attorney, King County, letter to community members, "Stay Out of Drug Areas (SODA): Your Support Needed," posted April 8, 2008. Interestingly, the neighbors who posted responses were largely unreceptive to the idea. See millerparkseattle.blogspot. com/2008/04/stay-out-of-drug-area-soda-program-your.html.

27. On this dynamic more broadly, see Steve Herbert, *Citizens, Cops and Power: Recognizing the Limits to Community* (Chicago: University of Chicago Press, 2006).

28. For a more detailed examination of the territorial power of the police, see Steve Herbert, *Policing Space: Territoriality and the Los Angeles Police Department* (Minneapolis: University of Minnesota Press, 1997).

29. In the North Precinct station, out of which this officer works, a SOAP board includes pictures of several dozen women who possess SOAP orders. The board seeks to assist officers in spotting prohibited individuals as a prelude to an arrest.

30. For his part, an officer in the West Precinct NCI unit was ecstatic with this program. He clearly valued his ability to use SODA orders as levers when he encountered people on the street. He also kept a binder of laminated sheets of papers, each containing dozens of names of people and the restrictive orders placed on them.

31. Letter from Assistant Chief Harv Ferguson to Councilmember Nick Licata re: "Proposed Amendment to Parks Exclusion Ordinance," September 29, 1998. Available at the Seattle city archive.

32. Carr, 2007 *Annual Report*, p. 15. According to this report, 192 defendants had at least one SODA violation; 624 had none.

33. Carr, 2007 *Annual Report*, p. 15.

CHAPTER 5

1. See, for example, Ellen O'Neill-Stephens, Senior Deputy Prosecuting Attorney, King County, letter to community members, "Stay Out of Drug Areas (SODA): Your Support Needed," posted April 8, 2008. Interestingly, the neighbors who posted responses were largely unreceptive to the idea. See millerparkseattle. blogspot.com/2008/04/stay-out-of-drug-area-soda-program-your.html.

2. Letter from Assistant Chief Harv Ferguson to Councilmember Nick Licata re: "Proposed Amendment to Parks Exclusion Ordinance," September 29, 1998. On file in the Seattle city archive.

3. Letter to "concerned citizens" from Mark Sidran, Seattle city attorney, dated May 7, 1999. On file in the Seattle city archive.

4. Mitch Duneier, *Sidewalk* (New York: Farrar, Strauss and Giroux, 1999).

5. Leonard C. Feldman, *Citizens without Shelter: Homelessness, Democracy, and Political Exclusion* (Ithaca, N.Y.: Cornell University Press, 2004).

CHAPTER 6

1. Katherine Beckett, *Making Crime Pay* (New York: Oxford University Press, 1997); Jonathan Simon, *Governing through Crime: How the War on Crime Transformed American Democracy and Created a Culture of Fear* (New York: Oxford University Press, 2007); Bruce Western, *Punishment and Inequality* (New York: Russell Sage, 2006).

2. Ian Loader, "Policing, Recognition and Belonging," *Annals of the American Academy of the Political and Social Science* 205 (May 2006): 202–221, p. 203, emphasis in original.

3. See Leonard Feldman, *Citizens without Shelter: Homeless, Democracy and Political Inclusion* (Ithaca, N.Y.: Cornell University Press, 2006).

4. There is, of course, the possibility that attorneys could initiate proactive civil litigation to challenge the use of trespass admonishments; because we are aware of no concerted efforts to do this, we do not explore this possibility here.

5. The literature on these courts is now quite large. Useful introductions include Greg Berman, John Feinblatt, and Sarah Glazer, *Good Courts: The Case for Problem-Solving Justice* (New York: Free Press, 2005); Michael Dorf and Jeffrey Fagan, "Problem-Solving Courts: From Innovation to Institutionalization," *American Criminal*

Law Review 40 (2003): 1501–1512; Peggy Hora, William Schma, and John Rosenthal, "Therapeutic Jurisprudence and the Drug Court Movement: Revolutionizing the Criminal Justice System's Response to Drug Abuse and Crime in America," *Notre Dame Law Review* 74 (1999): 439–555; and David Wexler and Bruce Winick, *Law in a Therapeutic Key* (Durham, N.C.: Carolina Academic Press, 1996).

6. Indeed, the evidence suggests that individuals who display signs of mental illness are more likely to be arrested than those who do not and if convicted are more likely to do more time in prison. See Linda Teplin, "The Criminalization of the Mentally Ill," *Psychologic Bulletin* 94 (1993): 54–67; Paula Ditton, *Mental Health and Treatment of Inmates and Probationers* (Washington, D.C.: U.S. Department of Justice, 1999).

7. David Rottman and Pamela Casey, "Therapeutic Jurisprudence and the Emergence of Problem-Solving Courts," *National Institute of Justice Journal* (July 1999): 12–19; David Wexler, "Reflections on the Scope of Therapeutic Jurisprudence," *Psychology, Public Policy and the Law* 2 (1996): 220–224.

8. Eric Turpin, Henry Richards, David Wertheimer, and Carole Bruschi, *Mental Health Court: Evaluation Report* (Seattle, Wash.: City of Seattle Municipal Court, 2001).

9. Pamela Casey and David Rottman, "Therapeutic Jurisprudence in the Courts," *Behavioral Sciences and the Law* 18 (2000): 445–457.

10. Henry Steadman, Susan Davidson, and Collie Brown, "Mental Health Courts: Their Promise and Unanswered Questions," *Psychiatric Services* 52 (2001): 457–458.

11. Casey and Rottman, "Therapeutic Jurisprudence in the Courts."

12. Bob Ferguson, "The Jail as Mental Institution," *Seattle Times*, January 11, 2007, available at seattletimes.nwsource.com/html/opinion/2003518876_bobferguson11.html.

13. National Institute of Drug Abuse, *Principles of Drug Addiction Treatment* (Washington D.C., 1999); Washington State Institute for Public Policy, *Mentally Ill Misdemeanants: An Evaluation of Change in Public Safety Policy* (Olympia: Washington State Institute for Public Policy, 2004).

14. Robert Barnoski and Steve Aos, *Washington State Drug Courts for Criminal Defendants: Outcome Evaluation and Cost-Benefit Analysis* (Olympia: Washington State Institute for Public Policy, 2003).

15. Turpin et al., *Mental Health Court: Evaluation Report.*

16. Seattle Municipal Court, *Seattle Community Court: Nineteen Months in Review* (December 2006); Washington State Institute for Public Policy, "Washington State's Drug Courts for Adult Defendants: Outcome Evaluation and Cost-Benefit Analysis," March 2003.

17. Dorf and Fagan express considerable caution about early evaluations of problem-solving courts, few of which they consider adequately done. From their viewpoint, the jury remains out on the question of efficacy. See Dorf and Fagan, "Problem-Solving Courts." Similarly, the U.S. General Accounting Office concluded in 2002, "Although DOJ points out in its comments that a number of individual program evaluation studies have been completed, no national impact evaluation of these programs has been done to date. We continue to believe that until post-program follow-up data on program participants are collected across a broad range of programs

and also included within the scope of future program and impact evaluations (including non-program participant data), it will not be possible to reach firm conclusions about whether drug court programs are an effective use of federal funds or whether different types of drug court program structures funded by DCPO work better than others. Also, unless these results are compared with those on the impact of other criminal justice programs, it will not be clear whether drug court programs are more or less effective than other criminal justice programs. As such, these limitations have prevented firm conclusions from being drawn on the overall impact of federally funded drug court programs." U.S. General Accounting Office, *Drug Courts: Better DOJ Data Collection and Evaluation Efforts Needed to Measure Impact of Drug Court Programs* (GAO-02-434; Washington, D.C.: Government Printing Office, April 2002), 20–21.

18. C. West Huddleston, Karen Freeman-Wilson, and Donna Boone, *Painting the Current Picture: A National Report Card on Drug Courts and Other Problem Solving Court Programs in the United States* (Washington, D.C.: Bureau of Justice Assistance, 2004).

19. Seattle Municipal Courts, *Seattle Community Court: Nineteen Months in Review* (December 2006).

20. Substance Abuse and Mental Health Administration, *National Treatment Improvement Evaluation Study: Final Report* (Washington D.C., March 1997); Washington State Institute for Public Policy, *Washington State's Drug Courts for Adult Defendants: Outcome Evaluation and Cost-Benefit Analysis* (March 2003), table 3.

21. Moreover, over 20 million people need but cannot receive drug or alcohol treatment in this country. Substance Abuse and Mental Health Administration, *Results from the 2007 National Survey on Drug Use and Health: National Findings* (Washington D.C., 2007).

22. Candace McCoy, "Review: Good Courts: The Case for Problem-Solving Justice," *Law and Politics Book Review* 16 (2006), 964–969, available at www.bsos.umd.edu/gvpt/lpbr/subpages/reviews/berman-feinblatt1206.htm.

23. James L. Nolan Jr., *Reinventing Justice: The American Drug Court Movement* (Princeton, N.J.: Princeton University Press, 2001).

24. Committee to End Homelessness, King County, *A Roof over Every Bed in King County: Our Community's Ten-Year Plan to End Homelessness* (Seattle: Committee to End Homelessness, King County).

25. Steadman et al., "Mental Health Courts."

26. Seattle Municipal Courts, *Seattle Community Court: Nineteen Months in Review* (December 2006).

27. Seattle City Attorney's Office, *Annual Report 2007*, 15.

28. Craig Reinarman and Harry G. Levine, *Crack in America: Demon Drugs and Social Justice* (Berkeley: University of California Press, 1997), 356.

29. For general overviews of harm reduction, particularly as it relates to intravenous drug use, see G. Alan Marlatt, *Harm Reduction: Pragmatic Strategies for Managing High-Risk Behaviors* (New York: Guilford Press, 2002); G. Alan Marlatt, "Harm Reduction: Come as You Are," *Addictive Behaviors* 21 (1996): 779–788; Ethan Nadelmann, "Thinking Seriously about Alternatives to Drug Prohibition," *Daedalus*

121 (1992): 85–132; Robert MacCoun, "Toward a Psychology of Harm Reduction," *American Psychologist* 53 (1998): 1199–1208; and Don Des Jarlais, Samuel Friedman, and Thomas Ward, "Harm Reduction: A Public Health Response to the AIDS Epidemic among Injecting Drug Users," *Annual Review of Public Health* 14 (1993): 413–450.

30. Lisa Sanchez, "Boundaries of Legitimacy: Sex, Violence, Citizenship and Community," *Law and Social Inquiry* 22 (1997): 543–580.

31. Lisa Maher and David Dixon, "Policing and Public Health: Law Enforcement and Harm Minimization in a Street-Level Drug Market," *British Journal of Criminology* 39 (1999): 488–512.

32. G. Pearson, "Drugs and Criminal Justice: A Harm Reduction Perspective," pp. 15–29 in *The Reduction of Drug-Related Crime,* edited by P O'Hare, R. Newcome, A. Matthews, and E. Drucker (London: Routledge, 1992).

33. Vancouver, British Columbia, hosts the only safe injection site in North America. In a recent court ruling mandating that the site remain open, the judge ruled it needed to be understood as a health care facility, not a haven for illegal activity. Said the judge, "While there is nothing to be said in favour of the injection of controlled substances that leads to addiction, there is much to be said against denying addicts health-care services that will ameliorate the effects of their condition." CBC News, "Vancouver Safe-Injection Site Supporters Pleased by Court Decision," May 28, 2008, www.cbc.ca/canada/british-columbia/story/2008/05/27/bc-safe-injection-ruling-reaction.html.

34. Stanley Tsemberis, "Housing First," in *Encyclopedia of Homelessness* (Thousand Oaks, Calif.: Sage, 2004), 277–280; Stanley Tsemberis, "Pathways to Housing: A Supported Housing Program for Street Dwelling Individuals with Psychiatric Disabilities," *Psychiatric Services* 51 (2000): 487–493; R. Greenwood, N. Schaefer-McDaniel, G. Winkel, and S. Tsemberis, "Decreasing Psychiatric Symptoms by Increasing Choice in Services for Adults with Histories of Homelessness," *American Journal of Community Psychology* 36, no. 3/4 (2006): 223–238.

35. See National Alliance to End Homelessness, *A Plan, Not a Dream: How to End Homelessness in Ten Years* (Washington, D.C.: National Alliance to End Homelessness, 2000), available at www.endhomelessness.org/section/tools/tenyearplan. It is worth noting that in Seattle at least, there is considerable controversy over the manner in which Housing First rhetoric is folded into discussions of ending homelessness. This rhetoric is frequently deployed by many centrally involved in King County's ten-year plan. Many homeless advocates, however, complain that only low-income housing that includes social services is being discussed in the creation and implementation of King County's ten-year plan. Given scarce resources, this may mean a decline in simple shelter. For this reason, some decry that Housing First as implemented may not hold true to the priority of providing shelter before any other form of service.

36. See www.desc.org/documents/1811_First_Year_Preliminary_Findings.pdf.

37. National Law Center on Homelessness and Poverty, *Model Approaches to Homelessness* (2007).

38. Bernard Harcourt, *The Illusion of Order: The False Promise of Broken Windows Policing* (Cambridge, Mass.: Harvard University Press, 2001).

39. For an insightful and thorough discussion of the manner in which homeless people and encampments are typically portrayed by Seattle media, see faculty. washington.edu/stygall/homelessmediacoveragegroup. Metaphors of filth, disease, and contagion are most frequently used in these media portrayals, which only makes it harder to view the homeless in an inclusive fashion.

40. Wesley Skogan, *Disorder and Decline: Crime and the Spiral of Decay in America* (Berkeley: University of California Press, 1990).

Selected Bibliography

Adame, Jaime, "Operation Safe Housing," *Gotham Gazette*, August 17, 2004.

Adams, Kenneth, "The Effectiveness of Juvenile Curfews at Crime Prevention," *Annals of the American Academy of Political and Social Science* 587 (2003): 136–159.

Adamson, Christopher R., "Punishment after Slavery," *Social Problems* 30, no. 5 (June 1983): 493–507.

Adler, Jeffrey S., "A Historical Analysis of the Law of Vagrancy," *Criminology* 27, no. 2 (1989): 209–229.

Allan, Edward L., *Civil Gang Abatement: The Effectiveness and Implications of Policing by Injunction* (New York: LFB Scholarly Publications, 2004).

Alschuler, Albert, and Steven J. Schulhofer, "Antiquated Procedures or Bedrock Rights? A Response to Professors Meares and Kahan," *University of Chicago Legal Forum* (1998): 215.

American Prosecutors Research Institute, *Unwelcome Guests: A Community Prosecution Approach to Street level Drug Dealing and Prostitution* (2004).

Anderson, Elijah, *Streetwise: Race, Class and Change in an Urban Community* (Chicago: University of Chicago Press, 1990).

Andreas, Peter, *Border Games: Policing the U.S.-Mexico Divide* (Ithaca, N.Y.: Cornell University Press, 2001).

Andrews, Mildred, *Pioneer Square: Seattle's Oldest Neighborhood* (Seattle: University of Washington Press, 2005).

Armstrong, Michael F., "Banishment: Cruel and Unusual Punishment," *University of Pennsylvania Law Review* III, no. 6 (April 1963): 758–786.

Ascher, Charles S., and James M. Wolf, "'Red Light' Injunction and Abatement Acts," *Columbia Law Review* 20 (1920): 605–608.

Associated Press, "High Court Refuses to Review Cincinnati's Anti-Trespass Law," April 29, 2002.

Austin, James, and John Irwin, *It's about Time: America's Imprisonment Binge* (Belmont, Calif.: Wadsworth, 2000).

Austin's Tenants' Council, "Suit Results in Changes to Criminal Trespass Policy," *Housing Rights Advocate* 20 (Fall 2001): 1–2.

Barak, Gregg, *Gimme Shelter: A Social History of Homelessness in Contemporary America* (Westport, Conn.: Praeger, 1992).

Barber, Michael, "Battle Street Crime Harder, City Urged," *Seattle Times*, August 27, 1986.

Barnoski, Robert, and Steve Aos, *Washington State Drug Courts for Criminal Defendants: Outcome Evaluation and Cost-Benefit Analysis* (Olympia: Washington State Institute for Public Policy, 2003).

Bauman, Zygmunt, "Social Issues of Law and Order," *British Journal of Criminology* 40 (2000): 205–221.

Bawarshi, Anis, et al., "Media Analysis of Homeless Encampment Sweeps," 2008, faculty.washington.edu/stygall/homelessmediacoveragegroup.

Becker, Howard S., *Outsiders: Studies in the Sociology of Deviance* (New York: Free Press, 1963).

Beckett, Katherine, *Making Crime Pay: Law and Order in Contemporary American Politics* (New York: Oxford University Press, 1997).

Beckett, Katherine, *Race and Drug Law Enforcement in Seattle*, report prepared for the ACLU Drug Law Reform Project and the Defender Association, September 9, 2008.

Beckett, Katherine, and Steve Herbert, "The Punitive City Revisited: The Transformation of Urban Social Control." Pp. 106–122 in *After the War on Crime: Race, Democracy, and a New Reconstruction*, edited by Mary Louise Frampton, Ian Haney Lopez, and Jonathan Simon (New York: New York University Press, 2008).

Beckett, Katherine, and Steve Herbert, "Dealing with Disorder: Social Control in the Post-Industrial City," *Theoretical Criminology* 12 (2008): 5–30.

Beckett, Katherine, and Theodore Sasson, *The Politics of Injustice*, 2nd ed. (Beverly Hills, Calif.: Sage Publications, 2004).

Beier, A. L., *Masterless Men: The Vagrancy Problem in England 1560–1640* (New York: Methuen, 1985).

Berman, Greg, John Feinblatt, and Sarah Glazer, *Good Courts: The Case for Problem-Solving Justice* (New York: Free Press, 2005).

Bernd, Belina, "From Disciplining to Dislocation: Area Bans in Recent Urban Policing in Germany," *European Urban and Regional Studies* 14 (2007): 321–336.

Birkland, David, "Loitering Law Is Resulting in 'Crack' Down," *Seattle Times*, September 18, 1987, E3.

Bishop, Todd, and Christine Frey, "Resurgent Downtown Still Faces Challenges," *Seattle Post-Intelligencer*, February 10, 2003.

Black, Donald, *The Behaviour of Law* (New York: Academic Press, 1976).

Blasi, Gary, "Policing Our Way out of Homelessness? The First Year of the Safer Cities Initiative on Skid Row," 2007, www.sfgov.org/site/uploadedfiles/mocj/CommInvlv_News/blasi_study.pdf.

Boland, Barbara, and Kerry Murphy Healey, *Prosecutorial Responses to Heavy Caseloads* (Washington, D.C.: National Institute of Justice, 1993).

Borrelli, Matthew D., "Banishment: The Constitutional and Public Policy Arguments against this Revived Ancient Punishment," *Suffolk University Law Review* 36 (2002–2003): 470.

Bowling, Benjamin, "The Rise and Fall of New York Murder: Zero Tolerance or Crack's Decline?" *British Journal of Criminology* 39, no. 4 (1999): 531–554.

Brandt, Steve, "Lurking Law under Scrutiny," *Minneapolis Star Tribune*, May 21, 2008.

Brenner, Neil, and Nik Theodore, *Spaces of Neoliberalism* (Oxford: Blackwell, 2002).

Burney, Elizabeth, *Crime and Banishment: Nuisance and Exclusion in Social Housing* (Winchester: Waterside Press, 1999).

Burney, Elizabeth, *Making People Behave: Anti-Social Behaviour, Politics, and Policy* (Cullompton: Willan 2005).

Burt, Martha, "Causes of the Growth of Homelessness During the 1980's," *Housing Policy Debate* 2, no. 3 (1991).

Burt, Martha, *Over the Edge: The Growth of Homelessness in the 1980s* (New York: Russell Sage Foundation, 1992).

Carnoy, Martin, *The New Global Economy in the Information Age: Reflections on Our Changing World* (University Park: Penn State University Press, 1993).

Carr, Thomas A., "Seattle Community Court," *Seattle City Attorney's Liaison Links*, spring 2006.

Carr, Thomas A., Seattle City Attorney, "2007 Annual Report," www.seattle.gov/law/docs/AnnualReport2007.pdf, 14–15.

Casey, Pamela, and David Rottman, "Therapeutic Jurisprudence in the Courts," *Behavioral Sciences and the Law* 18 (2000): 445–457.

Center for Civic Innovation at the Manhattan Institute, *Broken Windows Probation: The Next Step in Fighting Crime* (1999).

Chambliss, William, "A Sociological Analysis of the Law of Vagrancy," *Social Problems*, 12, no. 1 (1964): 67–77.

Chan, Sharon Pian, "Downtown Struggling with Safety Perceptions," *Seattle Times*, April 27, 2006.

Cheh, Mary M., "Constitutional Limits on Using Civil Remedies to Achieve Criminal Law Objectives," *Hastings Law Journal* 42 (1991): 1325–1348.

Christopherson, Susan, "The Fortress City: Privatized Spaces, Consumer Citizenship." Pp. 409–447 in *Post-Fordism: A Reader*, edited by Ash Amin (London: Blackwell, 1994).

City of New York (press release), "Mayor Michael R. Bloomberg Announces Operation Safe Housing," June 24, 2004.

City of Seattle, Department of Design, Construction and Land Use, "Monitoring our Progress: Seattle's Comprehensive Plan" (March 2003).

Cohen, Stanley, *Visions of Social Control* (Cambridge: Polity Press, 1985).

Committee to End Homelessness, King County, *A Roof over Every Bed in King County: Our Community's Ten-Year Plan to End Homelessness* (Seattle: Committee to End Homelessness, King County).

Congress of the United States, *Meeting our Nation's Housing Challenges*, Report of the Bipartisan Millennial Housing Commission (Washington, D.C.: U.S. Government Printing Office, 2002).

Crawford, Adam, "From the Shopping Mall to the Street Corner: Dynamics of Exclusion in the Governance of Public Space," presented to the World University Network, University of Leeds, June 2008.

Crawford, Adam, and Stuart Lister, *The Use and Impact of Dispersal Orders* (Bristol: Polity Press, 2007).

Cresswell, Tim, *In Place/Out of Place: Geography, Ideology and Transgression* (Minneapolis: University of Minnesota Press, 1996).

Curtis, Richard, "The Improbable Transformation of Inner-City Neighborhoods: Crime, Violence and Youth in the 1990s," *Journal of Criminal Law and Criminology* 88, no. 4 (1997): 1233–1277.

Des Jarlais, Don, Samuel Friedman, and Thomas Ward, "Harm Reduction: A Public Health Response to the AIDS Epidemic among Injecting Drug Users," *Annual Review of Public Health* 14 (1993): 413–450.

Ditton, Paula, *Mental Health and Treatment of Inmates and Probationers* (Washington, D.C.: U.S. Department of Justice, 1999).

Dolbeare, C. N., I. B. Saraf, and S. Crowley, *Changing Priorities: The Federal Budget and Housing Assistance, 1976–2005* (Washington, D.C.: National Low Income Housing Coalition, 2004), www.nlihc.org/doc/cp04.pdf.

Dorf, Michael, and Jeffrey Fagan, "Problem-Solving Courts: From Innovation to Institutionalization," *American Criminal Law Review* 40 (2003): 1501–1512.

Dubber, Markus Dirk, *The Police Power: Patriarchy and the Foundations of American Government* (New York: Columbia University Press, 2005).

Duneier, Mitch, *Sidewalk* (New York: Farrar, Strauss and Giroux, 1999).

Eck, John E., and Edward R. Maguire, "Have Changes in Policing Reduced Violent Crime? An Assessment of the Evidence." Chapter 7 in *The Crime Drop in America*, edited by Alfred Blumstein and Joel Wallman (Cambridge: Cambridge University Press, 2000).

Ellickson, Robert C., "Controlling Chronic Misconduct in City Spaces: Of Panhandlers, Skid Rows, and Public-Space Zoning," *Yale Law Journal* 105, no. 5 (1996): 1165–1214.

Emery, Julie, "Drug-Infested Areas Off-Limits to Offenders," *Seattle Times*, September 16, 1991, B5.

Fallows, James, "Saving Salmon, or Seattle," *Atlantic Monthly*, 286 (2000): 20–24.

Feldman, Leonard C., *Citizens without Shelter: Homelessness, Democracy and Political Exclusion* (Ithaca, N.Y.: Cornell University Press, 2004).

Felt, Chandler, "Seattle's Rich Areas Get Richer; Gentrification Widens 'Neighborhood Gap,' Census Shows," *Seattle Times*, September 17, 2002, A1.

Fernandez, Manny, "Barred from Public Housing, Even to See Family," *New York Times*, October 1, 2007, A1.

Flanagan, Peter M., "Trespass-Zoning: Ensuring Neighborhoods a Safer Future by Excluding Those with a Criminal Past," *Notre Dame Law Review* 79 (2003): 327–379.

Flint, John, and Judy Nixon, "Governing Neighbours: Anti-Social Behaviour Orders and New Forms of Regulating Conduct in the UK," *Urban Studies* 43 (2006): 939–956.

Fogleson, Robert, *Big-City Police* (Cambridge, Mass.: Harvard University Press, 1977).

Foote, Caleb, "Vagrancy-Type Law and its Administration," *University of Pennsylvania Law Review* 104 (1956): 603.

Foscarinis, Maria, "Downward Spiral: Homelessness and its Criminalization," *Yale Law and Policy Review* 14 (1996): 1–63.

Foscarinis, Maria, "The Federal Response: The Stewart McKinney Homeless Assistance Act." Pp. 160–171 in *Homelessness in America*, edited by J. Baumohl (Phoenix: Oryx Press, 1996).

Gabbard, Wesley, Bryan Ford, and James May, "The Stewart B. McKinney Homeless Assistance Act: A Historical Overview," *Journal of Social Distress and the Homeless* 15 (2006): 99–116.

Garland, David, *The Culture of Control* (Chicago: University of Chicago Press, 2001).

Gerard, John Sheehan, "Seattle Parks Banishment Ordinance: Second Analysis and Report.," Seattle, ACLU (1998), www.aclu-wa.org/Publication/banishment_ordinance.html.

Gibson, Timothy, *Securing the Spectacular City: The Politics of Revitalization and Homelessness in Downtown Seattle* (Lanham, Md.: Lexington Books, 2004).

Gilderbloom, John, and Richard Applebaum, *Rethinking Rental Housing* (Philadelphia: Temple University Press, 1988).

Godes, Kerry, "Drug-Loitering Law to Get Public Hearing," *Seattle Post-Intelligencer*, May 23, 1990, B1.

Goldstein, Elena, "Kept Out: Responding to Public Housing No-Trespass Policies," *Harvard Civil Rights–Civil Liberties Journal* 38 (2003).

Gordon, Diana R., *The Return of the Dangerous Classes: Drug Prohibition and Policy Politics* (New York: Norton, 1994).

Greenberg, Greg A., and Robert A. Rosenheck, "Jail Incarceration, Homelessness, and Mental Health: A National Study," *Psychiatric Services* 59, no. 2 (February 2008): 170–177.

Greene, Judith, "Zero Tolerance: A Case Study of Police Policies and Practices in New York City," *Crime and Delinquency* 45 (1999): 171–182.

Greenwood, R., N. Schaefer-McDaniel, G. Winkel, and S. Tsemberis, "Decreasing Psychiatric Symptoms by Increasing Choice in Services for Adults with Histories of Homelessness," *American Journal of Community Psychology* 36, no. 3/4 (2006): 223–238.

Gregory, Mary, Wiemer Salverda, and Stephen Brazen, *Labour Market Inequalities: Problems and Policies of Low-Wage Employment in International Perspective* (Oxford: Oxford University Press, 2000).

Groth, Paul, *Living Downtown: The History of Residential Hotels in the United States* (Berkeley: University of California Press, 1994).

Hackworth, Jason, *The Neoliberal City: Governance, Ideology, and Development in American Urbanism* (Ithaca, N.Y.: Cornell University Press, 2007).

Harcourt, Bernard E., *The Illusion of Order: The False Promise of Broken Windows Policing* (Cambridge, Mass.: Harvard University Press, 2001).

Harcourt, Bernard E., and Jens Ludwig, "Broken Windows: New Evidence from New York City and a Five-City Social Experiment," *University of Chicago Law Review* 73 (2006): 271.

Harris, Lasana T., and Susan T. Fiske, "Dehumanizing the Lowest of the Low: Neuroimaging Responses to Extreme Out-Groups," *Psychological Science* 17, no. 10 (2006): 847–854.

Harrison, Bennett, *The Great U-Turn: Corporate Restructuring and the Polarizing of America* (New York: Basic Books, 1988).

Harvey, David, *The Condition of Postmodernity: An Enquiry into the Origins of Cultural Change* (Oxford: Blackwell, 1991).

Harvey, David, *A Brief History of Neoliberalism* (New York: Oxford University Press, 2005).

Herbert, Steve, *Policing Space: Territoriality and the Los Angeles Police Department* (Minneapolis: University of Minnesota Press, 1997).

Herbert, Steve, "The Trapdoor of Community," *Annals of the Association of American Geographers* 95, no. 4 (2005): 850–865.

Herbert, Steve, *Citizens, Cops, and Power: Recognizing the Limits to Community.* (Chicago: University of Chicago Press.

Hill, Gordon, "The Use of Pre-Existing Exclusionary Zones as Probationary Conditions for Prostitution Offenses: A Call for the Sincere Application of Heightened Scrutiny," *Seattle University Law Review* 28 (2005).

Hopper, K., and N. G. Milburn, "Homelessness among African Americans: A historical and contemporary perspective." Pp. 123–131 in *Homeless in America,* edited by J. Baumohl (Phoenix: Oryx, 1996).

Hora, Peggy, William Schma, and John Rosenthal, "Therapeutic Jurisprudence and the Drug Court Movement: Revolutionizing the Criminal Justice System's Response to Drug Abuse and Crime in America," *Notre Dame Law Review* 74 (1999): 439–555.

Huddleston, C. West, Karen Freeman-Wilson, and Donna Boone, *Painting the Current Picture: A National Report Card on Drug Courts and Other Problem Solving Court Programs in the United States* (Washington, D.C.: Bureau of Justice Assistance, 2004).

Hunt, Alan, *Governing Morals: A Social History of Moral Regulation* (Cambridge: Cambridge University Press, 1999).

Hyla, Adam, "Yesler Terrace: Future in Question," *Real Change* (Seattle), March 23–29, 2005, 5.

Innes, Martin, *Understanding Social Control: Deviance, Crime and Social Order* (New York: McGraw-Hill, 2003).

Isaacs, S. L., and J. R. Knickman, eds., *To Improve Health and Health Care*, vol. 7 (San Francisco: Jossey-Bass, 2004).

Isin, Engin Fahri, *Democracy, Citizenship, and the Global City: Rights, Democracy and Place* (New York: Routledge, 2000).

Johnson, Bruce D., Andrew Golub, and Eloise Dunlap, "The Rise and Decline of Hard Drugs, Drug Markets, and Violence in Inner City New York." Chapter 6 in *The Crime Drop in America*, edited by Alfred Blumstein and Joel Wallman (Cambridge: Cambridge University Press, 2000).

Joint Center for Housing Studies of Harvard University, *The State of the Nation's Housing 2003* (Cambridge, Mass.: Harvard University Press, 2004).

Karman, Andrew, *New York Murder Mystery: The True Story of the Crime Crash in New York City* (New York: New York University Press, 2000).

Kelling, George L., and Catherine M. Coles, *Fixing Broken Windows: Restoring Order ad Reducing Crime in Our Communities* (New York: Free Press, 1996).

King, Ryan S., and Marc Mauer, *Distorted Priorities: Drug Offenders in State Prisons* (Washington, D.C.: Sentencing Project, 2002).

Lamb, H. Richard, "The Deinstitutionalization of the Mentally Ill," *Hospital and Community Psychiatry* 35 (1984): 899–907.

Lamb, H. Richard, and Linda Weinberger, "Persons with Severe Mental Illness in Jails and Prisons: A Review," *Psychiatric Services* 49 (1998): 483–492.

Lane, Polly, "Downtown Merchants Want Action on Crime," *Seattle Times*, April 23, 1993.

Lange, Greg, "Police Arrest Vagrants," *Seattle Times*, January 4, 1901, 7.

Larner, Wendy, "Neo-Liberalism: Policy, Ideology, Governmentality," *Studies in Political Economy* 63 (2000): 5–25.

Le, Phuong Cat, and D. Parvaz, "Census 2000: Seattle's Rich Areas Get Richer," *Seattle Post-Intelligencer*, September 17, 2002.

Lees, Loretta, Tom Slater, and Elvin Wyly, *Gentrification* (New York: Routledge, 2008).

Leonard, V. A., *Survey of the Seattle Police Department* (Seattle, Wash., 1945).

Levy, B. D., and J. J. O'Connell, "Health Care for Homeless Persons," *New England Journal of Medicine* 350 (2004): 2329–2332.

Lily, Dick, "Mayor's Plan to Reduce Police Force Draws Fire—Downtown Group Opposes Plan," *Seattle Times*, May 11, 1991.

Link, B. G., E. Susser, A. Stueve, et al., "Lifetime and Five-Year Prevalence of Homelessness in the United States," *American Journal of Public Health* 84 (1994): 1907–1912.

Loader, Ian, "Policing, Recognition and Belonging," *Annals of the American Academy of the Political and Social Science* 205 (May 2006): 202–221.

Lofland, Lyn, *A World of Strangers: Order and Action in Urban Public Space* (New York: Basic Books, 1973).

Lyons, William, *The Politics of Community Policing: Rearranging the Power to Punish* (Ann Arbor: University of Michigan Press, 1999).

MacCoun, Robert, "Toward a Psychology of Harm Reduction," *American Psychologist* 53 (1998): 1199–1208.

Maher, Lisa, and David Dixon, "Policing and Public Health: Law Enforcement and Harm Minimization in a Street-Level Drug Market," *British Journal of Criminology* 39 (1999): 488–512.

Manning, Peter, "Theorizing Policing: The Drama and Myth of Crime Control in the NYPD," *Theoretical Criminology* 5 (2001): 315–344.

Marlatt, G. Alan, "Harm Reduction: Come as You Are," *Addictive Behaviors* 21 (1996): 779–788.

Marlatt, G. Alan, *Harm Reduction: Pragmatic Strategies for Managing High-Risk Behaviors* (New York: Guilford Press, 2002).

Mauer, Marc, and Ryan S. King, *A 25-Year Quagmire: The "War on Drugs" and its Impact on American Society* (Washington, D.C.: Sentencing Project, 2007).

McCoy, Candace, "Review: Good Courts: The Case for Problem-Solving Justice," *Law and Politics Book Review,* 16 (2006): 964–969.

McCurdy, Robert, "The Use of the Injunction to Destroy Commercialized Prostitution in Chicago," *Journal of Criminal Law* 19 (1929): 513–517.

Meares, Tracey L., and Dan M. Kahan, "The Wages of Antiquated Procedural Thinking: A Critique of *Chicago v. Morales,*" *University of Chicago Legal Forum* (1998): 197.

Merry, Sally Engle, *Urban Danger: Life in a Neighborhood of Strangers* (Philadelphia: Temple University Press, 1981).

Millie, Andrew, "Anti-Social Behaviour, Behavioural Expectations and an Urban Aesthetic," *British Journal of Criminology* 48 (2008): 379–394.

Mitchell, Don, "The Annihilation of Space by Law: The Roots and Implications of Anti-Homeless Laws," *Antipode* 29 (1997): 303–335.

Mitchell, Don, *The Right to the City: Social Justice and the Fight for Public Space* (New York: Guilford Press, 2003).

Mitchell, Don, "Property Rights, the First Amendment, and Judicial Anti-Urbanism: The Strange Case of *Hicks v. Virginia,*" *Urban Geography* 26, no. 7 (2005): 565–586.

Mitchell, Katharyne, and Katherine Beckett, "Securing the Global City: Crime, Consulting, Risk and Ratings in the Production of Urban Space," *Global Legal Studies* 15, no. 1 (2008): 75–99.

Morgan, Murray, *Skid Road: An Informal Portrait of Seattle* (Seattle: University of Washington Press, 1982).

Morris, Martina, and Bruce Western, "Inequality at the Close of the Twentieth Century," *Annual Review of Sociology* 25 (1999): 623–652.

Moser, Sandra, "Anti-Prostitution Zones: Justifications for Abolition," *Journal of Criminal Law and Criminology* 91 (summer 2001): 1101.

Murakami, Kery, "Seattle Tourist Boom! Record Numbers of Visitors Pouring In," *Seattle Post-Intelligencer,* July 25, 2006.

Nadelmann, Ethan, "Thinking Seriously about Alternatives to Drug Prohibition," *Daedalus* 121 (1992): 85–132.

National Alliance to End Homelessness, *A Plan, Not a Dream: How to End Homelessness in Ten Years* (Washington, D.C., 2000).

National Coalition for the Homeless, *A Dream Denied: The Criminalization of Homelessness in U.S. Cities* (January 2006).

National Institute of Drug Abuse, *Principles of Drug Addiction Treatment* (Washington, D.C., 1999).

National Law Center on Homelessness and Poverty, "Model Approaches to Homelessness" (2007).

National Low Income Housing Coalition, "The Crisis in America's Housing: Confronting Myths and Promoting a Balanced Housing Policy" (Washington, D.C., 2005), www.nlihc.org/doc/housingmyths.pdf.

Neckerman, Kathryn M., and Florencia Torche, "Inequality: Causes and Consequences," *Annual Review of Sociology* 33 (2007): 335–357.

Nelson, Robert T., "Council Passes Drug-Loitering Law amid Boos," *Seattle Times*, June 26, 1990, B3.

Nolan, James L. Jr., *Reinventing Justice: The American Drug Court Movement* (Princeton, N.J.: Princeton University Press, 2001).

Novak, William J., *The People's Welfare: Law and Regulation in Nineteenth Century America* (Chapel Hill: University of North Carolina Press, 1996).

Parascandola, Rocco, "Trespass Arrests under Attack," *Newsday*, April 13, 2007.

Parent, Dale, and Brad Snyder, "Police-Corrections Partnerships," *Issues and Practices in Criminal Justice* series, National Institute of Justice (1999).

Pearson, G., "Drugs and Criminal Justice: A Harm Reduction Perspective." Pp. 15–20 in *The Reduction of Drug-Related Crime*, edited by P. O'Hare, R. Newcome, A. Matthews, and E. Drucker (London: Routledge, 1992).

Peck, Jamie, and Adam Tickell, "Neoliberalizing Space," *Antipode* 34 (2002): 380–404.

Raco, Mike, "Remaking Place and Securitizing Space: Urban Regeneration and the Strategies, Tactics and Practices of Policing in the UK," *Urban Studies* 40 (2003): 1869–1887.

Ramsay, Peter, "The Theory of Vulnerable Autonomy and the Legitimacy of the Civil Prevention Order," Law, Society & Economy Working Papers 1 (2008).

Reichert, Kent, "Police-Probation Partnerships: Boston's Operation Night Light." Forum on Crime and Justice, University of Pennsylvania, Jerry Lee Center of Criminology, March 2002.

Reinarman, Craig, and Harry G. Levine, *Crack in America: Demon Drugs and Social Justice* (Berkeley: University of California Press, 1997).

Roberts, Dorothy, "Race, Vagueness, and the Social Meaning of Order-Maintenance Policing," *Journal of Criminal Law and Criminology* 89 (1999): 775–836.

Rottman, David, and Pamela Casey, "Therapeutic Jurisprudence and the Emergence of Problem-Solving Courts," *National Institute of Justice Journal* (July 1999): 12–19.

Sampson, Robert, and Stephen Raudenbush, "Systematic Social Observation of Public Spaces: A New Look at Disorder in Urban Neighborhoods," *American Journal of Sociology* 105 (1999): 603–665.

Sanchez, Lisa, "Enclosure Acts and Exclusionary Practices: Neighborhood Associations, Community Police, and the Expulsion of the Sexual Outlaw." Chapter 6 in *Between Law and Culture: Relocating Legal Studies*, edited by David Theo Goldberg, Michael Musheno, and Lisa C. Bower (Minneapolis: University of Minnesota Press, 1997).

Sanchez, Lisa, "Boundaries of Legitimacy: Sex, Violence, Citizenship and Community," *Law and Social Inquiry* 22 (1997): 543–580.

Santos, Fernanda, "From Jail, a Panhandler Fights New York's Loitering Law as a Violation of Free Speech," *New York Times*, May 30, 2007.

Sassen, Saskia, *The Global City* (Princeton, N.J.: Princeton University Press, 2002).

Schellinger, Lisa, "Drug War Now Has Borders," *Seattle Post-Intelligencer*, December 12, 1990.

Schneider, Cathy, and Paul E. Amar, "The Rise of Crime, Disorder and Authoritarian Policing: An Introductory Essay," *NACLA Report on the Americas* 37, no. 2 (2003): 12–15.

Scull, Andrew T., *Decarceration: Community Treatment and the Deviant* (Englewood Cliffs, N.J.: Prentice Hall, 1977).

Seattle Displacement Coalition, "The Continuing Loss of Affordable Housing in Downtown Seattle," 2007, www.zipcon.net/~jvf4119/downtownhousing.htm.

Seattle/King County Coalition on Homelessness, "2008 One Night Count of People Who are Homeless in King County, Washington," 2008.

Seattle Municipal Courts, "Mental Health Court Results: A One Year Snapshot," 2007, http://www.seattle.gov/courts/comjust/mhresults.htm.

Seattle Municipal Courts, *Seattle Community Court: Nineteen Months in Review* (December 2006).

Sewell, Abby, "How Well Do Drug-Free Zones Really Work?" *Portland Alliance*, November 2005.

Simon, Jonathan, *Governing through Crime: How the War on Crime Transformed American Democracy and Created a Culture of Fear* (New York: Oxford University Press, 2007).

Skogan, Wesley, *Disorder and Decline: Crime and the Spiral of Decay in America* (Berkeley: University of California Press, 1990).

Smith, Neil, *The New Urban Frontier: Gentrification and the Revanchist City* (New York: Routledge, 1996).

Smith, Neil, "Global Social Cleansing: Postliberal Revanchism and the Export of Zero Tolerance," *Social Justice* 28, no. 3 (2001): 68–75.

Snider, William Garth, "Banishment: The History of Its Use and a Proposal for Its Abolition under the First Amendment," *North East Journal on Criminal and Civil Confinement* 24 (summer 1998): 455.

Soukup, Tamara, "Parking Lot Trespass Program," Seattle City Attorney's *Liaison Links*, spring 2005.

Soukup, Tamera, "Attempted Possession of Narcotics," Seattle City Attorney's *Liaison Links*, spring 2006.

Spradley, James, *You Owe Yourself a Drunk: An Ethnography of Urban Nomads* (Boston: Little, Brown, 1970).

Steadman, Henry, Susan Davidson, and Collie Brown, "Mental Health Courts: Their Promise and Unanswered Questions," *Psychiatric Services* 52 (2001): 457–458.

Stewart, Gary, "Black Codes and Broken Windows: The Legacy of Racial Hegemony in Anti-Gang Civil Injunctions," *Yale Law Journal* 107, no. 7 (May 1998): 2249–2280.

Substance Abuse and Mental Health Administration, *National Treatment Improvement Evaluation Study: Final Report* (Washington D.C., March 1997).

Substance Abuse and Mental Health Administration, *Results from the 2007 National Survey on Drug Use and Health: National Findings* (Washington D.C., 2007).

Suk, Jeannie, "Criminal Law Comes Home," *Yale Law Journal* 116, no. 2 (2006): 2–70.

Sullivan, Jennifer, "Police to Increase Patrols Downtown," *Seattle Times*, August 17, 2007.

Tabachnick, Cara, "Jump in Trespassing Arrests Draws Anger," *Newsday*, April 10, 2007.

Taylor, Ralph, *Breaking away from Broken Windows* (Boulder, Colo.: Westview Press, 2000).

Teplin, Linda, "The Criminalization of the Mentally Ill," *Psychologic Bulletin* 94 (1993): 54–67.

Thrush, Coll, *Native Seattle: Histories from the Crossing-Over Place* (Seattle: University of Washington Press, 2007).

Tonry, Michael, *Thinking about Crime: Sense and Sensibility in American Penal Culture* (Oxford: Oxford University Press, 2004).

Tsemberis, Stanley, "Pathways to Housing: A Supported Housing Program for Street Dwelling Individuals with Psychiatric Disabilities," *Psychiatric Services* 51 (2000): 487–493.

Tsemberis, Stanley, "Housing First." Pp. 277–280 in *Encyclopedia of Homelessness* (Thousand Oaks, Calif.: Sage, 2004).

Turpin, Eric, Henry Richards, David Wertheimer, and Carole Bruschi, *Mental Health Court: Evaluation Report* (Seattle, Wash.: City of Seattle Municipal Court, 2001).

U.S. General Accounting Office, *Drug Courts: Better DOJ Data Collection and Evaluation Efforts Needed to Measure Impact of Drug Court Programs* (GAO-02-434; Washington, D.C.: U.S. Government Printing Office, April 2002).

von Mahs, Jurgen, "The Sociospatial Exclusion of Single Homeless People in Berlin and Los Angeles," *American Behavioral Scientist* 48 (2005): 928–960.

Wacquant, Loic, "The New 'Peculiar Institution': On the Prison as Surrogate Ghetto," *Theoretical Criminology* 4, no. 3 (2000): 377–389.

Wacquant, Loic, "Toward a Dictatorship over the Poor? Notes on the Penalization of Poverty in Brazil," *Punishment and Society* 5, no. 2 (2003): 197–205.

Wacquant, Loic, *Urban Outcasts: A Comparative Sociology of Advanced Marginality* (Cambridge: Polity Press, 2008).

Walker, Samuel, *A Critical History of Police Reform* (Lexington, Ky.: Lexington Books, 1977).

Washington State Institute for Public Policy, *Washington State's Drug Courts for Adult Defendants: Outcome Evaluation and Cost-Benefit Analysis* (Olympia: Washington State Institute for Public Policy, March 2003).

Washington State Institute for Public Policy, *Mentally Ill Misdemeanants: An Evaluation of Change in Public Safety Policy* (Olympia: Washington State Institute for Public Policy, 2004).

Wells, Robert Marshall, "Up Town—For One End of Downtown Seattle, 1998 Was a Glittering Triumph. For the Other End, the Hard Work Has Just Begun," *Seattle Times*, January 24, 1999.

Werdegar, Matthew Mickle, "Enjoining the Constitution: The Use of Public Nuisance Abatement Injunctions against Urban Street Gangs," *Stanford Law Review* 51, no. 2 (January 1999): 409–448.

Western, Bruce, *Punishment and Inequality* (New York: Russell Sage, 2006).

Western Regional Advocacy Project, *Without Housing: Decades of Federal Housing Cutbacks, Massive Homelessness and Policy Failures* (San Francisco: Western Regional Advocacy Project, 2006), wraphome.org/wh/index.php.

Wexler, David, "Reflections on the Scope of Therapeutic Jurisprudence," *Psychology, Public Policy and the Law* 2 (1996): 220–224.

Wexler, David, and Bruce Winick, *Law in a Therapeutic Key* (Durham, N.C.: Carolina Academic Press, 1996).

White, Ahmed A., "A Different Kind of Labor Law: Vagrancy Law and the Regulation of Harvest Labor, 1913–1924," *University of Colorado Law Review* 75 (2004): 667.

Wilson, James Q., and George F. Kelling, "The Police and Neighborhood Safety," *Atlantic Monthly* (May 1982): 28–38.

Wolch, Jennifer, and Michael Dear, *Landscapes of Despair: From Deinstitutionalization to Homelessness* (Princeton, N.J.: Princeton University Press, 1987).

Wright, James, and Julie Lam, "Homelessness and the Low-Income Housing Supply," *Social Policy* 17 (1999): 48–53.

Wyly, Elvin, and Daniel Hammel, "Islands of Decay in Seas of Renewal: Urban Policy and the Resurgence of Gentrification," *Housing Policy Debate* 10 (1999): 711–771.

Yeamans, Robin, "Constitutional Attacks on Vagrancy Laws," *Stanford Law Review* 20 (1968): 782–793.

Yoo, Christopher S., "The Constitutionality of Enjoining Street Gangs as Public Nuisances," *Northwest University Law Review* 89 (1994): 212.

Zielinski, Danielle, "No Trespass: A Public Housing Solution and Problem," 2005, docket.medill.northwestrn.edu/archives/000131print.php.

Zimring, Franklin, *The Great American Crime Decline* (New York: Oxford University Press, 2007).

Index

Note: Page numbers in italics indicate figures or tables.

CPSIA information can be obtained at www.ICGtesting.com
Printed in the USA
BVOW01s1541261113

337360BV00003B/5/P